Divorce and After

CONTRIBUTORS

Jessie Bernard

Paul Bohannan

Ernest S. Burch, Jr.

Ronald Cohen

Paul Gebhard

Herma Hill Kay

Margaret Mead

Arthur A. Miller, M.D.

Max Rheinstein

Divorce and After

EDITED BY
Paul Bohannan

Anchor Books
DOUBLEDAY & COMPANY, INC.
GARDEN CITY, NEW YORK

Divorce and After was originally published in hardcover by Doubleday & Company, Inc., in 1970.

Anchor Books Edition: 1971

CONTENTS

IV. Divorce Around the World

V. Reform

I
Introduction

1

No News, but
New Ideas

JESSIE BERNARD

I. "No News Is Good News"

Because the research required to give us the facts is so time-consuming, we tend always to be somewhat behind actual events in our knowledge about our social world. Much of our thinking about divorce is, therefore, out of date, relating to the way things used to be rather than to the way they are. It may therefore be surprising to learn that the "news" about divorce today is that it is no longer news.

Either because other issues so far overshadow it or because it has at last become assimilated—in the sense that provision is made for the problems it raises and therefore consensus with respect to it achieved—or because of both, divorce per se has ceased to be a salient issue in the United States.[1] All jurisdictions make provision for divorce and all permit a variety of grounds for it. There is relatively little heat in whatever current discussion of divorce there is. We seem, in brief, to have come to terms with it.

Assimilation does not mean that there is not widespread concern about marital breakdown, especially with respect to children if they are involved; but the old disapproval of divorce and the punitive attitude toward those who dissolved their marriages has all but disappeared. Nor does acceptance imply that the wrenching of relationships, which divorce sanctions, is actually encouraged or that it is rewarded. It is not likely that divorce will ever become matter-of-fact, nor that it will ever become painless or casual and nonchalant. Not many women will ever agree that divorce can be fun. It will probably always be an extremely painful experience for most people, as breaking close ties always is, even outside of marriage. Assimilation means only that we recognize its inevitability in many cases and try to mitigate some of its worst consequences.

The process of assimilation is not complete as yet; but the general outlines are becoming clear. As recently as the 1950s, sociologists were emphasizing the "unstructured" nature of the postdivorce situation in our society, especially for women. But at the same time, forces were at work, slowly in some cases, rapidly in others, to change the situation. One was practical and had the effect of helping the divorced woman carry her bread-and-butter burdens; one was psychological and had the effect of helping her bear the emotional load.[2] The first supported her by making participation in the labor force more feasible; the other by allaying such emotional stresses and strains as feelings of guilt or blame or shame.

Along with this process of assimilation of divorce, and equally newsworthy, is the new conception of marriage which has emerged along with it as reflected in the substantive and procedural grounds for divorce. By specifying the conditions acceptable for ending a marriage, that is, acceptable grounds, divorce tells us the minimum requirements deemed necessary for a marriage. Other reflections of the new conception of marriage appear in discussions of such practices as premarital and extramarital sexual relations and in the great increase not only in working wives, but also increases in working mothers. The new conception of marriage, thus revealed, holds that people are bound to one another by ties of love, affection, companionship—even duty and obligation—rather than by legal force. The "companionate," as Burgess and Locke noted a generation ago, is taking the place of the "institution."

I wish to explore both of these items of "non-news." The first part of this paper deals with the ways which help divorced people, especially women, meet their new situation, and the second with the new conception of marriage, which divorce practices and procedures now reveal.

II. The Mitigation of Divorce

BREAD-AND-BUTTER PROBLEMS

LABOR FORCE PARTICIPATION. The practical provisions for divorced women in our society did not come in response to their needs. They came, rather, in response to the needs of women in general, especially to those of working women. But in the process of providing for them, women in the status of divorce were also accommodated. If married women could participate in the labor force, so also could divorced women. If the children of married working mothers could be taken care of in day-care centers or by mothers' helpers, so also could the children of divorced mothers. The institutional provision —the day-care center—which makes it possible for a married mother to work, helps the divorced mother as well. In brief, the provision for women in the status of divorce was not designed precisely for that purpose; it came as part of the general change in family life and the life-pattern of women in general.

In a generation when the only place of one sex was in the home, divorce required provision for the support of former wives. Alimony was the legal recognition that a man still had an obligation to support a woman even though he was no longer married to her. In a generation accustomed not only to the labor-force participation of women but also to outside work by wives and even mothers, the concept of alimony (as distinguished from child support) has lost favor.[3] Increasingly, divorced women support themselves by their own employment; less and less do they depend on alimony.

Recent trends in the employment of women are spectacular. One of the most striking phenomena in recent years has been the extraordinary rate at which women return to the labor force after marriage. The overall labor-force participation of women increased from 25.7 per cent in 1940 to 42.0 per cent in 1969; of married women living with husbands, from 14.7 per cent to 36.7 per cent[4]; in 1967, 71.2 per cent of women sixteen years of age and over in the status of divorce were in the labor force.[5]

At the turn of the century the average woman was destined to spend about eleven years in the labor force, all of it before marriage. At mid-century she was destined to spend about twenty-five years in the labor force; almost all of this time is after marriage. The general pattern in labor-force participation became one in which there was a decline when children were small but a return when the last child entered school; the mother was then in her early or mid-thirties. The average (median) divorcee at the time of divorce (31.4 years of age) is at an age when even many still-married women—including mothers—re-enter the labor force. The divorced woman is therefore often doing something she might have done anyway, even without a divorce. (Entering the labor force might have been an alternative or prelude to divorce.) The proportion of women in the divorced status who are in the labor force is, of course, always higher than that of married women with husbands present. But the important fact is that if almost two-fifths of married women with husbands present are in the labor force, the almost three-fourths (71.2 per cent) of women in divorced status who are in the labor force are in no sense in a peculiar or exceptional position.

About a third (32.9 per cent) of white employed women fourteen years of age and over, who were in the status of divorce in 1960, were in clerical occupations; this was the same as for all white employed women. Of employed women, 5.8 per cent were in the status of divorce; this was exactly the same as the proportion of clerical workers who were in this marital status.[6] Here too, then, the divorced woman was in no sense different from women in other marital statuses.

EMPLOYED MOTHERS. Because the pattern of reproduction during the 1940s and 1950s had been one in which children came early in the marriage, there was an increase in the proportion of divorces in which children were involved—from 42 per cent in 1948 to 45.5 per cent in 1953, 60.2 per cent in 1962, and 62.1 per cent in 1966.[7] As a result, both the total number of children involved in divorce and the average number per divorce have been rising. The total number doubled between 1953 (330,000) and 1966 (669,000). The average number of children per divorce increased by about a third (0.85 in 1953 and 1.34 in 1966).[8] The presence of these children enormously complicates the postdivorce adjustment of the mother, who is usually given custody of the children.[9]

The increase in the number of children involved in divorce just happened to coincide with an increase in labor-force participation by mothers in general. "Few, if any, single changes in family life have as profoundly affected so many families in so few years as the movement of mothers into paid employment. . . . Neither the general public nor social scientists were prepared for reports which began to appear in 1955 and the following years that more than a third of the mothers of school-age children were employed."[10] The proportion of married women with children under eighteen who were in the labor force more than quadrupled between 1940 and 1967, from 8.6 per cent to 38.2 per cent. The proportion of mothers who are in the labor force has increased about 1 percentage point per year since 1948.[11] For the most part, care of the children of working mothers was provided by mother-substitutes hired by the mothers themselves, and, for the most part, the mothers were satisfied with it.[12]

But as the number of working mothers rose, especially among low-income families—and women in divorced status are in low-income brackets with a median income in 1960 of $2640—the provision for child care came to be increasingly seen as a community function. Among social workers a movement for making such care available, either at child-care centers or at home by the new profession of "mothers' helpers," grew. Although such facilities were far from adequate in the 1970s, they were on their way to becoming standard services. Here again, then, provision for working mothers in general had the effect of serving the needs of women in the status of divorce also.

LIVING ARRANGEMENTS. One of the restraints on divorce which used to be cited as a deterrent was the absence of suitable living arrangements for divorced women. Unmarried women in earlier days were the maiden aunts living in their brother's or sister's home and so, also, presumably, would a divorced woman have to be. The problem of living arrangements per se is no longer a deterrent to divorce (if, in fact, it ever really was). In 1960 practically all women in the status of divorce (96.1 per cent) were, like practically all other women, living in households. Only a fifth of them (20.1 per cent) were relatives of the head of the household. (Only 13.4 per cent had gone home to mother.) Two thirds (66.6 per cent) were either themselves heads of households (37.2 per cent) or living as primary individuals (29.3 per cent).[13]

SOCIAL LIFE. Not really a bread-and-butter problem, but related in a way, has been the problem of social life for those living in the status of divorce. In a society which tends to organize social life on the basis of couples, the man or woman, but especially the woman, without a spouse is in an awkward position. Here again the divorced woman's problem results not from her status per se. Widowed and unmarried women have the same problem. It is a result of singleness, not of divorced status. Even here institutional provision is coming to be made on a do-it-yourself basis.

Parents Without Partners, Inc., for example, organized in 1957 and incorporated in 1958, is composed mainly of divorced persons. The preamble of its constitution shows its character:

> . . . The single parent in our society is isolated to some degree. The difficulties of providing both for ourselves and our children a reasonable equivalent of normal family life, is increased by that isolation. The established pattern of community life lacks both means of communication and institutions to enable us to resolve our special problems and find normal fulfillment.
>
> Therefore, in the conviction that we can achieve this and through working together, through the exchange of ideas, and through the mutual understanding, help and companionship which we find with one another, we have established Parents Without Partners, Inc. to further our common welfare and the well-being of our children.[14]

In brief, so far as such practical concerns as labor-force participation and living arrangements were con-

cerned, the women in the status of divorce were in no
way marked, peculiar, or disadvantaged. As our society
worked out an overall accommodation to the new life
career-patterns of women in general, it included the divorced woman along with all the others. Provision for
supplying a satisfying social life was also being made.
Divorced women still suffer from a truncated social life
which is based on married couples; but even here, progress is being made.

Guilt, Shame, and Blame

Along with these bread-and-butter changes have come
others more directly and exclusively relevant to the
women in divorced status. They are attitudinal and ideo-
logical and their general effect is to mitigate against feelings of guilt, blame, or shame in connection with divorce.

Attitudinal Changes: Public Opinion Polls. One
of the crudest indexes of this attitudinal change is supplied by popular polls. In the United States in 1936, 77
per cent of the respondents did not think divorce should
be made easier in their state; in 1945, about 66 per cent
seemed to be in this category, 35 per cent feeling divorce
laws were not strict enough and 31 per cent considering
them fair.[15] Polls are, however, very crude and especially so in this case where the formulation of the question differed at the two points in time. Today, polls
would almost certainly show acceptance by even larger
proportions.

Ideology of the Avant-Garde. More subtle is an
analysis by Melvin Tumin, which illuminates the contribution of the vanguard in directing attitudinal
changes. He points out that some social problems are
more popular with theorists than others; they like them
better. He asks why, for example, sociologists are "almost uniformly against poverty, mental illness, and ra-

cial discrimination . . . somewhat less than uniformly against war, and in some important sense . . . *for* such things as divorce, adultery, prostitution, crime, delinquency, and interracial disorders."[16] He notes, for example, that in the case of some problems, including divorce: ". . . sociological analyses . . . often show either a cool detachment and implied lack of concern about the problematic aspects . . . ordinarily attributed to them by the laymen of our society; or sociologists tend to display an almost whimsical kind of affection, guided by a thoroughly sympathetic understanding of how people could get involved in these normally disapproved patterns of behavior. Sometimes the attitude is not only 'Well, what could you expect, given the situation of these people and the structure of society?' but also includes a kind of militant applause for these types of reactions to the implied malfunctioning of the society."[17] Again, "when it comes to divorce . . . we often imply that sociologically speaking, we are a lucky society to experience only as little of these matters as we do."[18] He reminds us that we are very adroit in locating positive functions for divorce and the other favored problems. "Divorce and adultery are simply evil-sounding terms for expressions of spirit that rise above the ordinary limitations of unjustified normative restraints. . . . In effect, then, I am contending we like some problems more than others because we don't think they are really problems. . . . We see them as indirect expressions of laudable human spirit and verve and honesty or straightforwardness breaking through the hypocritical bounds of our ordinary norms . . . [and] we tacitly applaud these problems."[19] Specifically with respect to divorce: ". . . we rarely deplore [it] because we feel it is not only natural and expectable but a rather good institution, all things considered. Our tendency to press for far more liberal divorce laws is evidence in point. Our informal and perhaps unjustified sneers at marriage counseling also testify to our endorsement of the importance of the freedom to divorce."[20]

The shock value of Tumin's analysis should not distract us from recognition of its validity. It is true that social and behavioral scientists tend to find important functional values in divorce and in this sense their thinking constitutes an *apologia* for it.

RESEARCH. Much of the research related to divorce tends to come up with findings that mitigate its seriousness both for the individuals involved and for society as a whole. Thus a very considerable research literature leads to the conclusion that children in conflicted homes suffer more than children in divorced homes.[21] To a woman concerned about the effect of divorce on her children, such findings are reassuring and guilt-assuaging.

The research on "causes" of divorce has been in the direction of also relieving feelings of shame. In general, two approaches have tended to vie for acceptance. One characterized psychologists, the other, sociologists. There was evidence to support both.

The most extreme form of the psychological approach was that represented by Edmund Bergler who insisted that "divorce won't help." Some people, he argued, were incapable of sustaining a marital relationship. Divorce and remarriage meant only the replaying of the old record on a different instrument. The only cure was psychoanalysis to remove the basic flaw which, in effect, required divorce. The alleged defect might range from a relatively manageable neurosis to a full-blown psychosis.[22]

Less extreme, but still, however subtly, shaming in effect, was the school of thought represented by Lewis Terman. He introduced the concept of *marital aptitude*. Some people, he pointed out, were quite normal, even above normal, in most respects, but they lacked the interests required for domesticity. He developed an instrument for the measurement of marital aptitude based on his own researches. And, sure enough, among his subjects, those who rated low in marital aptitude had a higher divorce rate than those who rated high.[23]

Both the Bergler and the Terman approaches looked to the individual for causes—and found them. The school of thought represented by the sociologists Burgess and Cottrell looked for causes in the relationship itself, in what might be called the "team factor." Homogamy and heterogamy were among the variables they emphasized. The approaches were not mutually exclusive. Thus Bergler also looked into the relationship, but he insisted that it was impossible for one partner to be normal; neurotics had an unfailing instinct that led them to seek as mates the neurotics they needed for their own neurosis. Burgess and Cottrell, like Terman, also examined the personalities of their subjects, noting especially the conventional aspects of socialization. All researchers were looking for factors which made some people "divorce-prone"; they just looked for different things.

There was evidence for both schools of thought. If one examines people in the status of divorce at any one time, the catalog of pathologies is impressive. Their longevity is relatively low; mortality and morbidity—including alcoholism—rates are high. So also are mental illness and suicide rates. Granted that some of the disabilities result from rather than cause the divorce—for rates are high for the widowed population also, though not as high as those for the divorced—not all can be so considered. Especially since further evidence for lack of marital aptitude among the divorced comes also in the form of unsuccessful remarriage, which seems to buttress Bergler's dictum. It is hard to escape the feeling that in this population the incidence of pathologies of one kind or another is high.[24] Research of this kind tended to raise doubts of personal adequacy among the divorced; their sense of failure was deepened; they were shamed by it.

We now know the evidence was defective. One major defect lay in the fact that it was based on persons currently in the status of divorce. Another was that in emphasizing the failures among the remarried, it did not report the successes among them. Divorced persons who remain in divorced status may, indeed, be victims of pathologies which make them unfit for marriage; but most divorced persons remarry,[25] and are therefore not represented in the population currently in divorced status. And although it is true that their divorce rate is higher than for those in first marriages, a majority of the remarriages of divorced persons succeed as well as first marriages.[26] There was nothing wrong with them in their first marriage except a team factor. They were neither psychotic nor neurotic; they were not lacking in marital aptitude: they were simply married to the wrong mates. Given congenial or compatible mates, they were quite able to sustain a good marital relationship. At any rate, divorce was nothing to be ashamed of. This kind of research on the factors associated with divorce, like that on the effects of divorce on children, had the result, if not necessarily the intent, of easing the emotional load of the divorced.[27]

No amount of research can wholly eliminate the emotional price exacted by divorce. All it can do is help lighten the load. The sense of failure, which many divorced persons experience, is hard to relieve; only success can overcome it. But research can mitigate the accompanying feeling of guilt and shame.

In addition to the reassuring effect of research on divorced persons themselves, the relevance of research lies in the effect it has on those who have to deal with divorce—as counselors, lawyers, judges—and who lean heavily on its results, as lobbyists do also. We stated above that the assimilation of divorce into the social system did not mean that it was actively encouraged, certainly not that it was positively championed. Still, the net effect of current trends is clearly in that direction.

THE CONCEPT OF THE NO-FAULT DIVORCE. Perhaps the trend which contributes most to the mitigation of the trauma of divorce is one in the direction of revamping the theoretical and moral structure on which divorce procedures have been based. In the past, the conceptualization of divorce was in terms of a battle between an innocent party and a guilty one. This so-called adversary theory defined divorce action as one in which one party had to be vilified and the other—usually the wife—had to be proved blameless and grievously wronged. In order to assess blame, the unspeakable secrets of the marriage had to be revealed to the public. Everyone could feel the shame; two miserable people could experience guilt.

The adversary theory of divorce still prevails in theory, but it is so contrary to the current trends in thinking about marriage that in actual practice it is greatly mollified.[28] Procedural requirements soft-pedal the public display of dirty linen. Some jurisdictions require reconciliation attempts which must, of necessity, play down blame and emphasize understanding. The whole tenor of current court procedures is in the direction of making divorce psychologically and emotionally easier by robbing it of the stigma of blame. Divorce, it is felt, should not be punitive but, if possible, even therapeutic.[29]

There is now a movement to replace the received, but long since outgrown, adversary theory with one more conformable to the exigencies of the current scene so that the charades which are designed to circumvent the theory will no longer be necessary. Indicative of this trend in judicial and legal thought is the work of a special committee on divorce of the National Conference of Commissioners on Uniform State Laws. In 1967 the Ford Foundation made a grant to this conference to look into the whole matter of updating family law. Robert Levy was charged with preparing a monograph on divorce legislation. After a prodigious survey and analysis of the relevant legal and sociological literature on the subject, he recommended a set of criteria or specifications which, on the basis of his research, a uniform law should meet, including:

> Of all the currently feasible alternative approaches to the grounds for divorce, the "breakdown of marriage" notion has the fewest drawbacks, and the risks the approach entails can be minimized by adding specific legislative provisions directed at those risks. Although some provisions to safeguard the economic welfare of the wife and of children of the family may be needed, the protective devices should not include authorizing the judge to deny a divorce to which the party or parties would otherwise be entitled. Nor should the judge be given any "general discretion" to deny a divorce on social policy grounds.[30]

The net effect of these recommendations so far as divorce itself is concerned—quite aside from all the support and custodial provisions that must be made—is to reduce it to a legal recognition that a marriage has in fact broken down. Proof of such a breakdown need be no more than separation. If two people cannot bear to live with one another—or, indeed, if one cannot bear to live with the other—that in itself proves that a marriage no longer exists. The reasons why they cannot live together is of no concern to the world; it is no one's business but theirs.

On the basis of these recommendations, a uniform law was drawn up to serve as a pattern for the several states in the hope that in time they would enact one as similar to the model as their local situation warranted. If or when they do, the goal of a no-fault divorce would be achieved.

No one, we repeat again, can take the sting or heartache out of divorce. That can perhaps never be institutionalized, as bereavement can. The circumstances of divorce do not lend themselves to simple rites of passage which make possible a once-for-all change in personal relations. But, by and large, divorce is no longer, at least in modern social circles, an unprepared-for event, one that leaves those involved directly or indirectly in awkward positions, and not knowing what to do. It can be taken in stride. The divorced woman—with or without children—has a great deal of company as she enters the labor force; and for both her and her former husband the load of guilt, shame, and blame are greatly mitigated.

III. Accepted and Alleged Grounds for Divorce as Indicators of a New Conception of Marriage

Part and parcel of the attitudinal changes with respect to divorce is the emergence, noted previously, of a new conception of marriage itself, which they reflect. Divorce (like adultery, insanity, or drunkenness) is a legal rather than a psychological concept. As such it is a process of changing the legal obligations and privileges of a man and a woman toward one another. It is simply a way of permitting them to renege on a promise, of releasing them from a commitment. It tells us little or nothing about the breakdown of the relationship; but it does tell us how a society thinks about the relationship. Thus the grounds accepted for divorce give us some insight, if only in a negative way, into the conception of marriage held in any given society. Changes in laws are usually very slow in coming about; often they are reflections of *faits accomplis* rather than blueprints or plans for the future. The grounds accepted for divorce in most American jurisdictions have not changed drastically for decades; what does change is the interpretation of the grounds and ease of proving them to a court.

Monogamic marriage as institutionalized in the West specifies that by and large it should be a lifelong com-

mitment to one partner; the partners must promise to remain together till death do them part. Divorce, by
specifying the exceptions which are permitted, the conditions which abrogate the promise short of death, and
the grounds on which the relationship may be dissolved,
makes clear what people have a right to expect and what
they do not have to accept. Provision for divorce does
not, of course, forbid people to endure anything. No
society requires that divorces be sought or granted simply
because grounds exist. If a woman is willing to endure
drunkenness, infidelity, cruelty, or what-have-you, the
law does not compel her to sue for divorce; it will not
force one on her. The law is permissive rather than com-
pulsive. Fortunately so, perhaps, since conditions which
some court somewhere would accept as grounds for divorce probably occur at some time or another in almost
every marriage. If the mere existence of adultery, for example, required divorce, then more than half of all
marriages would end in divorce.[31] One of the partners,
theoretically *not* both, must want a divorce before it will
be granted. Obviously, many partners do not want divorce even when grounds are present.

But by providing divorce as an alternative, the law
specifies the options available for those who do want a
divorce. Four kinds of grounds are especially indicative
of the conception of marriage which now prevails as il-
lustrative of what is not acceptable: adultery, cruelty,
incompatibility, and voluntary separation.

ADULTERY. The almost universal acceptance of adultery as a ground for divorce makes clear that spouses
have a right to demand sexual monopoly from their partners. Sex favors are an exclusive prerogative. Since there
is hardly any likelihood at all that adultery will soon, or
ever, cease to be an accepted basis for divorce, we may
conclude that even the modern conception of marriage
implies that if a spouse insists on sexual fidelity, the
court will back him (her) up. But what is interesting is

the marked decline in the use of adultery as a basis for divorce. It was once the most widely alleged ground; it is now relatively minor, very few divorces being granted on the basis of it today—only 1.6 per cent in 1963, the last year for which data are available.[32]

Three of the many possible reasons for the decline in alleged adultery in divorce suits are (1) adultery has declined, (2) adultery is no longer minded or objected to by spouses, or (3) adultery is no longer alleged because lesser grounds are more available.

The first must be rejected out of hand. In a chapter whose main thesis has to do with the stability or lack of change in sexual patterns over a period of time, Kinsey and his associates reported enormous increases in extramarital relations among men in a younger as compared with those in an older generation at all ages and at all except the college educational levels.[33] The generational changes appear to be even more striking in the case of wives than of husbands. By the age of forty-five, for example, the proportion of women who had experienced extramarital relations was almost twice as high among women born in the twentieth century (40 per cent) as it was among those born in the nineteenth (21 per cent).[34] Clearly the decline in the allegations of adultery in recent divorce suits does not reflect a decline in extramarital relationships.

The second possible reason suggested above—that spouses today no longer view adultery as seriously as in the past—is documentable in at least some cases if not in most. Of special relevance is the fact that in the half (49 per cent) of the cases reported by Kinsey and his associates in which the husband knew or suspected extramarital relations of the wife, most such incidents (58 per cent) resulted in no difficulty (42 per cent) or only minor difficulty (16 per cent) in the marriages.[35] In some cases, reportedly, they were welcomed. In fact, the Kinsey data showed "a not inconsiderable group of cases in

the sample in which the husbands had encouraged their
wives to engage in extramarital activities."[36] The group
included some abnormal types, to be sure, but "in some
instances it represented a deliberate effort to extend the
wife's opportunity to find satisfaction in sexual relations."[37] John Cuber has also shown high incidence of
adultery in a relatively high socioeconomic class level.[38]
Probably the greatest understatement of the century is
that of Kinsey and his associates that we have in spouse-
encouraged adultery "a notable break with the centuries-
old cultural tradition."

Still there is evidence that fidelity is prized among
young people at least for the duration of a relationship.
Even the relationships not legally sanctioned that are
reported among the avant-garde on some campuses, demand fidelity as long as they last. Such relationships imply a serious, if not necessarily a lifelong commitment.
Frivolous or fly-by-night, or certainly promiscuous, relationships are not approved. If a relationship rests on the
modern design and is voluntary, not dependent on outside sanctions, fidelity may be a matter of course. Outside involvements *ipso facto* mark the end, or at least the
weakening, of the relationship. Apparently a sexual monopoly is more important to young than to older men and
women.[39]

The third reason suggested above—that adultery is not
needed so much as a ground today—rests on a "sociological law" to the effect that (except when divorce is being
used by a spouse for punitive purposes) the grounds alleged in a divorce suit will tend to be the least serious
that a court will accept.[40] Adultery, which involves scan-
dal and a third party, will according to this "law" not be
used if a less serious ground is possible. The fact that in
the nineteenth century adultery was the most common
ground used suggests that courts would not settle for anything but the most serious offense. And, as a corollary,
the fact that, despite the incidence of adultery in at least

half of all marriages today, adultery is the least often alleged among all grounds suggests that other grounds are now acceptable.

As a contrapuntal aspect of this hesitancy to use the ground of adultery in divorce, there is also, perhaps, a hesitancy to admit that adultery meant so much to the "innocent" partner. The attitude toward adultery, which seems to characterize the modern conception of marriage, illustrates well Tumin's thesis presented earlier. The very fact that a researcher undertakes to study the problem scientifically marks the first step in de-tabooing it. He must at once proclaim his disinterested, objective, non-moralistic stance by calling the object of his study extra-marital relations rather than use the legal and pejorative term, adultery. The end result tends to be, as in the case of Kinsey and his associates, either a defense of or even an advocacy of extramarital relations.[41] And some writers go even farther; the "wronged party" is judged to be guilty rather than the adulterer. The man or woman who alleges and proves adultery in a divorce suit can be sure of getting a divorce, but he can also be sure of getting little sympathy from his world. If all marriages in which adultery occurs do not necessarily end in divorce, it is equally true that more than the reported number do. Both facts give us insights into the modern conception of marriage.

CRUELTY. Cruelty was infrequently alleged in the nineteenth century. Courts would not have viewed it as a justifiable basis for dissolving a relationship unless it was extremely serious, threatening life and limb. They would certainly not have been hospitable to the concept of general indignities and mental suffering which are currently included in the concept of cruelty. The allegation of cruelty has increased, however; since 1922 it has been the most commonly alleged ground for divorce; in 1963, the last year for which data are available, 53.7 per cent of all divorce suits were based on it.[42]

As with the case of adultery, we may ask why this increase. Among the reasons we might invoke are the following possibilities: (1) husbands (and wives) have become more cruel in recent years; (2) husbands (and wives) are less willing to take cruelty from one another; (3) there are more occasions for the exercise of cruelty; or (4) it is more acceptable to courts and easier to prove.

Although there are no Kinsey-type data to document a trend in the incidence of marital cruelty, there is no evidence that men and women have—on the basis of any definition—become crueler in this day and age as compared with the past. We may therefore reject the first of the reasons suggested above.

It is, on the other hand, easy to believe that husbands and wives—more especially wives—are less willing to take any cruelty from their spouses than in the past. Standards and expectations are higher. And, as the trends noted above make life for the divorced woman easier, the wife is in a better position to protect herself against cruelty. She has alternatives not formerly open to her. She doesn't have to take cruelty.

The modern conception, furthermore, increases the occasions for cruelty. We referred above to the current conception of marriage as a "companionate" as contrasted to an "institution." The terminology is not correct, but the difference is real. Two patterns of marital relationships have been distinguished: one (corresponding to the "institution") may be labeled a parallel or segregated[43] type of relationship and one an interacting (or "companionate") one. In the parallel pattern, husbands and wives perform their separate but interdependent roles without expecting a great deal of interpersonal interaction. Each knows what is expected in the marital-role pattern and goes about doing it without discussion. There may, of course, be a great deal of affection, but it is not likely to be expressed, certainly not often verbally. Such a pattern tended to prevail in rural America in the nineteenth century; it tends to characterize blue-collar marriage even now.[44] Men today tend to find it more congenial than do women, and the modern conception of marriage leans markedly in the direction of the interactional or "companionate" pattern.

But such a pattern is much more difficult to maintain than the older one.[45] By increasing the volume of interpersonal contact between the spouses, it multiplies the occasions for hurting one another. Women, especially the more highly educated, are not satisfied with token interaction; they want more interpersonal response. Deprivation may very well look to them like cruelty. Both the quality and the quantity of the relationship are vulnerable to charges of cruelty. Thus an increasing number of acts or non-acts may be so defined.

Courts are apparently willing to go along with the new conception of cruelty in marriage and are therefore quite easily convinced. Cruelty is easier to prove than it used to be. From time to time the press regales the public with seemingly trivial evidence of mental cruelty accepted by some court somewhere: the husband did not notice a new dress, the wife was embarrassed by her husband in front of friends, unkind words were spoken. In this respect, courts follow a similar extension of the concept of cruelty now in process in, let us say, the civil rights movement. (The term "police brutality," for example, has come to include verbal acts as well as acts of physical force.) Perhaps no other ground so clearly reflects the changing conception of marriage today as does cruelty. Spouses do not even have to accept unkindness from one another. Our standards of marital relations have risen.

INCOMPATIBILITY. So far only three states—Alaska, New Mexico, and Oklahoma—accept incompatibility, which usually, though not necessarily always, refers to sexual incompatibility as a ground for divorce. It is as though we feared to take this major step in the direction of giving up the concept of blame. At any rate, despite the fact that marriage counselors find sexual incompatibility basic in many divorces, it is not specified as such as a ground in most jurisdictions. We do not yet view sexual compatibility—short of impotence and frigidity—as an intrinsic factor in marriage; thus no jurisdiction openly concedes that its absence justifies divorce. It seems that if a man can perform the sex act and if his wife is capable of responding, neither is entitled to a divorce no matter how unsatisfactory the sexual relationship between them is to either or both.

In actual practice, though, under some other rubric, grounds are found to cover this particular circumstance and the marriage is permitted to dissolve.

In one way or another, however, incompatibility is probably accepted as grounds for divorce, either by collusion or by way of some other legal dodge of one kind or another. Cruelty is probably the commonest cover for incompatibility. Most legislators have not yet been ready to recognize the new conception of marriage by making incompatibility the basis for divorce. In the jurisdictions which do accept incompatibility, it is very extensively used. In New Mexico, for example, it is used in seven-eighths of all divorces.[46]

VOLUNTARY SEPARATION: THE CONCEPT OF THE NO-FAULT DIVORCE. The final step toward the modern conception of marriage, acceptance of divorce by mutual consent, in which no grounds would be necessary, nothing would have to be proved, no villains or victims would be required, but only proof that the marriage had, in effect, ended—is now in process of being taken. If or when states accept the model no-fault divorce law proposed by the National Conference of Commissioners on Uniform State Laws, marriage will become completely voluntary, lasting legally only so long as it meets the needs of both partners.

In the meanwhile, voluntary separation is a near approximation and is available in twenty-one jurisdictions. Overall, it is not widely used; but in some jurisdictions it is used as a step in most divorces.[47] The acceptance of voluntary separation as a justification for divorce, that is divorce by mutual consent or no-fault divorce, is perhaps the most revolutionary change in the whole concept of marriage. It means, in effect, that the partners do not really have a lifelong commitment, that the relationship has to last only as long as both partners want it to last. They do not have to prove anything, not even incompatibility. Even if only one partner wants it, as Goode has shown in his analysis of the strategy of divorce, it would be possible, for if either partner really wants a divorce badly enough, he can almost always maneuver the other into accepting it also.[48] It is perhaps fear of precisely this hazard that makes legislators hesitate to legitimize mutual consent. But if one party is adamant in his or her insistence on divorce, the marriage has actually broken down; living together under legal duress does not reconstitute the marriage. The no-fault divorce recognizes this bitter reality.

The apparent reluctance of legislators to increase the grounds for divorce, associated with the apparent willingness of courts to accept more circumstances as justifying it, illustrates the process by which changes in marriage are institutionalized with a minimum of shock. We have here an almost classic example of growing popular change, as distinguished from enacted change.[49]

Trends

The relevant objective facts about divorce trends in the United States can be summarized briefly. The long-time trend over many decades was up, reaching a peak in 1946 when many hasty wartime marriages were, apparently, dissolved; after that, it fluctuated around 9 per thousand (based on number of married women fifteen years and over) or 2 per thousand (based on the total population).[50] In 1958 it reached a postwar low (8.9 and 2.1), but since that time it has risen. In 1968 there were 2.9 divorces per one thousand of the population.[51]

It is hazardous, however, to project future trends on the basis of the past. Quite equivocal conclusions may be arrived at on the basis of what we know from past research. If, for example, we based our projection on one set of data, we could with some confidence look for a declining rate. We know, to illustrate, that a low divorce rate has been associated with high levels of education, with the more prestigeful occupations, with good income. An increasing proportion of the population does have higher

FIGURE I

Divorce Rates, United States, 1920–68 (Source: Monthly Vital Statistics Report, Public Health Service, January 6, 1969)

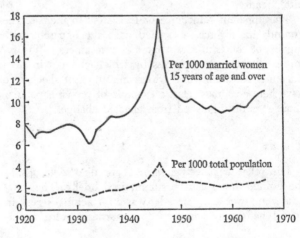

education, white-collar occupations, high incomes. We should, therefore, project a declining divorce rate.

On the other hand, we know that, in the past, divorces declined during depressions and rose in times of prosperity. Prosperity, or, to use the current term, "affluence," is confidently predicted for the future and should, if the past is a guide, bring with it more divorce. As should also the trend toward the companionate or interactional pattern of marriage, which makes such great demands on the relationship. There are, in brief, reasonable bases for projecting contradictory, perhaps mutually canceling, trends.

Quite aside from the hazards involved in projecting future trends on the basis of past records is the fact that many variables do not seem to have the same significance now as in the past. Religious differences, for example, which past studies have tended to find related to marital instability do not seem to play a large part in divorce at the present time.[52] Nor do education, occupation, and income seem to have the same meaning as in the past.

Further, nothing is more frequently commented on than the nihilistic, even anarchistic attitudes which characterize—even when they do not typify—the college population today. On the more avant-garde campuses, young people live together in serious, responsible relationships without benefit of clergy or city hall, faithful to one another as long as the relationship itself lasts. It is hard to imagine a generation, which resists even minor restrictions on its freedom by academic rules, accepting major restrictions on its freedom by legislated rules. They jealously, as well as zealously, fight to protect their private lives from outwardly imposed controls. It is not hard to imagine them picketing a legislature that attempted to make divorce difficult.[53] Still, Kinsey and his associates reported a probable decline in adultery in his younger, as contrasted with his older, college-educated-male generation.

No more than religion and education, are occupation and income the same kinds of variables as they were in the past. They could once be taken as measures of social class in the sense of class cultures. In these different class cultures, sex *mores* were quite different.[54] Adultery, for example, was accepted, even expected, by young wives in the lower classes.[55] Since sex patterns seem to be well established by adolescence, should we expect upwardly mobile men and women to bring this pattern with them when they enter the middle-class culture by way of occupation and income?

David Mace is of the opinion that we are well on the way to a general consensual, if not legal, acceptance of a new kind of marriage; a serious, responsible, long-time relationship not necessarily, like legal marriage, based on a lifetime commitment but on personal compatibility. Such relationships do not contemplate the birth of children. He does not see these relationships as supplanting marriage as now conceived, but they would be available as acceptable alternatives for those who preferred them. What increase in this kind of relationship would do to divorce rates remains to be seen. It is conceivable that as such relationships became more common, legal ones would be entered into only by those who did, in fact, want a lifelong commitment.

Difficult as it is, in brief, to project trends on the basis of the past, it is almost certain that there will not be a reversal in the current trend toward the assimilation of divorce. Its acceptance is a *fait accompli*. It will, no doubt, continue to be regretted. Though defended, it is not likely to be positively prized. It can be expected to become even more matter-of-fact, noted by state and by associates, but little more. The whole trend in current social life is in the direction of demands for *laissez faire* in personal relationships.[56] The issues that do arise will tend to be in the direction of making divorce as non-

traumatic as possible for partners and for children. The
idea of forcing people to remain together is repugnant
to the present world view.

FIGURE 2

Aggregate Articles on Divorce: Per Year, 1900–65

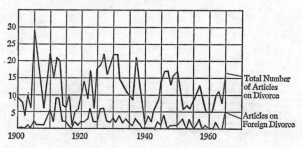

II
Process

There is a legal aspect, a personal aspect, and a community aspect to every divorce. All must be carefully investigated. Bohannan's article analyzes the six aspects of the personal experience of divorce (including the legal experience and the community experience) that every divorcee must undergo in one order or another and at one intensity or another. Doctor Miller examines the psychic reasons that communities and friends react as they do to divorces.

2

The Six Stations
of Divorce

PAUL BOHANNAN

Divorce is a complex social phenomenon as well as a complex personal experience. Because most of us are ignorant of what it requires of us, divorce is likely to be traumatic: emotional stimulation is so great that accustomed ways of acting are inadequate. The usual way for the healthy mind to deal with trauma is to block it out, then let it reappear slowly, so it is easier to manage. The blocking may appear as memory lapses or as general apathy.

On a social level we do something analogous, not allowing ourselves to think fully about divorce as a social problem. Our personal distrust of the emotions that surround it leads us to consider it only with traditional cultural defenses. Our ignorance masquerades as approval or disapproval, as enlightenment or moral conviction.[1]

The complexity of divorce arises because at least six things are happening at once. They may come in a different order and with varying intensities, but there are at least these six different experiences of separation. They are the more painful and puzzling as personal experiences because society is not yet equipped to handle any of them well, and some of them we do not handle at all.

I have called these six overlapping experiences (1) the emotional divorce, which centers around the problem of the deteriorating marriage; (2) the legal divorce, based on grounds; (3) the economic divorce, which deals with money and property; (4) the coparental divorce, which deals with custody, single-parent homes, and visitation; (5) the community divorce, surrounding the changes of friends and community that every divorcee experiences; and (6) the psychic divorce, with the problem of regaining individual autonomy.

The first visible stage of a deteriorating marriage is likely to be what psychiatrists call emotional divorce. This occurs when the spouses withhold emotion from their relationship because they dislike the intensity or ambivalence of their feelings. They may continue to work together as a social team, but their attraction and trust for one another have disappeared. The self-regard of each is no longer reinforced by love for the other. The emotional divorce is experienced as an unsavory choice between giving in and hating oneself and domineering and hating oneself. The natural and healthy "growing apart" of a married couple is very different. As marriages mature, the partners grow in new directions, but also establish bonds of ever greater interdependence. With emotional divorce, people do not grow together as they grow apart—they become, instead, mutually antagonistic and imprisoned, hating the vestiges of their dependence. Two people in emotional divorce grate on each other because each is disappointed.

In American society, we have turned over to the courts the responsibility for formalizing the dissolution of such a marriage. The legislature (which in early English law usurped the responsibility from the church, and then in the American colonies turned it over to the courts) makes the statutes and defines the categories into which every marital dispute must be thrust if legal divorce is possible. Divorce is not "legalized" in many societies but may be done by a church or even by contract. Even in our own society, there is only one thing that a divorce court can do that cannot be done more effectively some other way —establish the right to remarry. As long as your spouse lives, you cannot legally remarry until you are legally divorced. Because of the legal necessity of this one aspect, several other aspects of divorce are customarily taken care of by lawyers and judges. However, legal divorce itself does nothing but create remarriageability.

The economic divorce must occur because in Western countries husband and wife are an economic unit. Their unity is recognized by the law. They can—and in some states must—own property as a single "legal person." While technically the couple is not a corporation, they certainly have many of the characteristics of a legal corporation. At the time the household is broken up by divorce, an economic settlement must be made, separating the assets of the "corporation" into two sets of assets, each belonging to one person. This is the property settlement. Today it is vastly complicated by income tax law. A great deal of knowledge is required to take care of the tax positions of divorced persons—and if the lawyer does not have this knowledge, he must get assistance. Although the judges may ratify the property settlement, they usually do not create it unless the principals and lawyers cannot do so.

The coparental divorce is necessary if there are children. When the household breaks up, the children have to live somewhere. Taking care of the children requires complex arrangements for carrying out the obligations of parents.

All divorced persons suffer more or less because their community is altered. Friends necessarily take a different view of a person during and after divorce—he ceases to be a part of a couple. Their own inadequacies, therefore, will be projected in a new way. Their fantasies are likely to change as they focus on the changing situation. In many cases, the change in community attitude—and perhaps people too—is experienced by a divorcee as ostracism and disapproval. For many divorcing people, the divorce from community may make it seem that nothing in the world is stable.

Finally comes the psychic divorce. It is almost always last, and always the most difficult. Indeed, I have not found a word strong or precise enough to describe the difficulty or the process. Each partner to the ex-marriage, either before or after the legal divorce—usually after, and sometimes years after—must turn himself or herself again into an autonomous social individual. People who have been long married tend to have become socially part of a couple or a family; they lose the habit of seeing themselves as individuals. This is worse for people who married in order to avoid becoming autonomous individuals in the first place.

To become an individual again, at the center of a new community, requires developing new facets of character. Some people have forgotten how to do it—some never learned. The most potent argument against teen-age marriages is that they are likely to occur between people who are searching for independence but avoiding autonomy. The most potent argument against hurried remarriage is the same: avoidance of the responsibilities of autonomy.

Divorce is an institution that nobody enters without great trepidation. In the emotional divorce, people are likely to feel hurt and angry. In the legal divorce, people often feel bewildered—they have lost control, and events sweep them along. In the economic divorce, the reassignment of property and the division of money (there is *never* enough) may make them feel cheated. In the parental divorce they worry about what is going to happen to the children; they feel guilty for what they have done. With the community divorce, they may get angry with their friends and perhaps suffer despair because there seems to be no fidelity in friendship. In the psychic divorce, in which they have to become autonomous again, they are probably afraid and are certainly lonely. However, the resolution of any or all of these various six divorces may provide an elation of victory that comes from having accomplished something that had to be done and having done it well. There may be ultimate satisfactions in it.

Divorce American style is a bewildering experience—so many things are happening at once. We have never been taught what we are supposed to do, let alone what we are supposed to feel. I know a divorced man who took great comfort in the fact that one of his business associates asked him, when he learned of his divorce, "Do I feel sorry for you or do I congratulate you?" He thought for a moment and said—out of bravado as much as conviction—"Congratulate me." It was, for him, the beginning of the road back.

The Emotional Divorce and the Problem of Grief

One of the reasons it feels so good to be engaged and newly married is the rewarding sensation that, out of the whole world, you have been selected. One of the reasons that divorce feels so awful is that you have been deselected. It punishes almost as much as the engagement and the wedding are rewarding.

The chain of events and feelings that lead up to divorce are as long and as varied as the chain of events that lead up to being selected for marriage. The difference is that the feelings are concentrated in the area of the weak points in the personality rather than the growing points of the personality.

Almost no two people who have been married, even for a short time, can help knowing where to hit each other if they want to wound. On the other hand, any two people—no matter who they are—who are locked together in conflict have to be very perceptive to figure out what the strain is really all about. Marital fights occur in every healthy marriage. The fact of health is indicated when marital disputes lead to a clarification of issues and to successful extension of the relationship into new areas. Difficulties arise only when marital conflict is sidetracked to false issues (and sometimes the discovery of just what issue is at stake may be, in itself, an adequate conclusion to the conflict), or when the emotional pressures are shunted to other areas. When a couple are afraid to fight over the real issue, they fight over something else—and perhaps never discover what the real issue was.

Two of the areas of life that are most ready to accept such displacement are the areas of sex and money. Both sex and money are considered worthwhile fighting over in American culture. If it is impossible to know or admit what a fight is all about, then the embattled couple may cast about for areas of displacement, and they come up with money and sex, because both can be used as weapons. Often these are not the basis of the difficulties, which lie in unconscious or inadmissible areas.

These facts lead a lot of people to think that emotional divorce occurs over money or over sexual incompatibility just because that is where the overt strife is allowed to come out. Often, however, these are only camouflage.

MONEY AND THE EMOTIONAL DIVORCE. One of the most tenacious ideas from our early training is "the value of a dollar." When in the larger society the self is reflected in possessions, and when money becomes one mode of enhancing the self—then we have difficulty with anybody who either spends it too lavishly or sits on it more tightly than we do.

Money is a subject about which talk is possible. Most

middle-class couples do talk about money; most of them, in fact, make compromises more or less adequate to both. But in all cases, money management and budgeting are endlessly discussed in the American household. If communication becomes difficult, one of the first places that it shows up is in absence of knowledge about the other person's expenditures.

I interviewed one divorced woman who blamed her ex-husband's spending practices and attitude toward money as a major factor in their divorce. She said that he bought her an expensive car and asked her to leave it sitting outside the house when she was not driving it. *She* announced that *he* could not afford it. He asked her to join a golf club. She refused, although she was a good golfer and liked to play—because *she* told him *he* could not afford it. Whenever he wanted to use her considerable beauty and accomplishments to reflect a little credit on himself for being able to have captured and kept such a wife, she announced that he could not afford it. After the divorce, it continued. Then one day, in anger, she telephoned him to say that she was tired of making sacrifices—this year she was going to take the children on a transcontinental vacation and that he would simply have to pay for the trip. He did not explode; he only thought for a minute and said that he guessed that would be all right, and that he would whittle down his plans for the children's vacation with him, so that it would come within the budget.

This woman told this story without realizing what she had revealed: that her husband was not going to push himself or them into bankruptcy; that he did indeed know how much things cost, and that he could either afford or otherwise manage what he wanted to give her. There was doubtless a difference of opinion about money —she, it appears, preferred to save and then spend; he preferred, perhaps, to spend and then pay. She, for reasons I cannot know from one extended interview, did not recognize his feelings. She *did* announce to him, every time that he wanted to spend money on her, that he was inadequate. I suspect it was her own fear that she would let him down. Without knowing it, she was attacking him where it hurt him and where her housewifely virtue could be kept intact, while she did not have to expose herself or take a chance.

I am not saying that there are not spendthrift husbands or wives. I am saying that if differences that lie beyond money cannot be discussed, then money is a likely battleground for the emotional divorce.

SEX AND THE EMOTIONAL DIVORCE. Among the hundreds of divorcees I have talked to, there is a wide range of sexual attitudes. There were marriages in which sexual symptoms were the first difficulties to be recognized by the couple. There were a few in which the sexual association seemed the only strong bond. I know of several instances in which the couple met for a ceremonial bout of sexual intercourse as the last legitimate act before their divorce. I have a newspaper clipping that tells of a man who, after such a "last legal assignation," murdered his wife before she became his ex-wife. And I know one divorce that was denied because, as the judge put it, he could not condone "litigation by day and copulation by night."

Usually, when communication between the spouses becomes strained, sexual rapport is the first thing to go. There are many aspects to this problem: sexual intercourse is the most intimate of social relationships, and reservations or ambivalences in the emotions are likely to show up there (with unconscious conflicts added to conscious ones). The conflicts may take the extreme form of frigidity in women, impotence in men. They may take the form of adultery, which may be an attempt to communicate something, an unconscious effort to improve the marriage itself. It may be an attempt to humiliate the spouse into leaving. Adultery cannot sensibly be judged without knowing what it means to a specific person and to his spouse in a specific situation. Adultery is a legal ground for divorce in every jurisdiction in the United States, and indeed in most of the record-keeping world.

Because sexuality is closely associated with integration of the personality, it is not surprising that disturbance in the relationship of the spouses may be exposed in sexual symptoms. Except in some cases in which the marriage breaks up within a few weeks or months, however, sexual difficulties are a mode of expression as often as they provide the basic difficulty.

GROWING APART. Married people, like any other people, must continue to grow as individuals if they are not to stagnate. Only by extending themselves to new experiences and overcoming new conflicts can they participate fully in new social relationships and learn new culture. That means that no one, at the time of marriage, can know what the spouse is going to become. Moreover, it means that he cannot know what he himself may become.

Some of this growth of individuals must necessarily take place outside of the marriage. If the two people are willing and able to perceive and tolerate the changes in one another, and overcome them by a growing relationship directly with the other person, then the mutual rewards are very great, and conflicts can be resolved.

Inability to tolerate change in the partner (or to see him as he is) always lies, I think, at the root of emotional divorce. All marriages become constantly more attenuated from the end of the honeymoon period probably until the retirement of the husband from the world of affairs. That is to say, the proportion of the total concern of one individual that can be given to the other individual in the marriage decreases, even though the precise quantity (supposing there were a way to measure it) might become greater. But the ties may become tougher, even as they become thinner.

When this growing apart and concomitant increase in the toughness of the bonds does *not* happen, then people feel the marriage bonds as fetters and become disappointed or angry with each other. They feel cramped by the marriage and cheated by their partner. A break may be the only salvation for some couples.

In America today, our emotional lives are made diffuse by the very nature of the culture with which we are surrounded. Family life, business or professional demands, community pressures—today all are in competition with one another for our time and energies. When that happens, the social stage is set for emotional divorce of individual couples, because the marriage relationship becomes just another competing institution. Sometimes emotional divorce seems scarcely more than another symptom of the diffuseness.

EMOTIONAL DIVORCE AND GRIEF. Emotional divorce results in the loss of a loved object just as fully—but by quite a different route of experience—as does the death of a spouse. Divorce is difficult because it involves a purposeful and active rejection by another person, who, merely by living, is a daily symbol of the rejection. It is also made difficult because the community helps even less in divorce than it does in bereavement.

The natural reaction to the loss of a loved object or person (and sometimes a hated one as well) is grief. The distribution of emotional energy is changed significantly; new frustration must be borne until new arrangements can be worked out. Human beings mourn every loss of meaningful relationship. The degree depends on the amount of emotional involvement. Mourning may be traumatic—and it may, like any other trauma, have to be blocked and only slowly allowed into awareness. Mourning may take several months or years.

Divorce is even more threatening than death to some people, because they have thought about it more, perhaps wished for it more consciously. But most importantly—

there is no recognized way to mourn a divorce. The grief
has to be worked out alone and without benefit of traditional rites, because few people recognize it for what
it is.

When grief gets entangled with all the other emotions
that are evoked in a divorce, the emotional working
through becomes complicated—in a divorce one is very
much on his own.

The Legal Divorce and the Problem of Grounds

Judicial divorce, as it is practiced in the United States
today, is a legal post-mortem on the demise of an intimate
relationship. It originated in Massachusetts in the early
1700s as a means for dealing with the problems that
emotional divorce caused in families, at the same time
that all going households could continue to be based on
holy matrimony. Legal divorce has been discovered and
used many times in the history of the world, but this
particular institution had no precursors in European
history. The historical period in which it developed is
important. In those days it was considered necessary that
the state could profess its interest in the marriage and the
family only in the guise of punishing one of the spouses
for misconduct. Thus, the divorce itself was proclaimed
to be the punishment of the guilty party. Whether divorce as a punishment was ever a commonsensical idea is
a moot point—certainly it is not so today. Yet, our law
still reflects this idea.

Thus, if the state is to grant divorces to "innocent"
spouses as punishment to offending spouses, it must le-
galize certain aspects of the family—must, in fact, establish minimal standards of performance in family roles.
Marriages break down in all societies; we have come, by
state intervention, to solve some of these breakdowns
with the legal institution of divorce. Until very recently,

no country granted its citizens the clear right to divorce, as they have the clear right to marry. The right is always conditional on acts of misbehavior of the spouse, as misbehavior has been legally defined and called "grounds." Whatever the spouse does must be thrust into the categories that the law recognizes before it can be grounds for divorce.

This way of handling divorce has some strange and unintended effects. It has made lawyers into experts in several aspects of divorce; there are no recognized experts in other aspects of divorce. Therefore, lawyers are called upon to assume responsibility for more and more aspects of the institution—and in many they have no training, in others there is no possible legal base from which they can operate. The difficulty in legal divorce in America seems to lie in two related situations: the uncertainty of the population and even of the legal profession about what the lawyers are supposed to do, and the absence of institutions paralleling the legal institutions to handle the non-legal problems.

DIVORCE LAWYERS AND WHAT THEY DO. If you want a physician, you look in the yellow pages and find them noted, most of them with their specialties spelled out. With lawyers it is not so—there is only a list. It is an unfortunate by-product of the ethical commitment of the American Bar Association not to advertise that attorneys cannot list their special competences. It is my opinion that, at least as far as family lawyers are concerned (the only exception now allowed is patent law), this ruling should be changed.

The legal profession is committed to the proposition that any lawyer—or at least any firm of lawyers—should be able to handle any sort of problem. Legally, divorce is indeed a simple matter; that is part of the trouble. Any competent lawyer can indeed write the papers and make the necessary motions. The difficulty comes in the counseling aspect of divorce practice.

Every divorcing person must find his lawyer—and it may be difficult. It may be done through friends, business associates, clergymen, but it is surprisingly often done in the yellow pages. Perhaps there is no other situation in our country today in which a person in emotional distress is so faced with buying a pig in a poke. Clients who are inexperienced may not realize that they can fire a lawyer faster than they can hire him. They worry along with a lawyer they neither like personally nor trust professionally.

Because lawyers are for the most part untrained in family psychology and sociology, and because there is no practice—not even the criminal law—in which they are dealing with people in such states of emotional upset, divorce becomes a "messy" or "dirty" kind of practice— these are their words. In the hierarchy of lawyers by specialties (and there is a rigid and fairly overt hierarchy), the divorce lawyer and criminal lawyer rank approximately at the bottom—allowing, of course, for such considerations as ethics, financial success, social rank, and the like. My own opinion is that the more emotional the problems a lawyer handles, the further down the lawyers' pecking order he ranks. Corporation lawyers are at the top; corporations have no emotions. Divorcees and criminals have little else.

Lawyers also dislike divorce practice because it is not lucrative. Many divorcees think lawyers take advantage and overcharge them. In most divorce cases, the legal fees—both of them—are paid by the husband, and are set by the judge at the time of the divorce hearing. Many lawyers think that the fees that the court sets are ridiculously low—another reason that they do not like to take divorce cases. Many lawyers make additional charges for the many other services they perform for divorcees. Divorce lawyers tend to work on an hourly rate, though probably all of them adjust the rate to the income of their client.

Most divorcees, on the other hand, do not appreciate how much work their lawyers actually put in. Because the court hearing seldom takes more than a few minutes, and because the papers are often not a thick bundle, the assumption is that comparatively little effort went into it. The divorce lawyers I know earn their fees; the good ones always contribute a lot of personal advice, care, and solace without charge.

Many divorce cases do not end when the decree is final. Money must be collected; ex-husbands may use non-payment of alimony as the only sanction they have over ex-wives; financial positions and obligations change. For these and many other reasons, the divorcee may come back to the lawyer sooner or later. One divorced woman summed it up, "Every divorcee needs a good firm of lawyers."

But the greatest difficulty arises from the fact we started with: divorce lawyers are forced, in the nature of the law, to put the "real situation," as they learn it from their clients, into language that the law will accept. If a divorce action is to go to court, it must first be couched in language that the courts are legally permitted to accept. Both marriage counselors and lawyers have assured me that reconciliation is always more difficult after grounds have been discussed and legal papers written than when it is still in the language of "reasons" and personal emotion. Legal language and choice of grounds are the first positive steps toward a new type of relationship with the person one of my informants called "my ex-to-be." Discussion of grounds often amounts, from the point of view of the divorcing person, to listing all the faults that the spouse ever committed, then picking one. Since everyone has faults, this is not difficult to do. (There is an old joke that goes the rounds of divorce lawyers about the conscientious young man who came to his lawyer and said he wanted a divorce, but was not sure he had grounds. The cynical lawyer raised his eyes and asked, "Are you married?")

We all know that grounds and reasons may be quite different. The divorcing person usually feels that he should not "tattle" and selects the "mildest" ground. Yet, every person who institutes a suit for divorce must wonder whether to use "adultery" if in fact it occurred, or to settle for the more noncommittal "mental cruelty." Does one use drunkenness when divorcing an alcoholic? Or desertion? Or does one settle for "incompatibility?"

WHAT THE COURT DOES. The judges in a divorce court are hard-working men who must become accustomed to a veritable chaos of emotional confusion. Some of them do the job well, with great knowledge and commitment. Others feel that they have themselves been sentenced, that no human being should be asked to stand very much of it, and hope to be in some other court soon.

The usual divorce in court takes only a few minutes —sometimes as little as two or three and seldom more than fifteen or twenty. Many divorcees are disturbed to discover this fact, having thought all their grievances would be heard and, perhaps, they would "get some justice." Many report, "It's a weak-kneed system. I don't feel that it really did the job." Others are constantly aware that they perjured themselves—about grounds, about residence, perhaps about facts. Some divorcees feel virtuous for using "mental cruelty" as a ground and tell all their friends "the real reason"—thereby alienating friends. Others take a pragmatic attitude about the legal proceedings: "What do I care? I got what I wanted, didn't I?"

The court action seems short and ineffective at the time—not traumatic. Most divorcees, in retrospect, cannot remember the details of it; in part, I think, because there is little to be remembered. Divorce dockets are crowded in all American cities. Judges do not have time to give each case the thought and time the divorcing parties think it deserves—realizing that one's monumental troubles are not worth the court's time can often act as a restorative, but sometimes as a depressant. Many judges agree that they would like to have more time to make specific investigations and suggestions in each case —to convince themselves that attempts have been made to discover whether these two people should in fact be divorced—whether divorce is a reasonable solution to their problems. Though judges do take time with some cases, most would like to be able to take more.

One of the reasons that the divorce institution is so hard on people is that the legal processes do not provide an orderly and socially approved discharge of emotions that are elicited during the emotional divorce and during the early parts of preparation for the legal processes. Divorces are "cranked out" but divorcees are not "cooled out."

The Economic Divorce and the Problem of Property

The family household is the unit of economic consumption in the United States. As such, middle-class households must have a certain amount of domestic-capital equipment besides personal property such as cars and television sets. In most households, these items "belong to the family," even though they may be legally owned in the name of one of the spouses. There are (at the time of writing) six states in the United States that declare all property owned by either spouse to be "community property" except for what they owned before the marriage and what they inherit. California is the most thorough and noteworthy example of a community-property state; many states are in process of changing their laws—some of them toward stricter community-property principles, some for a "better break" for one partner or the other. Any list is soon out of date.

Behind the idea of fair settlement of property at the

time of divorce is the assumption that a man cannot earn money to support his family if he does not have the moral assistance and domestic services of his wife. The wife, if she works, does so in order to "enhance" the family income (no matter how much she makes or what the "psychic income" to her might be). Therefore, every salary dollar, every patent, every investment, is joint property.

In most states, the property settlement is not recorded in the public records of divorce, so precise information is lacking. However, in most settlements, the wife receives from one-third to one-half of the property. As one sits in a divorce court, however, one realizes that in many divorces the amount of property is so small as to need no settlement or even to cause any dispute. Judges regard settlement as the province of lawyers, and generally agree that the lawyers have not done their jobs if the matter comes to court.

Many wives voluntarily give up their rights to property at the time they become ex-wives. Some are quite irrational about it—"I won't take *anything* from *him!*" Sometimes they think (perhaps quite justly) that they have no moral right to it. Others, of course, attempt to use the property settlement as a means of retaliation. The comment from one of my informants was, "Boy, did I make that bastard pay." It seems to me that irrational motives such as revenge or self-abnegation are more often in evidence than the facts of relative need, in spite of all that judges and lawyers can do.

The property of the household is never, in the nature of household living, separable into two easily discernible parcels. Even in states that lack common-property laws, the *use* of property is certainly common within the household and subject to the rules of the household, of course, but (except for clothes or jewelry or tools) usually not the exclusive property of any specific member of the household. Whose, for example, is the family car?

Whose is the hi-fi? Whose is the second-best bed? And whose is the dog?

ALIMONY. The word "alimony" is derived from the Latin word for sustenance, and ultimately from the verb which means "to nourish" or "to give food to." The prevailing idea behind alimony in America is that the husband, as head of the family, has an obligation to support his wife and children, no matter how wealthy the wife and children may be independently.

At the time of divorce, the alimony rights of the wife are considered to be an extension of the husband's duty to support, undertaken at the time of marriage. Therefore, alimony means the money paid during and after the divorce by the ex-husband to the ex-wife (rarely the other way around).

There is, however, another basis on which some courts in some American jurisdictions have looked on alimony —it can be seen as punishment of the husband for his mistreatment of the wife. Where this idea is found, the wife cannot be entitled to alimony if she is the "guilty party" to the divorce. In most states, the amount of alimony is more or less directly dependent on whatever moral or immoral conduct of the wife may come to the attention of the court. A woman known to be guilty of anything the court considers to be moral misconduct is likely to be awarded less than an "innocent" wife. The law varies widely on these matters; practice varies even more.

The most important thing about the award and payment of alimony is that it is done on the basis of a court order. Therefore, if it is not paid, the offending husband is in contempt of court. The institution of divorce is provided, as we have seen before, with only one formal sanction to insure the compliance of its various parties. And that is the court.

The amount of alimony is set by the court, on the basis of the wife's need and the husband's ability to pay.

Both her education and training and his may be taken into account; the state of health may be relevant. Sometimes the length of the marriage is a consideration—a short period entitling the wife to less alimony. The age of the children, the moral behavior of each spouse, the income tax position—all these things and undoubtedly many more will affect the court's decision about alimony.

Either ex-spouse may petition the court to have alimony arrangements changed, upon any change in either the ex-wife's need or the ex-husband's ability to pay. It cannot, however, be changed on the basis of the postmarital behavior of either party. Some courts listen with sympathy to an ex-husband's request to reduce alimony at the time of his remarriage; almost all alimony is arranged so that it stops entirely at the time of the ex-wife's remarriage.

CHILD SUPPORT. Courts and citizens are both much clearer about child support than they are about alimony. The principle is obvious to all: as long as he is able to do so, the responsibility for supporting children lies with their father. Whether a man is morally and legally obliged to support his children depends only on one factor: his ability to do so. In assessing child support payments, the court looks simply at his ability to pay, including his health, and to the needs of the child. The amount may be set by the court; it is always ratified by the court.

The principles behind the idea of child support are simple. However, the functioning of the child support aspects of the divorce institution are anything but simple. The difficulty arises, again and as usual, because of the lack of sanctions aside from the court, and from the further fact that court action is expensive and usually slow. The father who does not pay the stipulated child support is in contempt of court, and can be brought back into court on that basis. In order to avoid clogging the courts, some states have found various ways in which the payments can be made to the state and forwarded to the mother or other guardian of the children. This, too, is expensive. There seems to be no really adequate means, as yet, of dealing with men who do not make support payments.

Some mothers try to stop the visitation of fathers who do not make support payments—and some courts uphold them. Although most divorced parents realize that "fighting through the children" is harmful to the children, not all succeed in avoiding it.

The Coparental Divorce and the Problem of Custody

The most enduring pain of divorce is likely to come from the coparental divorce. This odd word is useful because it indicates that the child's parents are divorced from each other—not from the child. Children do not always understand this: they may ask, "Can Father divorce *me*?" This is not a silly or naïve question; from the standpoint of the child what was a failure in marriage to the parents is the shattering of his kinship circle.

The children have to go somewhere. And even when both parents share joint legal custody of the child, one parent or the other gets "physical custody"—the right to have the child living with him.

The word "custody" is a double-edged sword. It means "responsibility for the care of" somebody. It also means "imprisonment." The child is in the custody of his parents—the criminal is in the custody of the law. When we deal with the custody of children in divorces, we must see to it that they are "in the care of" somebody, and that the care is adequate—we must also see that the custody is not punitive or restricting.

Legal custody of children entitles the custodial parent to make decisions about their life-styles and the things they can do which are developmentally important to them—educational and recreational and cultural choices. In the common law, the father had absolute property rights over the child—the mother had none, unless she inherited them at the death of the father. About the time judicial divorce was established in America, custody preferences shifted until the two parents were about equal. With the vast increase in the divorce rate in the early third of the twentieth century, the shift continued, giving the mother preference in both legal and physical custody. We rationalize this practice by such ideas as mother love, masculine nature, or the exigencies of making a living.

Custody of the children, once granted to the mother, will be taken away from her by the courts *only* if she can be shown to be seriously delinquent in her behavior *as a mother*. Her behavior *as a wife* may be at stake in granting the divorce or in fixing the amount of the alimony— but not in granting custody. A woman cannot be denied her rights as a mother on the basis of having performed badly as a wife, or even on the basis of her behavior as a divorcee if the children were not threatened physically or morally. Similarly, a man cannot be penalized as a father for his shortcomings as a husband.

The overriding consideration in all cases is that the court takes what action it considers to be "in the best interests of the child." The rights of children as human beings override, in our morality and hence in our law, all rights of the parents as parents, and certainly their rights as spouses. We have absolutely inverted the old common law.

It is generally considered that a child's best interests lie with his own parents—but if they do not, what is called "third-party custody" can be imposed by the court. Courts do not like to separate children from at least one parent—but sometimes there is no alternative "in the best interests of the child."

A man is always, either by statute law or by common

law, obliged to take financial responsibility for his minor children. If there are overriding circumstances that make it impossible for him to work, then that responsibility devolves on their mother. Sometimes a mother refuses her ex-husband the right to support his children as a means to deny him the right to see them—some men accept this, but few would be forced by a court to accept it if they chose to question its legality.

The rights of the parent who has neither legal nor physical custody of the child are generally limited to his right of visiting the child at reasonable times. This right stems from parenthood and is not dependent on decrees issued by a court. The court may, of course, condition the rights of visitation, again in the best interests of the child.

CHILDREN AND ONE-PARENT HOUSEHOLDS. Children grow up. The association between parent and child and the association between the parents change with each new attainment of the child. The child grows, parents respond—and their response has subtle overtones in their own relationship. In divorce, their responses must necessarily be of a different nature from what it is in marriage. In divorce, with communication reduced, the goals of the spouses are less likely to be congruent—the child is observed at different times and from different vantage points by the separated parents, each with his own set of concerns and worries.

Coparental divorce created lasting pain for many divorcees I interviewed—particularly if the ex-spouses differed greatly on what they wanted their children to become, morally, spiritually, professionally, even physically. This very difference of opinion about the goals of living may have lain behind the divorce. It continues through the children.

The good ex-husband/father feels, "My son is being brought up by his mother so that he is not my son." A divorced man almost always feels that his boy is being made into a different kind of man from what he himself is. Often, of course, he is right. The good ex-wife/mother may be tempted to refuse her ex-husband his visitation rights because, from her point of view, "He is bad for the children." This statement may mean no more than that the children are emotionally higher strung before and after a visit, and therefore upset her calm. But the mother may think the father wants something else for the children than she does, thus putting a strain on her own efforts to instill her own ideals and regulations.

It is difficult for a man to watch his children develop traits similar, if not identical, to those he found objectionable in their mother and which were among those qualities that led to the emotional divorce. The child becomes the living embodiment of the differences in basic values. A man may feel that "she" is bad for the children even when he has the objectivity to see also that the children will not necessarily develop unwholesome personalities, but only different personalities from those they might have developed through being with him.

The problem for the mother of the children is different—she has to deal with the single-parent household, making by herself decisions, which she almost surely feels should be shared. She does not want somebody to tell her what to do, as much as somebody to tell her she is right and make "sensible suggestions." Like most mothers, she wants support, not direction.

There is a traditional and popular belief that divorce is "bad for children." Actually, we do not know very much about it.

Although social scientists no longer put it this way, there is still in the general population a tendency to ask whether divorce "causes" juvenile delinquency. Obviously, if the child's way of dealing with the tensions in the emotional divorce of his parents is to act out criminally, he has turned to delinquency. But other children react to similar situations with supercompliance and perhaps ultimate ulcers. The tensions in divorce certainly tell on children, but the answers the children find are not inherent in the institution of divorce.

The more fruitful question is more difficult: "How can we arm children to deal with themselves in the face of the inadequacies and tensions in their families, which may lead their parents to the divorce court?" At least that question avoids the scapegoating of parents or blaming it all on "society"—and it also provides us a place to start working, creating new institutions.

TELLING CHILDREN ABOUT DIVORCE. It is a truism today that parents should be honest with their children, but parents apparently do not always extend this precept to being honest with their children about divorce. One of the most consistent and discouraging things found in interviewing American divorced persons came in response to my question, "What have you told your child about the nature of divorce in general and your own in particular?" The question was almost always followed by a silence, then a sigh, and then some version of, "I haven't told them much. I haven't had to. They know. You can't kid kids."

It is true, generally, that children are not easily deceived. But it is not true that they know instinctively why something is happening. Children today are comparatively sophisticated about divorce—until they are involved in it.

Children who live in and with the institution of divorce have a lot to learn that other children may never have to learn. The most important ideas to be communicated to them deal with the nature of the new life they will lead. It may be reasonable, in some cases, not to acquaint them with the facts of the emotional and legal divorces. But the new situation—custody, visitation, the new division of labor in the household—can be explained quite clearly so that the child can do his adjusting to a fairly predictable situation.

Of equal importance, they must be taught purposefully and overtly some of the culture of the family that does not occur in the ex-family. That is to say, children in divorce must pick up by instruction what they would have learned by habituation or osmosis in an unbroken healthy home.

The children must learn how to deal with the "broken orbit" of models for the roles they will play in life. A boy cannot become fully a man—or a girl a woman—if they model themselves only on the cues they pick up from one sex alone. A woman cannot teach a boy to be a man, or a girl a woman, without the help of men. And a man cannot teach either a boy to be a man or a girl to be a woman without the help of women.

All of us interact with members of both sexes. Our cues about the behavior of men come from the responses of women, as well as from the responses of men. Children—like the rest of us—must have significant members of both sexes around them.

Obviously, children of even the most successful homes do not model themselves solely on their parents, in spite of the importance parents have as models. There are television models (boys walk like athletes or crime busters); there are teachers, friends, storekeepers, bus drivers, and all the rest. But the child who lives in a one-parent home has to adjust to a different mixture of sex-role models. The big danger may be not so much that a boy has no father model in his home, but that his mother stops his walking like Willie Mays or a television cowboy because she doesn't like it. And worst of all, she may, without knowing it, try to extinguish in him the very behavior patterns he has learned from his father: especially, if she does not want to be reminded of his father.

Children who live in one-parent homes must learn what a husband/father is and what he does in the home

—and they have to learn it in a different context from children of replete homes. They must learn what a wife/ mother is in such a home. Children are taught to be husbands and wives while they are still children. In the one-parent home the children have to be taught actively and realistically the companionship, sexual, coparenting, and domestic aspects of marriage.

It is important to realize that these things can be taught. Yet, it is in this very process of teaching the child that the parent may reveal a great deal of bitterness and hostility toward the ex-spouse. The good parent has to teach the child without denigrating or idealizing the other parent.

A noted psychoanalyst has told me that in her opinion there are only two things children learn in two-parent homes that cannot be taught in one-parent homes; one is the undertone of healthy sexuality that is present in a healthy home. Nothing appears on the surface save love —but the sexual tone of married love permeates everything. Even in the most loving one-parent home this is something that can, perhaps, be explained to children, but something that they will have trouble feeling unless they experience it elsewhere. The other thing that is difficult to teach, she says, is the ambivalence of the child toward both parents. When the relationship of father-child is none of the business of the child's mother, or the relationship of mother-child outside the ken and respon-sibility of the child's father, then the illusion can be maintained by the child that father is wholly right and mother wholly wrong, or father wholly unjustified and mother completely innocent. It is seldom true.

In short, the ex-family must do many of the things that the family ordinarily does, but it does them with even more difficulty than the family. It is in the coparen-tal aspects of the divorce that the problems are so long-lasting—and so difficult. And the reason, as we have seen, is that a child's mother and father are, through the child, kinsmen to one another, but the scope of activities in their relationship has been vastly curtailed.

The Community Divorce and the Problem of Loneliness

Changes in civil status or "stages of life" almost invariably mark changes in friends and in significant communities. We go to school, and go away to college. We join special-interest groups. When we are married, we change communities—sometimes almost completely except for a few relatives and two or three faithful friends from childhood or from college.

When we divorce, we also change communities. Divorce means "forsaking all others" just as much as marriage does, and in about the same degree.

Many divorcees complain bitterly about their "ex-friends." "Friends?" one woman replied to my question during an interview, "They drop you like a hot potato. The exceptions are those real ones you made before marriage, those who are unmarried, and your husband's men friends who want to make a pass at you."

The biggest complaint is that divorcees are made to feel uncomfortable by their married friends. Little need be said about this here because Doctor Miller's chapter in this report covers the matter decisively.

Like newly marrieds, new divorcees have to find new communities. They tend to find them among the divorced. Morton Hunt's book, *The World of the Formerly Married,* provides a good concise report on these new communities. Divorcees find—if they will let themselves—that there is a group ready to welcome them as soon as they announce their separations. There are people to explain the lore that will help them in being a divorcee, people to support them emotionally, people to give them information, people to date and perhaps love as soon as they are able to love.

America is burgeoning with organizations of divorced people. The largest, and a vastly admirable organization, is *Parents Without Partners,* which has many branches throughout the country. Here, as Doctor Bernard mentioned in the first section, a divorced person can find information and friends. The character of this organization varies from one of its chapters to another. I know one chapter—over a third of its membership widows—that is quiet to the point of being sedate. I know other chapters that devote themselves to public works, large-scale picnics and parties that include all their children, and the kind of "discussion" of their problems that enables people "to get to know each other well enough to date seriously rather than experimentally."

There are, of course, some people who avoid other divorcees. Such people tend to disappear into the population at large, and hence are more difficult to find when we study their adjustments.

But the community divorce is an almost universal experience of divorcees in America. And although there are many individuals who are puzzled and hurt until they find their way into it, it is probably the aspect of divorce that Americans handle best.

The Psychic Divorce and the Problem of Autonomy

Psychic divorce means the separation of self from the personality and the influence of the ex-spouse—to wash that man right out of your hair. To distance yourself from the loved portion that ultimately became disappointing, from the hated portion, from the baleful presence that led to depression and loss of self-esteem.

The most difficult of the six divorces is the psychic divorce, but it is also the one that can be personally most constructive. The psychic divorce involves becoming a whole, complete, and autonomous individual again—

learning to live without somebody to lean on—but also without somebody to support. There is nobody on whom to blame one's difficulties (except oneself), nobody to shortstop one's growth, nobody to grow with.

Each must regain—if he ever had it—the dependence on self and faith in one's own capacity to cope with the environment, with people, with thoughts and emotions.

WHY DID I MARRY? To learn anything from divorce, one must ask himself why he married. Marriage, it seems to me, should be an act of desperation—a last resort. It should not be used as a means of solving one's problems. Ultimately, of course, most people in our society can bring their lives to a high point of satisfaction and usefulness only through marriage. The more reason, indeed, we should not enter it unless it supplies the means for coping with our healthy needs and our desires to give and grow.

All too often, marriage is used as a shield against becoming whole or autonomous individuals. People too often marry to their weaknesses. We all carry the family of our youth within ourselves—our muscles, our emotions, our unconscious minds. And we all project it again into the families we form as adults. The path of every marriage is strewn with yesterday's unresolved conflicts, of both spouses. Every divorce is beset by yesterday's unresolved conflicts, compounded by today's.

So the question becomes: How do I resolve the conflicts that ruined my marriage? And what were the complementary conflicts in the spouse I married?

Probably all of us marry, at least in part, to defend old solutions to old conflicts. The difficulty comes when two people so interlock their old conflicts and solutions that they cannot become aware of them, and hence cannot solve them. Ironically, being a divorced person has built-in advantages in terms of working out these conflicts, making them conscious, and overcoming them.

WHY WAS I DIVORCED? Presumably the fundamental

cause of divorce is that people find themselves in situations in which they cannot become autonomous individuals and are unwilling to settle for a *folie à deux.* Divorcees are people who have not achieved a good marriage—they are also people who would not settle for a bad one.

A "successful" divorce begins with the realization by two people that they do not have any constructive future together. That decision itself is a recognition of the emotional divorce. It proceeds through the legal channels of undoing the wedding, through the economic division of property and arrangement for alimony and support. The successful divorce involves determining ways in which children can be informed, educated in their new roles, loved and provided for. It involves finding a new community. Finally, it involves finding your own autonomy as a person and as a personality.

AUTONOMY. The greatest difficulty comes for those people who cannot tell autonomy from independence. Nobody is independent in the sense that he does not depend on people. Life is with people. But if you wither and die without specific people doing specific things for you, then you have lost your autonomy. You enter into social relationships—and we are all more or less dependent in social relationships—in order to enhance your own freedom and growth, as well as to find somebody to provide for your needs and to provide good company in the process. Although, in a good marriage, you would never choose to do so, you *could* withdraw. You could grieve, and go on.

These are six of the stations of divorce. "The undivorced," as they are sometimes called in the circles of divorcees, almost never understand the great achievement that mastering them may represent.

3

Reactions of Friends
to Divorce

ARTHUR A. MILLER, M.D.

I. Introduction

When a couple divorces or is in the process of divorcing,
their friends have various reactions. The friends' feelings
and thoughts can lead to actions, which may play a
significant role in the subsequent course of the divorce.
These reactions can determine whether or not the divorce
occurs, what form it takes, and the behavior of the divorcees after the divorce. Therefore, it is important to
explore the reactions of friends and the source and meaning of such reactions. This paper will include some remarks about friendship groups, a discussion of the
feelings and thoughts of friends of divorcees, and a consideration of the actions of divorcees' friends, based on
their feelings, thoughts, and fantasies.

The term "divorce" designates a group of interpersonal
situations, which have the common feature of a dissolution of a marriage. They differ, however, according to
many variables, including the age of the divorcees, the
duration of the marriage, the number and ages of the

children, and the manner of divorcing. Friends respond differently according to these variables and their pattern: the "plot" of the divorce. This plot has meaning to them, because of their individual wishes and aims, their particular character structures, their relationships to the marriage or to one or both of the divorcees, and the state of their own marriages. Depending on the features of the troubled marriage and of the friend who reacts to it, the divorce can represent many things to the friend, such as the gratification of a conflictful wish, a threat, a disillusionment, a reason for feeling guilt or shame, an emotional loss, or a reassurance.

There are several phases of a divorce: the marriage, with its difficulties, the decision to separate, the process of divorcing, the period after the actual divorce. Friends' emotional needs, conflicts, and responses affect how they interact with the divorcees in these various phases. These responses can affect the possibility of preservation of the marriage or serve as a disrupting influence. The components of the situation being considered here are the divorcing couple, the phase of divorcing, and the context of friends and their reactions.

Divorce requires more than a reorientation to the former spouse. It is an event that can cause reverberations throughout a complex network of relationships, the friendship group. In some social orbits, people are replaceable units. In others, they are not replaceable at all, at least not without considerable disruption and emotional upheaval. The disruption, upheaval, reassessments, and reorganizations occur to the individuals involved. These phenomena, however, are affected by and can cause change in the characteristics of a friendship group.

News of a contemplated divorce, a separation, or an actual divorce, when introduced to friends of the divorcees, can evoke discussion, questions, emotions, attitudes, speculation, and often an impulse to direct involvement. Relatively casual and inadvertent observations of such responses, in social situations, led to striking impressions. These observations and impressions were supplemented by experiences during several years of consultation with caseworkers in family agencies. They have, in addition, been explored in greater depth in the course of psychoanalytic therapy, when patients have discussed their feelings, thoughts, and actions stimulated by hearing of the divorce of a friend. Such observations indicate that friends are often responded to in a twofold manner: in terms of the present realities of the relationship and according to transferences, i.e., patterns of relationship brought over from one's past. The transference significance of the divorce and the divorced people accounts for much that is irrational and inappropriate in friends' responses to a divorce. There are, however, significant emotional reactions based on the importance of the divorcees with regard to one's current emotional and social adaptation.

II. *Friends and Friendship Groups*

A friendship group has certain characteristics,[1] which reflect the character structures of the individuals involved but transcend the individuals. The group, being the orbit in which the individuals have significant and involved relationships, has a code of behavior, regarding what is sanctioned, preferred, and most adaptive for living within the group. The code is accepted and the forms of behavior are engaged in because, being the conditions for membership within this friendship group, they ensure the emotional gains obtained from the available relationships.

The group has a shared set of standards, which determines what kind of behavior is viewed as desirable and what is considered shameful. Although, in well-developed adults, such standards are largely internalized and autonomous, they are usually influenced by environmental conditions. The effect of external guidelines for behavior is intensified when the group is made up either of individuals with frankly pathological character structures or of those who have not emerged from an adolescent phase of character development. These ideals influence choices of behavior, including those which determine the behavior between married persons, whether problems in a marriage are dealt with by divorce, by other kinds of action, or by individually bearing the conflict with resulting neurotic symptoms. These ideals also determine whether friends interfere in a marriage, either to help or meddle, and whether friends foster the divorce or prevent it. When the code sanctions involved actions with one's friends, or when the lines of demarcation are blurred as to who belongs to whom and how much emotional or sexual fidelity is required, the task of working out problems within a marriage is complicated.

In some friendship groups, the standards of behavior are so loose and the point at which one might experience shame is so remote that a clearly defined marital relationship is difficult to maintain. Divorce may be accepted, even encouraged as a preferred form of behavior. Divorcees may both remain within the group and continue to share the same friends. Sometimes there is exchanging of partners and even subsequent reshuffling, with remarriage of those who had divorced one another. In other friendship groups, the standards might value such things as fidelity, sticking with a problem, and self-sacrifice for the sake of children rather than the pursuit of individual happiness. The accepted behavior is then such that it delays or precludes divorce as a way of conflict resolution. In such groups, the shame of having divorced can make the divorcees unacceptable to the group or burden their sense of self-esteem while they remain in the group.

In some social cliques divorce may become "contagious." Once one of the circle of friends has divorced, shame about divorcing is diminished. The standard of behavior might, in fact, swing in the opposite direction, where divorcing takes on a positive significance. When the standards are ambiguous, the divorced couple might be viewed in a critical light and become the scapegoats for their friends' struggles with their own internal ideals and acceptable forms for coping with conflict.

A group's code regulates not only what is to be aspired to, lest one feel shame, but also what kind of behavior is considered a transgression, evoking feelings of guilt. Although these prohibitions are internalized and become more or less autonomous, especially after adolescence, transaction between the internalized code and external conditions is frequent. In the psychology of groups, the members identify with one another and all put the group leader in the place of their own consciences.[2] In a group, people permit themselves behavior that they are not able to engage in, with impunity, when they function as individuals. In addition to the group conscience shaping the consciences of individuals involved, potentially guilt-provoking behavior and wishes may lose their sting because of the sharing of guilt. One feels he is not in the thing alone; others did it first, put him up to it, or he was innocently swept along by the tide. Such considerations fashion the form of expression of drives, sexual and aggressive. For example, groups vary as to how sexual fantasies and impulses toward someone else's spouse are to be expressed: friendliness, affection, casual kissing and embracing when greeting one another, or direct unbridled adulterous behavior. Marriages within the group may be threatened or safeguarded by the way in which sexual drives and aggressive drives (rivalry, envy) are expressed, i.e., repressed, veiled, sublimated, or expressed in a raw conflict-producing form.

What a group views as being acceptable behavior determines whether or not the divorcee is considered to be justified in objecting to the spouse's "transgressions." This refers not only to interactions between one of the spouses and friends, but also to the behavior between the spouses and with their children. Varying interpretations are accordingly given to behavior which might be considered selfish, inconsiderate, cruel, or unfair. Such evaluations consequently influence the behavior of friends within the group, the conflicts between spouses, the assessment of justification for divorce, and the reactions of friends to people who have divorced. The reactions include such questions as: Is divorce itself considered a transgression? Who is the guilty party? Is vengeance justified?

Friendship groups, thus, often become "stage settings" for one or several of the members to enact their individual conflicts. They require a cast of characters to do this. Usually without conscious awareness, they assign roles, which others often participate in because of a complementary form of conflict. Sometimes the person to whom the role is assigned does not really participate, the casting occurring only in the fantasy of the protagonist. This occurs particularly in people with a so-called "neurotic character," whose behavior is based on an unwitting re-enactment of experiences from their earlier life.[3] There is, for example, the person who re-enacts his childhood-determined drama of coming between a married couple. Another, because of his unresolved conflicts moves relentlessly toward being the loser.[4] Often the "oppressor" and "victim" find one another with an uncanny sort of attraction. The plots are many and varied.

Certainly, friendships are based largely on realistic, contemporary needs and mutuality of interests. All too often, however, a meshing of transferences are observable within a group of friends. Divorces can be the consequence of such enactments, which may be motivated by such things as sexual desires, wishes to hurt, need to be hurt, or the desire to be the preferred one—in fact, the gamut of unresolved conflicts regarding childhood wishes and the attempts to master the traumatic experiences of the past.

One form of drama resulting from intermeshing of neurotic transferences is that of rescuer and the one who needs to be rescued. This may occur, for example, when the divorcee becomes depressed or makes a suicide attempt. The friend may feel, however irrationally, responsible to the divorcee, or feel that he should be able to give him emotional support and be significant enough to him to forestall such suffering. The person who had a parent or sibling who was depressed, suicidal, or otherwise emotionally disturbed is particularly vulnerable to this. This is especially so when he felt in some way responsible for that state or dealt with the anxiety aroused by devoting himself to making the significant and needed person feel better. Frequently, people would rather think that the unhappiness of a loved and needed person is due to something they did or did not do rather than it being due to factors out of their control. Depression or a suicide attempt in a divorcee might cause alienation in the friend. He may be disillusioned by this manifestation of weakness or be concerned about the emotional demands that will be made on him. When, however, the friend needs to be a "rescuer," the circumstance suits him and mobilizes him to action. Such action can be very supportive and helpful to the divorcee. If, however, the rescuer is reluctant to relinquish his rescuee, the divorcee's recovery and forward movement from what would have otherwise been a transitional state is thwarted or at least complicated. Withdrawal, indifference, or a critical attitude of friends can add to the divorcee's suffering. But, an overly solicitous, infantilizing approach, often pursued to exploit the recipient for one's own emotional purposes, can be emotionally crippling or delay the convalescence from the divorce. It should be emphasized that the exploitation of the relationship for neurotic motives may be mutual. The friendship might have originated partly because of an intermeshing of transferences.

Friends seek and find one another for many reasons. We have noted the meshing of neurotic characters. In general a friend is chosen for the gratifications afforded, of aggressive as well as loving aims, for identity delineation and maintenance by mutual recognition, for a model according to which to develop, or for a source of self-esteem. In addition, a friendship is tolerable if the characteristics and behavior of the parties involved mutually support defenses against anxiety or do not arouse anxiety. A friend's response to a divorce has to be viewed in terms of whether the idea of divorce, the reasons for it, the way it is carried out, and the emotional consequences threaten the friend's psychological defenses against anxiety. His reactions in the face of the divorce can be seen as responses to the threat. When the balance of his emotional economy is disrupted, he reacts with intensification of characteristic defenses or new ones. This accounts for whether he suffers internally, takes flight, makes an active attempt to undo the possibility of divorce, denies that he is affected by it, or is tempted to get involved in the crosscurrents of emotion tensions by using the divorce as an opportunity to give expression to emotional conflicts and for gratification of poorly controlled impulses. The likelihood of anxiety being evoked in the friend is increased when the circumstances of the divorce and its emotional climate have a specific symbolic significance to him, evoking a recollection of or the emotions related to traumatic circumstances in his earlier life.

In-laws must also be considered in the network of relationships within which a divorce occurs. Although we are not considering the intricacies of motives for a marriage, it is frequently seen that in choosing a mate the relationships which come along with the acquisition of the mate can play a significant role. Some people marry to acquire a family, i.e., in the in-laws. One may be emotionally invested in the spouse's mother, father, or siblings. Over the years of the marriage, these relationships develop; ties are intensified, animosities occur. When the divorce occurs, the realignments of emotional ties occur with varying degrees of upheaval, depending on the length of the marriage and the history of the relationships.

III. Feelings and Thoughts of Friends of Divorcees

Let us turn now to a consideration of the feelings and thoughts of friends of divorcees and explore their possible sources. Some are obvious, whereas others are more subtle, both in appearance and significance. Some are in the range of normal reactions, while others are signs of emotional disturbance. Impressions derived from observation of people involved in divorces indicate that the following occur in their friends: (1) anxiety, (2) shame, (3) inordinate preoccupation with the divorce, (4) desire for a sexual relationship with one of the divorcees, (5) pleasure about the divorcee's suffering, (6) feelings of superiority, (7) surprise and incredulity, (8) experience of emotional loss and grief, (9) conflict over allegiances, (10) disillusionment about friendship, (11) crisis about personal identity, (12) preoccupation and curiosity about the settlement.

On hearing of a divorce, the friend may experience *anxiety* or fear. Perhaps he has found his own marriage somewhat less than satisfactory. The gratifications are less than he feels entitled to. The hopes he had are not being fulfilled, and, not realizing his ambitions, he feels himself to be suffering and stagnating. The source of such feelings might not be actually in the marriage, but they are ascribed to the marriage. He has avoided a direct examination of the situation and tried to make the best of it. His friends' divorce now presents him with a challenge. He is stirred, if only momentarily, to take another look at his marriage. His previous defenses—such as avoidance, rationalization, denial, substitute gratification —might be threatened. Therefore, he experiences anxiety. Most marriages, even if not really bad, have enough dissatisfactions and unfulfilled hopes built into the situation to make such stocktaking and anxiety a frequent phenomenon.

A related phenomenon is the experience of *shame*. Consider the marriage, for example, which is not really adequate and gratifying, but is painful, and complicates or deters one's growth and development. The confrontation with someone who is doing something about extricating himself from an undesirable situation can evoke a sense of shame. One feels inferior or inadequate for letting things go on, while someone else is able to do something about it.

At times, the friend is *inordinately preoccupied with the subject of the divorce*. He ruminates about it, talks about it at every opportunity, and seeks more information about the trouble the couple has had and the grounds for divorce. The associated feeling may be pleasure. Frequently, this occurs when the divorce comes as somewhat of a surprise to the couple's friends. Now that the separation or divorce has occurred and the conflicts causing it are known, the friend feels he has been let in on a secret. The previously closed door is open. He revels in his interest, being avid for more information. Such a reaction becomes more understandable if we recall how frequently a child feels left out of his parents' "secrets," and how his curiosity is aroused and handled by direct exploration, repression, displacement, or sublimation. The pleasure in response to such information might be mixed with guilt and anxiety: guilt because of the forbidden quality, anxiety because what goes on "behind the door" is not fully comprehensible to him, and his understanding of it is incomplete.

A frequently observed phenomenon in the life of a child is a jealousy of the relationship between his parents. He feels left out. Not only does he want to know what goes on between them, but he would like to separate them. Having, in the earliest years of life, related in a dyadic fashion, essentially to one significant person, he has progressed to an awareness of a triad. Within this triad, he suffers the emotional blow of not feeling central. Therefore, he is concerned with getting rid of one or the other of his parents. Wishing to replace the parent of the same sex is commensurate with his subsequent developmental prospects and tasks. Frequently, the child wishes to remove the parent of the opposite sex. The shape this conflict takes and the direction of the major emotional investment depends on many factors. In any event, the wish to separate one's parents is frequent. The divorce has a significance to the friend in these terms, when he has transferred this incompletely solved conflict onto the divorcee. He can react variously: with guilt for the forbidden wish, with pleasure over the fact of the separation, with an attempt to make reparation by trying to effect a reconciliation, or by playing a subtle role in fostering and facilitating the rift in the marriage.

When the couple is separated or divorced, friends' *fantasies and aspirations for a sexual relationship* with one of the partners can become intensified. Deterrents to such contact are diminished, now that he or she is free. The wishes may be acted on directly. At other times, there are involvements which only allude to the wishes. Frequently, the divorced person becomes a focus of attention and the recipient of direct or veiled seductive overtures. When there is guilt or anxiety about the wishes, the divorced friend may be avoided defensively.

All relationships have an element of ambivalence inherent in them. The *suffering and failure of the divorced ones may be a source of pleasure* to the friend. In addition to the natural increment of ambivalence, hostile wishes toward the divorcees may exist for more specific reasons. When the couple is favored with wealth, social position, or noteworthy talents, the failure of their marriage might be a compensation in the rivalry between friends. It is a balm to one's wounded self-esteem and often a rationalization for one's inadequacies to be able to feel that, although the divorcees have so much, they are "really not happy"—"unable to make a real relationship with a spouse," or have achieved what they have at the expense of a family life, love relationships, the spouse, or their children. When such responses are accompanied by feelings of guilt about the hostile envy and malevolent wishes, the friend experiences conflict about his pleasure, which can lead to compensatory reparational efforts.

Friends at times *feel superior to the divorcees.* They feel a pride in being able to endure in their own marriage. The persons who divorce are seen as quitters, weak, and inferior. Such an attitude depends on the friend's standards regarding the behavior toward which one should aspire. This is the other side of the coin of the aforementioned response of shame over staying with one's own marriage while someone else was courageous enough to do something about an unworkable situation.

Friends sometimes respond to a divorce with complete *surprise.* They had not imagined that the couple was having marital difficulty. Along with the surprise, there is *incredulity* and the protest that "It cannot be." The incredulity and resistance to facing the fact can have a general defensive significance—the avoidance of one or several of the emotional reactions already mentioned. Another, more specific, process can occur, related to the idealization of friends and their marriage.

Among the determinants of choice and maintenance of a relationship is the wish for proximity and interaction with someone who represents what one would like to be. This is a frequent mechanism during adolescence.[5] A person involved in his own developmental process may be aware that there are functions and characteristics which it would be reassuring to have. Prior to acquiring them and as a prelude to their becoming internalized by the process of identification, he seeks a relationship with someone who has or appears to have these characteristics. This person becomes a complement to his modes of function and sources of self-esteem. To be involved with this possessor of valued, admired characteristics provides a sense of strength, compensating for an inner sense of weakness. It is not, as in some relationships, that the friend is a strong protector or caretaker. Instead, the friend represents capability and mastery of self and environment. One feels strengthened in the reflection of this. In addition, his self-esteem may be enhanced by being associated with such an admirable person.

These processes, providing a buttress to feelings of mastery and self-esteem, are usually transitional phenomena during childhood and adolescence. Ideally, the process continues beyond the direct need for the other as a complement to one's undeveloped capacities. The "other" (his characteristics) serves as a model for the process of identification. If this occurs, the characteristics become integrated into one's self, diminishing the dependency on the ideal. However, many friendships are based on some stage in the process, short of internalization and development of an autonomous self. One might be in the midst of the internalizing process or fixated at some stage of it, with little likelihood of going beyond the need for association with the ideal person.

When the divorce occurs, the ideal may be shattered. The friend may have overvalued the marriage. That is, he admired and wished to have, or at least be in association with someone who had, the ability to have a good, effective, and gratifying relationship with spouse and children. The apparent ability to have an adult form of relationship was valued. The failure of this in the divorcees can make the friend despair of ever being able to achieve such a state of integration. The surprise about the divorce may be due to his having overidealized the married couple. He wanted so much to find an ideal, of someone who could do it, a source of overcoming his weakness, a supply of self-esteem, or a model with whom he could identify, that his wishes obscured his vision of the realities. He could not, or would not, see the signs that the marriage was something less than he felt he needed it to be. The undeniable fact of the divorce takes him by surprise. The incredulity and refusal to believe the facts are a reaction to the feeling of loss.

The idealization which accompanies this mechanism can burden a friendship. The recipient of the admiration might be denied the right to be himself rather than to conform to the fantasy of his friend. When the balloon of fantasy has been burst by the divorce, the disillusioned friend may turn away from the divorcees or the one who was especially idealized. The divorcee may find his sense of loss intensified, because, in addition to the loss of spouse, family life, and continued contact with his children, he does not have available emotional supplies and supports from friends.

Often, only when the structure of a relationship is threatened or shattered do the fantasies about the relationship become evident. The people involved were relating, to a significant degree, according to their individual wishes. When the structure changes, the absence of fantasied gratification becomes evident. Frequently, the reason for dissatisfaction is not known. The friend simply turns away, searching for others to fulfill his needs. The rapid shifts in relationships seen in adolescents is related to this.[6] The adolescent, searching for models, sources of strength or self-esteem, as well as for gratification of sexual and aggressive drives, may make intense rapid ties, which are abruptly broken off when the relationship evokes too much anxiety or does not serve the needs of his developmental struggle. Today's rapidly made, intense relationship, according to which one forms identifications, may be cast aside tomorrow if it is disturbing, disappointing, or unfulfilling.

All parties concerned in the context of the divorce may, to some degree, *experience an emotional loss and grief*. That marriage, that couple, might have had a great significance in one's emotional economy. The marriage as an entity may have been closely interwoven with one's pattern of pursuit of emotional supplies, gratifications, supports, and feelings of emotional security. The divorce means that this is excised. At least, a considerable reorganization of patterns of relationship has to occur.

When there is bitterness between the divorcees leading to alienation, friends are confronted often with a *conflict over allegiances*. Intense emotional conflicts can result for all concerned. The redistribution of allegiances may mean a loss of an emotionally significant friend. The friend of the divorcees, as well as the divorcees themselves, may have to experience a period of grief and undergo a process of mourning for what is felt to be lost. In addition, anxiety, guilt, and shame reactions might occur when a routine pattern of relationship is disrupted and one has to reassess feelings of rivalry, jealousy, envy, sexual desire, and preferences among friends.

Particularly vulnerable people, whose self-esteem depends greatly on external emotional supplies, may react strongly with feelings of *disillusionment about the untrustworthiness of friends and the impermanence of relationships*. Some might react with intense depression or a regression to a psychosis. What friends mean to one another emotionally is often not clearly known to the parties involved. Frequently, each one is not entirely conscious of the emotional significance of the relationship to him. The interpersonal upheaval related to a divorce can stir up emotional reverberations, when the lines of cleavage in the pre-existing relationship structure becomes evident.

A sense of personal identity depends on several factors.[7] Significant among these is the mutuality experienced in a given social context. What a person means to his friends and the reciprocal significance of the friends determines the delineation of the identity of those involved. The divorcees can experience a *crisis of personal identity;* at least, if not a crisis, a process of reorganization of the identity. Friends, who were enmeshed in a pattern of mutuality with "the marriage" and the individuals involved may also experience the need for reassessment of their identities. From the side of the divorcees, if there is evidence that the divorce has apparently affected the friend very little, a considerable reassessment of the emotional significance of the previous friendship may be aroused.

Attitudes toward change can play a role. Adverse reactions occur when there is anxiety about change. Change is, however, often sought or longed for. Consider, for example, the person who is bored and feels that he is restricted or not "making it." Often, the quest is for change in external circumstances and relationships rather than for change in himself, which would be necessary in order to deal effectively with the disturbed mood. The friend, then, is fascinated by or envious of the divorcees. He sees, or fantasies, that they are disencumbered and given an opportunity for new adventures in personal relationships. This quest for change can take various forms. Rather than effect changes in his wishes, aspirations, and defenses, he considers a geographical change, different employment, or altered marital status. Predisposed people, often in middle age, may be disquieted or "infected" by their friends' divorce.

Friends frequently become *preoccupied with curiosity and attitudes about the settlement.* Fantasies and aspirations may be stirred up. Conflicts about greed, rivalry, and exploitation are involved. All too frequently, the narcissism, which is ubiquitously present in varying degrees, causes a friend to consider, "But what does this mean to me?" He might side with the one who is most advantageous to him materially, socially, or emotionally. In other instances, his character leads him to identify with the one who has been "unfairly" dealt with and is at a disadvantage.

With whom does the friend identify? It can be with the husband, the wife, the children, or even with the "other" man or woman who might have lured one of the spouses from the marriage. If the husband or wife is identified with, responses vary according to the state in which they are thought to be. He (she) might seem fortunate to be free of a miserable relationship, pitiable because of dashed hopes, unfortunate because of the difficult time ahead without a spouse; justifiably indignant because of the awful behavior of the spouse, deservedly vengeful toward the spouse, lost and alone because of disrupted family life and complicated social relationships. Sometimes the friend's attitude toward the divorce is based on the fact that he sees it from what he believes to be the point of view of the children involved. Because of an attraction to one of the spouses, the friend might identify with the other man or woman, who came between the husband and wife.

IV. Actions of Friends, Based on Feelings and Thoughts

The foregoing remarks deal predominantly with the emotional reactions, thoughts, and fantasies of friends in response to news of a contemplated or actual divorce. In this section the consideration of the possible reactions will be discussed further, with more emphasis on the actions of friends based on their feelings, thoughts, and fantasies. We are concerned here largely with the questions: When and why do friends, subtly or overtly, unconsciously or consciously, act to subvert a marriage, cultivating and nurturing the divorce? When and why do they act to preserve the marriage?

Frequently, interested observers of an impending divorce express the wish that the couple will remain together. Religious, social, and historical factors, as well as concern about the children's welfare are among the possible determinants of such an attitude. From the psychological viewpoint, however, there appears to be still another determinant. An existing, continued marriage serves a defensive, inhibiting, and controlling function. The various emotional conflicts discussed above may be forestalled, attenuated, or obscured. The parties involved are then spared the conflictful impulses, fantasies, wishes, painful self-evaluation, anxiety, guilt, shame, grief, and mourning over a lost relationship, and are also spared the disruptions of the patterns of mutuality contributing to the identities of the involved parties.

The actual behavior with which friends respond to a divorce situation is related to their emotional reactions. There may be encouragement for the divorce to occur. Sometimes this encouragement is deliberate. Often, it is subtle. Frequently, the motive is unconscious, based on transferences to the couple or feelings that their divorce will represent some emotional or material advantage to oneself. Friends often become mediators, attempting to forestall the pending divorce and to achieve a reconciliation of a separated couple. The effectiveness of their actions and whether they do more harm or good depends on their motives. Although altruism is not unheard of in such situations, the personal significance of the situation to the friend is a potent factor.

The actions of friends are understandable in the light of the plot of the divorce: how the friends play a role in this, and whether a drama based on a character problem is being enacted.[8,9] The friend and the divorcees can be involved in a stereotyped repetitive pattern, based on unsolved childhood experiences, patterns which unconsciously bedeck every current situation in which the person finds himself. Accordingly, the friend enacts a role in relation to the divorcees. His personal plot may impel him to stir up trouble, to foster a divorce, to lure one or the other of the partners, to be the mediator, to save the marriage, to be a friend of the children involved, or be a "better" parent than the one who is absent because of the divorce. The friend might, consciously or unconsciously, set it up so that he can step in after the divorce. Under the guise of being a good Samaritan to the unfortunate divorcee, he seeks sexual satisfaction. Sometimes, it is not actual physical satisfaction he seeks, but instead he wishes to establish himself in an advantageous light compared to the absent spouse: to be understanding, kind, strong, available, in some way superior and preferable.

At times, friends do not become involved in any of these ways, but rather they withdraw. Such a phobic avoidance may be a protective posture to avoid conflictful feelings. The withdrawal often is not simply a calm avoidance, but the friend suffers emotionally, because of the conflicts stirred up by the divorce situation. Persons, objects, and situations are phobically avoided because they represent a temptation to a forbidden impulse and/ or a threat of suffering or harmful consequences for such impulses.[10] Contact with the divorcees might stir up personal conflicts in the friends (e.g. about their own marriages), a temptation to an affair, or guilt-provoking satisfaction at the sight of their troubles. At times, friends wish to avoid evidence of intense interpersonal conflict, hostility, despair, or loneliness. The divorced people are then left out in the cold as far as their friends, or some of their friends, are concerned. Although friends can be of great emotional aid during a divorce, in other cases their personally motivated interferences or withdrawals can increase the suffering and complicate the divorcees' adaptation to the divorce.

Some marital partners live in a state of emotional divorce. Though legally married and living together, they are emotionally estranged. Such marriages continue for many reasons. Among those that continue, sometimes it would be better, for the happiness and emotional development of all concerned, if there were an actual divorce. Friends can be determining factors of whether the issue is faced or the partners muddle along. Gratifications from friendships can make the state of emotional divorce tolerable. At times, the outward form of a marriage is retained because of the fear of the effect of divorce on friendships. The dislocations attendant to a divorce might threaten valued friendships and the marriage is maintained to avoid such a loss.

When one of the partners has a disturbance of sexuality, friendships can support or disrupt the marriage. There are those who continue in a marriage, which they can manage emotionally or use as a front, while they concomitantly pursue a homosexual relationship. The marriage can be disrupted by a homosexual third person. When there is a potency or frigidity problem or disproportionate appetites for sexual relations in marital partners, "friends" can be of service to the unsatisfied partner. The non-sexual advantages of the marriage may be preserved. These remarks are not made to advocate this as a form of problem solving, but to describe a frequent state of affairs. The forms that marriages actually take are manifold. Being drawn to the situation unwittingly, friends become essential characters in the setup; they make themselves available or seek to become involved because of their own emotional needs. The functions they serve will either facilitate the perpetuation of the marriage or activate the process of divorce.

People in the midst of marital turmoil, or in the process of divorcing, often consider their behavior in the light of how it will appear to friends. One might feel justified in the eyes of friends or fear that the spouse will appear in a better light. This attitude frequently is based on how it will appear, in terms of what will be publicly known, rather than what actually transpired within the marriage. The possibility of forestalling divorce, by getting at the real source of the trouble, can be diminished when one or both are swept along largely by the concern over how it will appear to others. Sometimes a divorce will be delayed until one of the partners has had time to provoke the other into behavior that justifies the first one's position. The divorcing is then conducted for an audience of friends. Complications occur when one of the spouses is known to be mentally ill, perhaps hospitalized, or physically handicapped. Such circumstances attract emotional responses and taking of sides by friends. What are considered just grounds vary from friend to friend and within various groups. These matters can have practical consequences after the divorce. Subsequent friendship alignments or opportunities for a new marriage can be affected.

Friends are often consulted when one or both partners are considering divorce. They can shift the balance toward decision to divorce or continuation of the marriage. The objectivity of friends in such situations should be suspect. Excluding instances of conscious, deliberately malicious, disruptive intentions, the network of interactions within a group of friends can be intricate, the motives not fully conscious, and the advice given based on self-interest. The friend's aims, conflicts, and characterological patterns for handling sexual, aggressive, and narcissistic strivings may make him a biased party and can cause him to be drawn into the conflict. Consequently, in the process of divorcing and after the divorce, the troubled couple may find their problem-solving attempts either supported or sabotaged by friends.

Should a separated person move in with a friend? There is no simple answer to this question. It, of course, depends on the friend and the nature of the friendship. A man separated from his wife may live with a bachelor friend and find this way of life attractive. He then delays facing up to the problems of his marriage. Sometimes, after a period of such bachelor existence, the veneer of glamour wears off. He misses the gratifications of a marriage and family, or he might feel shame on viewing himself as having regressed to a kind of adolescent existence. Friends living together during separation from their marriages can discover their individual problems, seeing them as they become manifest in the new situation.

The response of friends to a divorce affects the behavior of the children of the divorcees. When friends withdraw, children sometimes note their absence. This is experienced with perplexity, turmoil, guilt, or shame. The fabric of their existence is increasingly disrupted. The intensity of change to be mastered is increased. Parents' friends and their children often provide important relationships. Loss of these deprives the child of potential sources of self-esteem, gratifying companionship, and a sense of continuity, which plays a role in maintaining one's identity. When a child feels that his "badness" caused the divorce, the withdrawal of friends seems to attest to his suspicions about himself, increasing feelings of guilt. If added to the shame of an unsuccessful family there is a diminished status in the community, the child's emotional burden increases.

Friends can, of course, be helpful to the child. They might provide a substitute for the absent parent, giving emotional support, guidance, and necessary models for development. However, there is a danger of the friend exploiting the child emotionally, for his own needs. The child's resolution of conflicted feelings about his parents and their divorce and his subsequent development can be complicated if the friend uses his relationship with the child to relieve his own anxieties, to prove something, to compete with the absent parent, to gain some sexual or aggressive aim with the present parent, or to make himself emotionally indispensable to the child. In general, however, continued relationships with friends and their children can make the disrupted home a less lonely and sad one. Disrupted relationships, new relationships to master, and geographical uprooting, as when the remaining parent remarries, can prove to be traumatic to the child.

Friends often become involved in finding social contacts, potential new spouses for the divorcees. This can, of course, be based on a benevolent friendly intention to contribute to the divorcee's solution of his problems and future happiness. The friend may identify with the divorcee and empathically appreciate his plight. Sometimes the benevolence is accompanied by a wish to be in control of the divorcee's life. The friend becomes intensely preoccupied with the details of the divorcee's social life. He gains a vicarious experience. In addition, he may wish to be important or indispensable to his divorced friend. Thus, a relationship is maintained that satisfies, for the involved friend, veiled sexual and aggressive drives or an attempt to master the anxiety stirred in him by his friend's divorce. An unconscious or conscious sexual interest in the divorcee or the person to whom he introduces the divorcee can be gratified by such activity.

The divorcee might find that the emotional entanglements within his previous circle of friends is such that his chances of finding a mate there are minimal. If he remains in this group, he is exposed to the currents of his friends' attempts to cope with their own emotional conflicts. He becomes the object of pity, comforting concern, control, envy, or suspicion. An unattached person may be seen as being a threat to the continuing marriages. Such emotional complications may make it necessary for the divorcee to withdraw and find new friends. This can be a painful loss to all concerned. At other times, it is a relief to the divorcee and his friends, when the previous relationship was fraught with ambivalence. In some friendship contexts, a person's allotted and accepted role can be inimical to his most effective development. The reshuffling accompanying a divorce can grant him a valuable opportunity to extricate himself from such relationships and spur him to mobilize his developmental potential.

The divorce may have occurred because one spouse was lagging developmentally in comparison with the other spouse. The pattern of friendships can contribute to such a developmental lag. For example, a wife continues in a passive, daughterly role in her relationship with her husband and other aspects of her life. She has a woman friend who, unwittingly, supports and fosters this behavior in the wife. At times, a group of women friends engage in a pattern of subtle mother-daughter interactions with one another. The wife's regressed position may have complicated her relationship with her husband, who justifiably expected more from her. A divorce occurred. He may have left the circle of friends because he found the pattern of relationship stifling. The wife stayed with them, continuing in a situation deleterious to her growth. Sometimes, she is fortunate enough to make new relationships within which she can grow, avoiding perpetuation of the pattern and recurrence of marital difficulties.

III

Aftermath

There are two primary problems that result from a divorce—domestic problems and sexual problems. Gebhard gives some surprising facts about the latter. Mead and Bohannan address the difficulties that arise in households of remarriage and in groups of kinsmen in which divorce plays a significant part.

4

Postmarital Coitus Among Widows and Divorcees

PAUL GEBHARD

Introduction

The subject of postmarital coitus, that is coitus after the dissolution of marriage through death, separation, or divorce, has received very little scientific attention. In those few instances where data have been obtained concerning incidence and frequency of postmarital coitus, the focus generally has not been on the postmarital condition but upon the subject of remarriage.

This seeming lack of scientific interest in postmarital sexuality is rather remarkable in view of the increasing prevalence of divorce, but it may reflect the protective disinterest adopted by our society. We are quite concerned about sexuality in the young and seek to mold these hopefully still-plastic personalities into the ideal patterns that we ourselves failed to fully achieve. We are also quite concerned about sexuality in marriage; we view it as a force that can exert a powerful cohesive or disruptive influence upon this highly valued basic social unit. But postmarital sexuality lies in an embarrassing limbo. While we tell our unmarried young people that coitus is not necessary for emotional and psychological health, we change our story once they marry. Then our counselors, clinicians, and clergy join with the laymen in emphasizing that coital relationships with orgasm for both partners are a vital and necessary part of life—a goal to be achieved and maintained. This message is repeated ad infinitum in marriage manuals and articles in popular magazines. After proselytizing for sex among the married and stressing its intrinsic value, society cannot abruptly reverse its stand again when a death or divorce renders a person unmarried. On the other hand, society cannot discard conventional morality, which demands coitus be confined to those married to one another. The escape from this dilemma is the usual one: ignore and minimize the problem as much as possible, but if you are forced to take a position then condemn publicly and condone privately.

As a result of this socially useful hypocrisy, the previously married are allowed greater freedom than those who never married. Because of habituation to coitus and this greater social permissiveness, it is believed that the great majority of previously married women and virtually all of the men have postmarital coitus.[1] While this generality seems factually accurate, one may ask further socially important questions. What is the incidence of postmarital coitus at particular ages? The statement that four-fifths of the previously married females have such coitus does not tell us when they have it, or how soon after the end of the marriage it begins. What is the frequency? This is a significant question to ask of a group accustomed to regular marital coitus, and the answer may have great implications in regard to physical and psychological adaptation. What is the rate of female orgasm—is it depressed or elevated? Do widows and divorcees differ with respect to postmarital sexuality?

These questions and others have been largely left un-answered. Even the otherwise exhaustive book by Kinsey and his colleagues dealt only briefly with the previously married female and did not distinguish between the widowed and the divorced.[2] Since I was involved in this sin of omission, it is only fair that I belatedly try to rectify it. The purpose, then, of this chapter is to present factual data answering, insofar as possible, these questions con-cerning postmarital coitus while differentiating between the widowed and the divorced.

Method and Sample

This study is based upon 632 white females who were U.S. citizens, who had never been imprisoned, who were interviewed by the staff of the Institute for Sex Research between 1939 and 1956, and whose marriages had been terminated by death, separation, or divorce between ages twenty-one and sixty inclusive.

Virtually all of the marriages were legal; the few common-law marriages in the sample were cases where the couple had lived openly as man and wife for over one year. Separation was defined as living apart with the intention of divorcing or at least never again cohabiting. To be counted, a separation had to have existed at least two months. Divorces far outnumbered separa-tions: only seventy-two women had been separated but not divorced, and some of these were planning divorce. Annulments were considered as divorces.

Multiple divorces or separations complicated the analyses in roughly 11 per cent of the separated or di-vorced sample (hereafter referred to for simplicity as the divorced). In these cases all postmarital data were used although the individual was counted only once in the "ever-never" type of calculations—the multiple broken marriages were treated as one. For example, if a woman with two broken marriages had had extramarital coitus during one of them, she was counted simply as one woman who had extramarital coitus in a marriage. She was not counted again as a woman who had not had extramarital coitus in a marriage which later ended.

To make the distinction between the widowed and the divorced analytically clear, we placed in the divorced sample any widow with a prior or subsequent separation, annulment, or divorce. In brief, none of the women in our widowed sample had ever been separated or divorced by the time they were interviewed.

In addition to the "ever-never" type of calculations (such as the percentages who had *ever* had premarital, extramarital, and postmarital coitus), a number of calculations were made involving periods of life.[3] These "age-periods" are simply five- or ten-year segments of life. Through use of such age-periods one can answer questions as to whether or how often something occurred during a given period of life; for example, how many divorced women had coitus sometime between age twenty-six and age thirty? Such calculations are sometimes confusing to persons without statistical knowledge because women may be counted in some age-periods, but not in others. If a woman was age twenty-five at the interview, she obviously cannot be counted in age-period twenty-six to thirty or older. Similarly, if a divorced woman remarried at age twenty-six and stayed married she could not be counted thereafter in any calculations of postmarital behavior. However, if she was again divorced, she would immediately become eligible for being counted once more as a divorced person. Thus a young divorcee will appear in age-period twenty-one to twenty-five, remarry and disappear during age-periods twenty-six to thirty and thirty-one to thirty-five, and then reappear in age-period thirty-six to forty because she had her second divorce sometime in that thirty-six to forty period.

Incidence of Postmarital Coitus

The great difference in the postmarital sexual behavior of the widowed and the divorced is seen at once in the percentages who had experienced postmarital coitus. Eighty-two per cent of the divorced had had such coitus compared to 43 per cent of the widowed. One's first impulse is to say, "Well, I suppose most of the divorcees were reasonably young, whereas the widows were probably elderly." This simplistic explanation is destroyed when one calculates the incidence of postmarital coitus by age-period so that only the widowed and divorced of the same age are being compared. Table 1 reveals that at all ages the divorced have substantially more women having coitus than have the widowed. The difference is usually 15 to 33 percentage points, and in one age-period the figure for the divorced is double that of the widowed. During their twenties and thirties, roughly two-thirds to three-quarters of the divorced were having coitus in contrast to the one-third to one-half of the widowed. In their forties the divorced widen their lead: about three-fifths to two-thirds of them experiencing coitus as opposed to roughly one-quarter to one-third of the widowed. After age fifty the differences lessen as age exerts its leveling influence, but they are still very marked.

The largest proportion of divorced women having coitus occurs from ages thirty-one to forty; thereafter the percentages fall uninterruptedly and rather rapidly, but seem to stabilize at around 40 per cent from ages thirty-one to sixty.

Although their percentages are always lower, the widowed show a similar progression, reaching their peak in their late twenties and early thirties, declining in their late thirties and early forties, and seemingly stabilizing at a 23–26 per cent level thereafter.

Actually, of course, this "stabilizing" is only a lessening or pause in the rate of decline. We know from previous analyses of older postmarital (widowed and divorced combined) females that only about one-eighth were having coitus at age sixty and none at ages sixty-five or seventy. This is not to imply that sex ends at sixty-five; at that age fully half of the married females were continuing marital coitus.[4]

Returning to this matter of a pattern in incidence of postmarital coitus for both the widowed and divorced, we see an initial incidence that is fairly high (compared to the incidences of all age-periods) but which is followed by a maximum. From this maximum there is a relatively rapid decrease in the percentages, with this rate of decrease ultimately slowing. The reason for this pattern would seem to be that the initial incidence is moderately high because the women were accustomed to coitus and were young enough to be at their peak of physical attractiveness. The maximum incidence occurred somewhat later as (1) the trauma of death or divorce wore off, (2) there was a stronger motivation to remarry, and (3) there was a progressive erosion of sexual inhibition which occurs in most women as they near or enter their thirties. The subsequent decrease in the number of postmarital women having coitus seems due chiefly to a selective factor: the more sexually motivated and responsive females tend to marry and thereby leave an increasingly large proportion of less responsive females in the ranks of the postmarital women. About half of the divorcees and a quarter of the widows did remarry. We know that simple age is not the chief factor since 80 per cent of the married women in their late fifties still continue marital coitus.

It was unexpected that this sequential pattern just described exists so clearly as it does since women are divorcing or being widowed at all ages. It is unfortunate that time and energy did not permit me to tabulate the percentage of new divorcees and widows in each age-period. Nevertheless, the bulk of the divorces in our sample occurred between ages twenty-six and thirty while the widowing was more evenly spread, but was commonest among women in their thirties. At this juncture I should add that the youthfulness of our sample of widows is in part the result of World War II and the Korean War.

The enormous differences between the widowed and divorced in incidence of postmarital coitus seem to derive from several interrelated factors. Educational differences may be ruled out since in this sample the widowed and divorced were essentially equal in educational attainment (roughly 60 to 70 per cent of both groups had attended college). Religious differences, however, do appear to be a definite factor. The degree of devoutness rather than the denomination proved to be the critical matter.[5] In the various age-periods from 30 to 40 per cent of the widowed were labeled devout on the basis of church attendance as opposed to 15 to 29 per cent of the divorced. There was a moderate tendency for both groups to become more devout with increasing age. However, religious devoutness alone cannot explain the differences we see in incidence of postmarital coitus since the calculations showed that a marked change in coital incidence was not necessarily mirrored by a corresponding change in devoutness. For example, the percentage of devout widows remained between 36 and 41 per cent from age thirty-one to fifty, yet the incidence of coitus fell from 47 to 26 per cent. Obviously devoutness has only a more general repressive effect and can be overridden by other factors.

One important factor is prior experience in coitus outside of marriage. If one has had premarital or extramarital coitus one is more likely to engage in postmarital coitus. There is a substantial but not great difference between the widowed and the divorced in terms of premarital coitus: 28 per cent of the former having such experience versus 37 per cent of the latter. There is, however, a great difference in extramarital coitus. Only 8 per cent of the widowed while married had had coitus with a man other than their husband, while one-third of the divorced had this experience. The high incidence of post-marital coitus among the divorced is in no small part the continuation of extramarital coitus occurring in the last year of the marriage. Some 31 per cent of the divorced were having extramarital coitus in that final year.[6] In brief, women in unhappy marriages tend to take lovers and continue sexual relations with them through the breakup of the marriage and after the divorce. In this sense the divorced had a "head start" on the widows who had no ready-made sexual partners. To be sure, there is no lack of men willing to solace a new widow, but the great majority of women are interested in an emotional rather than a purely sexual relationship, and emotional relationships take time to develop—time that may be measured in years if the widow finds herself in an age or environmental situation where there are few eligible males.

The trauma of being widowed is probably a strong factor in delaying postmarital coitus. Even after the initial phase of acute grief has ameliorated, the widow may find it difficult to find a male who measures up to the image of her deceased husband, an image which tends to benefit from selective memory.

Remarriage as well as initial marriage is generally fore-shadowed by coitus with the future spouse. Many women who would ordinarily avoid coitus for moral (or other) reasons will have it when marriage seems impending. Consequently, the lower incidence of post-marital coitus among the widowed agrees with their lower rate of remarriage: only 27 per cent of the widows remarried while 47 per cent of the divorced did so. To put it simply, widows seem less motivated or less able than divorcees to remarry, and hence are less likely to engage in the coitus that generally precedes marriage. The widow more often than the divorcee will have a more comfortable financial position, having inherited all or most of the estate, and is also more apt to have a congenial social milieu of in-laws and married friends who are not only supportive, but who maintain the widow's patterns of behavior. Such a situation may be comforting, but it also muffles the motivation to seek a new husband aggressively. Lastly, there is in our culture a romantic ideal of "being loyal to the memory" of the deceased, a feeling that a second marriage is disloyal and in some vague way sexually immoral. This feeling, seldom openly expressed, is not infrequently held by the widow and/or her relatives and may exert more influence than she or they would be prepared to admit. Some of our case histories of widows have recorded upon them unsolicited comments such as, "I knew I'd never find another like him" (i.e., so I didn't do much hunting). Children may resent and interfere with a potential remarriage, feeling intensely loyal to the deceased. The divorcee, of course, has no such chains to the cemetery.

The restraint imposed by herself or by others upon the widow is clear in the calculations as to how long after the termination of marriage women waited before starting postmarital coitus. Of those divorced who had such coitus, a full three-quarters began within one year.[7] The same was true of only about half (52 per cent) of the widows. The difference is in part due to the divorced carrying over pre-existing affairs into postmarital life. One-eighth of the divorced waited from thirteen months up to three years; for the widowed the figure is 22.2 per cent. Nearly one-tenth (9.7 per cent) of the divorced and one-fifth (22.2 per cent) of the widowed experienced more than three years of abstinence before resuming coitus. From these figures it is clear that the widowed were far more tardy than the divorced in again developing a full heterosexual relationship.

Before closing this section on the incidence of postmarital coitus, note should be made of a curious phenomenon. Once a woman begins postmarital coitus she is extremely likely to have it with more than one man. This generalization applies to both the divorced and widowed, and may be the basis for the stereotypical concepts of the "merry widow" and "gay divorcee" as being somewhat promiscuous. Whereas a high proportion of never-married women have premarital coitus only with the fiancé whom they subsequently married,[8] relatively few women with postmarital coitus confine it to one fiancé. The percentage is nearly 16 per cent for the widowed and 12 per cent for the divorced. Sexually experienced women, many with at least an occasional desire for coitus, circulating in a world full of typically libidinous males, are not likely to find a permanent liaison or marriage with their first postmarital sexual partners. Of course nearly all of the women, widowed or divorced, who remarried and who had postmarital coitus had a portion of that coitus with their future husbands.[9] An exact tabulation of this figure was not made.

Frequency of Postmarital Coitus

The frequencies of postmarital coitus for the sample of widows are of limited value since the number of widows in any one age-period is small, and the number having coitus is smaller still. It was feasible only to calculate frequencies for age-periods twenty-six to thirty, thirty-one to thirty-five, thirty-six to forty, and forty-one to forty-five; in all other age-periods the number of widows having coitus is under fifteen. The larger sample of divorcees permits calculation through age-period forty-six to fifty, but not beyond. See Table 2.

The average (mean) frequencies of coitus among the divorced who had coitus varied from sixty-four to seventy-three times per year (1.23 to 1.40 per week) during their twenties and thirties. In their early forties the frequency dropped rather sharply to about fifty times per year and fell again, but only slightly, in their late forties to forty-five per year.

The picture for the widowed is rather similar, but on a much smaller scale. Their coital frequencies were forty-four per year (0.85 per week) in age-period twenty-six to thirty, forty-one in the following period, and thirty-six times per year in age-period thirty-six to forty—in brief, nearly a stable frequency over a fifteen-year span. Then, as with the divorced, age-period forty-one to forty-five is marked by a sharp decline in coital frequency, the average for the widowed being about twenty per year.

The explanations for the widowed having coital frequencies so far below those of the divorced are the same as those advanced in the discussion of the incidence of coitus: the divorced being more liberal in their sexual behavior due to their greater prior experience in premarital and extramarital coitus, many of the divorced bringing with them into postmarital life already established sexual relationships, the greater religious devoutness of the widows, et cetera. Religious devoutness is known to be associated with lower frequencies of other forms of non-marital coitus and the same seems true here.[10] Beyond these explanations already given, I must confess that I have an unproven impression, derived from hand-sorting the case histories for a few other items, that the widows as a whole are less sexually motivated than the divorced.[11] The widowed seem to have a larger proportion of women who could figuratively "take sex or leave it." This attitude has no necessary relationship to orgasmic capacity: such a woman can have marital coitus with orgasm for years, be widowed, and then live years of abstinence with little or no sexual frustration. This is incomprehensible to most males. What selective factors could be involved in why more women of this type are found among widows is a matter for conjecture. Perhaps the more responsive females are also more nervous, aggressive, and intolerant of marital problems, and hence divorce or cause their husbands to divorce them, while a more bland and unresponsive sort of female would be less aware of or more forgiving of male defects and hence live to be a widow. Or a cynic might say that males married to such women might court danger, holding their lives cheaply. In either case this is a matter calling for further investigation.

The decline of coital frequencies for both the widowed and divorced could be anticipated since the more sexually active tend to marry, and those remaining unmarried suffer a gradual loss of physical beauty, energy, and marriageability. However the rather abrupt drop in frequency in the early forties is puzzling, especially since there is no concomitant decrease of comparable magnitude in the percentage having coitus. The decrease may be in part attributable to the beginning of menopause in some females.[12] The males must share some of the responsibility for this decrease, especially since many of these women were involved with males older than themselves.

Orgasm and Postmarital Coitus

While religious scruples definitely influence the incidence and frequency of nonmarital coitus, they have been shown to have minimal effect upon the ability to experience orgasm in coitus either in or outside of marriage,[13] consequently degree of devoutness cannot be relied upon heavily to explain differences between the widowed and divorced in the percentage of their coitus resulting in orgasm for the female.

The smallness of the widowed sample made it necessary to use ten-year rather than five-year age-periods. Table 3 contains the data indicating that the widowed are quite as orgasmically responsive as the divorced and possibly more so during their twenties. It is interesting to note that the percentage of women reaching orgasm in virtually every coital act is higher for both the widowed and divorced than it is for married women.[14] This is to some degree the result of self-selection: while the temporarily unresponsive wife cannot always evade coitus, the widow or divorcee can do so more easily. In other words, the unmarried female is more likely to have coitus only when she wants it and hence her orgasmic response is greater.

The percentages fluctuate, but it appears that after age thirty about 50 to 60 per cent of all postmarital females reached orgasm in nearly every coital act (90–100 per cent). The divorced women show a trend to have an increasing number of women reaching orgasm nearly every time; such a trend was not evident among the widowed. To examine this matter better the divorced (who are sufficiently numerous for such an analysis) were divided into five-year age-periods. When this was done, a clear progression was seen in the percentage of high-orgasm (90 per cent or more) divorcees, the figure rising steadily from 36 per cent in age-period twenty-one to twenty-five to 65 per cent in age-period forty-one to forty-five (see Figure 3). Then in the following periods the figure drops to 57–58 per cent—this drop is probably the result of menopausal disturbance. The gradual increase with age in the proportion of divorcees reaching orgasm (nine times out of ten or better) suggests a rebound in responsiveness depressed by an unhappy marital situation. Data presented later in this section tend to substantiate this hypothesis. The absence of any trend toward increased responsiveness among widows suggests there was no orgasm-depressive situation to be overcome subsequently.

Conversely the divorced from age twenty-one to fifty show decreasing proportions of women having orgasm seldom or never. This trend is not seen among the widowed whose small numbers make the percentages unusably erratic.

Comparing the coital-orgasm rate in the postmarital period to that of the pre-existing marriage, one sees that it is usual for both the widowed and divorced to have a greater orgasmic response in postmarital life (Table 4). Of those having coitus, 57 per cent of the divorced and 48 per cent of the widowed had a higher percentage of orgasm during their postmarital life than in their former marriage. Marital orgasm rate exceeded the postmarital in 24 per cent of the widowed and 18 per cent of the divorced. While some of this postmarital superiority in female response can be attributed to these women being more able than wives to decide whether or not coitus will occur, several other variables are involved. The most obvious of these, and the one undoubtedly accounting for most of the difference between the widowed and divorced, is the divorced woman's rebound in responsiveness. It has been demonstrated that marital unhappiness is associated with a lower orgasm rate for wives.[15] Since most wives are unhappy in at least the terminal years of the majority of marriages which end in separation or divorce, one can reasonably assume their orgasm rates will be depressed. With the end of the marriage and the eventual formation of new and happier emotional relationships, the orgasm rate may be expected to increase.

This rebound explanation does not apply to all divorcees; one must seek yet other reasons for the higher postmarital-orgasm rate. The relaxation of inhibition which accompanies emotional maturation, which in turn follows on age and experience, is undoubtedly a factor.

Some of the improvement is due to novelty—the stimulation derived from a completely new sexual partner. Still another factor is probably experience with several partners: one learns more from several coital partners than from one, and orgasm is in part a learned response for the human female.

Summary

Despite the limitations of the sample and the crudity of the measures (e.g. not taking into account duration and frequency of coitus in calculating orgasm rate, nor distinguishing between "new" and "old" widows and divorcees in the age-periods), there were some valid and striking findings. Many of these were anticipated—for example, it is scarcely news that many divorcees have coitus—but such confirmations of folk knowledge are valuable since they are quantified rather than impressionistic. Other findings, particularly those based on comparisons of the widowed and divorced, are largely new contributions to knowledge. My attempts to explain various phenomena are sometimes based on varying amounts of factual evidence, but in other instances (hopefully evident to the reader) I indulged in conjecture. In either case the need for further and more detailed research is clear.

The more important findings are these:

(1) The majority of women whose marriages have ended have coitus while widowed, separated, or divorced.

(2) These women most commonly begin their postmarital coitus within one year after the end of the marriage.

(3) The average frequency of such coitus varies from

about thirty-six to seventy-three times a year up to age forty after which a marked decrease occurs.

(4) The women who have postmarital coitus generally experience orgasm in such coitus more often than they did in their coitus while married. As a whole, postmarital women have higher orgasm rates than wives of the same age.

(5) The divorced exceed the widowed in terms of prior nonmarital sexual experience, the per cent who have postmarital coitus, the frequency of postmarital coitus, and the speed with which such coitus is begun after the end of the marriage.

(6) Statistical tables follow.

TABLE 1

Age-Specific Incidence of Postmarital Coitus

AGE-PERIOD	DIVORCED		WIDOWED	
	% With Coitus	Total	% With Coitus	Total
21–25	73.4	177	42.1	19
26–30	70.3	236	54.8	42
31–35	78.3	207	47.2	53
36–40	77.9	154	35.8	53
41–45	68.6	118	34.7	49
46–50	59.0	61	26.5	49
51–55	39.4	33	26.3	38
56–60	42.9	14	23.5	34

TABLE 2

Average (mean) Frequency of Postmarital Coitus Among Females with Such Coitus

AGE-PERIOD	FREQUENCY PER WEEK	
	Divorced	Widowed
21–25	1.36	—*
26–30	1.36	0.85
31–35	1.23	0.78
36–40	1.40	0.69
41–45	1.01	0.39
46–50	0.88	—*
51–55	—*	—*
56–60	—*	—*

* The number of cases is less than fifteen so no calculation is feasible.

TABLE 3

Female Orgasm Rate in Postmarital Coitus

PERCENTAGE OF COITUS RESULTING IN ORGASM	AGE PERIODS							
	21–30		31–40		41–50		51–60	
	PERCENT OF FEMALES INVOLVED							
	Div.	Wid.	Div.	Wid.	Div.	Wid.	Div.	Wid.
0	23	10	15	7	11	20	17	28
1–39	14	13	11	12	8	4	17	0
40–89	20	7	19	26	19	14	6	22
90–100	42	70	56	56	62	62	61	50

Percentages are rounded to the nearest whole figure.

TABLE 4

Female Orgasm Rate in Postmarital Coitus Compared to Marital Coitus

ORGASM RATE	DIVORCED	WIDOWED
More in Post-marital Coitus	57%	48%
Same	25%	28%
More in Marital Coitus	18%	24%

Excluded from the above calculations were 8% of the total divorcees with postmarital coitus and 21% of the total widows with postmarital coitus where the orgasm rate was unknown or too complex to calculate.

FIGURE 3

Per Cent of Divorcees Reaching Orgasm in 90–100% of Their Postmarital Coitus

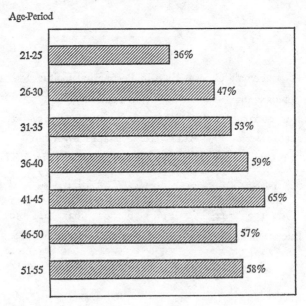

Age-Period

Age-Period	
21-25	36%
26-30	47%
31-35	53%
36-40	59%
41-45	65%
46-50	57%
51-55	58%

5

Anomalies in American Postdivorce Relationships

MARGARET MEAD

In human societies, we almost always find a contrast between life as people believe it to be, and life as it is lived by some, if not all, members of that society. People carry about with them a model of what each human relationship should be—how a mother should feel about her child, how a child should feel about its mother, how brothers and sisters should feel about each other, and what a marriage relationship should be like. These ideal patterns are almost always at least partially unattainable because of the vagaries and exigencies of human life. Often, the ideal is in conflict with reality: some women are childless, some children are orphans, some brothers have no sisters, some sisters have no brothers, and some wives or husbands do not live long enough to fulfill the roles which the marriage ceremonies have decreed they enact. People often cling in their minds to a pattern far removed from the realities of everyday life; the more remote their ideal is from reality, the more the conflicts that arise.

When I did my first field work, I still believed that such patterns would adjust themselves fairly rapidly, and that delinquent behavior, for example, could be defined as the disapproved behavior of a minority of young people in a society undergoing change. But later studies demonstrated that it was possible for nearly an entire people to live their lives in flagrant disregard of rules they continued to profess. The most disruptive people in a society can even be those who insist on rules that have become outmoded.

Something of this applies to the Mundugumor people of the Yuat River in New Guinea,[1] who had gradually evolved an elaborated form of marriage by brother and sister exchange. To marry "correctly," a man had to exchange his sister for the daughter of his mother's father's mother's father's sister's son's daughter's son's daughter, and his sister had to marry his wife's brother. As can be imagined, such a marriage required so many felicitous biological accidents, that it was virtually impossible for anyone to be married correctly. Nevertheless, the Mundugumor refused to accept as proper any substitution for this fantastically difficult arrangement, except in the case of individuals adopted as infants. As a result, a marriage that conformed to the rules was an enormous rarity. At the time I studied the Mundugumor, in 1932, there was not a single correct marriage in the entire village of Kenakatem. Obviously, their form of marriage was the inevitable consequence of an elaboration of some earlier and easier form of marriage with a cross-cousin. But instead of returning to a more simple form, there were enough Mundugumor who clung stubbornly to the unrealizable ideal, so that everyone was embarrassed and miserable. Since no one was in a correct relationship to his in-laws, everyone was uncomfortable. But instead of modifying the rules covering marriage, the Mundugumor continued to make them more complicated. Under their system, the only men who might have felt comfortable as peers were full brothers—as half brothers by different mothers were not members of the same "rope," or alternating descent group. But there was a rule that full brothers should not speak to each other except publicly, and then only in anger.

The Mundugumor had still another ideal—that of polygamy. Polygamy was important for any man of stature in the community. When such a man sought to acquire more wives for himself by exchanging women, he either pre-empted his brother's rights to his sisters, or exchanged daughters who rightfully should have served as marriage exchange for his sons. Clearly, the ideal of polygamy was inconsistent with the marriage system. But having numerous wives was considered such a sign of male prowess, that a man with only one wife treated her as if she were one among many. Consequently, the lone wife of an insignificant man had to struggle to please and allure him, behaving in exactly the same way as one of the ten wives of a man of importance. In this society, it was the virtuous and the conforming who did harm, who preserved an impossible system and condemned all others for marrying in various incorrect ways.

The Arapesh of New Guinea[2] present a sharp contrast to the Mundugumor, in that monogamy was the ideal, and the marriage arrangement did not depend upon the exchange of sisters—although some sort of balance between hamlets and villages in the number of women exchanged was judged desirable. The Arapesh marriage system depended upon the child betrothal of a prepubertal girl to a youth who hopefully would reach puberty several years ahead of her. The affianced girl was brought into the household of her future husband, and he, helping his fathers and brothers, "grew" her by providing her with food. Her dutifulness and his authority in the marriage depended on his being able to invoke the fact that he actually did "grow" her. Due to his wife's physical immaturity, and the belief that sex before maturity retarded growth, consummation of marriage was forbidden until both had attained their full growth. The assumption was that the marriage of this couple (whose relationship was cemented by long years of cherishing on the part of the husband, and equally long years of dependence on the part of the wife) would endure into old age, when neither surviving spouse would be young enough to consider marrying again.

This ideal flew in the face of the facts almost as much as did that of the Mundugumor. Children's ages were not recorded, and it frequently happened that a girl grew up "too fast," while the contracting parents-in-law watched aghast and saw the growth of the young husband terribly endangered by his wife's maturity. In such instances, the girl was sometimes hastily reassigned to a brother of the husband. Sometimes, too, the marriage was consummated too soon, and when the young couple failed to have children, this was regarded as the inevitable and dreadful consequence of premature intercourse. The Arapesh ideal of marriage fell short of realization in other ways. When young men died, the young girls they had cherished were assigned to men who had not reared them, and who could not make the customary claim to their affectionate submission. When older men died, their widows were assigned as second wives to young or middle-aged men, introducing a co-wife into a household in a society whose ideal included monogamy. When women from the fiercer tribes of the interior took refuge with these mountain people, the Arapesh—much as they disliked polygamy—could not resist keeping the women as prizes and assigning them to the more able men. Among the Arapesh, polygamous marriage introduced a singular bit of make-believe. The man had to treat each of his two wives (and occasionally three) as if she were his only wife; if he failed to do so, strife broke out.

An equally illuminating example of how a society can complicate relationships, to its own discomfort, is provided by Reo Fortune's study of the Dobuans.[8] In the Dobuan society, husband-and-wife pairs changed their dwellings yearly; one year was spent in the wife's village, the next in the husband's village, and so on. The stranger in the village, husband or wife, was subjected to suspicion and enmity from the "owners" of the village. In neither village could both the husband and wife feel at home. In a kind of complementary reprisal, the inside of each Dobuan house was guarded as jealously as a connubial bedroom. Beside each house, each wife watched over her cookpot, afraid of the poison of her neighbors.

These anomalies and difficulties sprang from a primitive people's inability to take into account such basic facts of life as relative age, sex, number of children, or death itself. And they sprang also from these people's tendency to complicate interrelationships in societies based on kinship. Such anomalies and difficulties dramatically demonstrate that in human societies, intelligence does not provide automatic self-correcting devices that can be relied upon to work out rules to keep things flowing smoothly. At the time I studied the Mundugumor, they were no longer even obeying the taboo against eating members of their own group, and only the arrival of colonial rule saved them from complete extinction. At the time Reo Fortune studied the Dobuans, women were actively attempting to prevent the birth of children. These are small-scale illustrations; but they serve to highlight the fragility of human institutions, even in the absence of drastic technological change, or violent conflict between societies of different complexity.

As the great religions spread over the face of the earth, crossing language boundaries and reaching peoples of very different cultural backgrounds and technological levels, the discrepancies between ideals and practices became a common expectation in all societies. In primitive societies, custom is sanctioned by tradition, but is subject to very rapid transformation, because there are no sacred texts to preserve the past, intact and static. The great religions are all associated with script. All have sacred texts in which the ideals that animated and continue to animate them are expressed—encased in the particular language and cultural forms of the period in which the sacred texts were written. Furthermore, in the great religions we have a different kind of association between ethics and custom than that which is found in many primitive societies. Monogamous marriage, matters of usury, the position of women, the observance of a day of rest, food taboos—all may become such an integral part of the religious belief, that abandonment of any detail of correct social custom becomes tantamount to the abandonment of a belief in God. Where religion and custom are so intertwined, the problem of adapting to new social, biological, and technological conditions becomes even more complicated. Such adaptations are difficult, whether within the Roman Catholic Church or within the Church of Latter Day Saints (in which continuing revelation is possible); whether among the Protestant sects (who must base consensus upon interpretation of the unchanging text of the Scriptures) or within the Eastern Orthodox churches, in which tradition is ambiguously paired with revelation as a guide to conduct.

Within different societies at the same time, and also throughout the course of industrial and postindustrial development, there have been periodic attempts to separate the essence of a religious belief from the temporary accretions with which it had been combined. In Europe, where it has been essential that the wife of a landowning peasant should have children, the churches have long coexisted with courtship customs which ensured that the girl had conceived before the marriage was consummated. These practices, of course, often resulted in illegitimate births. Among the great, although divorce was forbidden, annulment could be arranged. Such contradictions are commonplace, both within sacred and secular ideologies. Communism, like Roman Catholicism, also has mechanisms for adjusting dogma to fit changing conditions.

One set of such contradictions is introduced into contemporary society by divorce, and all the problems that result from any failure to observe the whole sequence of behaviors that are regarded as appropriate in Judaeo-Christian forms of marriage and parenthood. The ideal is clear and unequivocal. We are a society in which the union of a male and female institutes a new social unit, and the identity and care of the children depend upon the maintenance of that social unit. Neither the father's kin nor the mother's kin have any legal responsibility for the children, as long as the parents are alive. Only the succession of monogamous and permanent unions provides stability. Grandparents and children may be held responsible for each other, if the parents die, but brothers may not be held responsible for sisters, nor aunts and uncles for nephews and nieces. The large extended family, or clan, which takes responsibility for all the descendants of both male and female members, and thus provides for every child, does not exist in law, and is seldom found in fact.[4] Each American child learns, early and in terror, that his whole security depends on that single set of parents who, more often than not, are arguing furiously in the next room over some detail in their lives. A desperate demand upon the permanence and all-satisfyingness of monogamous marriage is set up in the cradle. "What will happen to me if anything goes wrong, if Mommy dies, if Daddy dies, if Daddy leaves Mommy, or Mommy leaves Daddy?" are questions no American child can escape.

In the past, the question of death was more salient, and the terrible fear of stepparents permeated our fairy tales, and still dominate the life stories of many older people. In the past, it must be remembered, we were essentially a people whose belief in monogamy was tempered by a high adult death rate. Men whose vigor outpaced the strength of their wives could expect that these women would die, and that they themselves would be free to marry younger women, and see them into an early grave, too—mothers of ten children, of whom three might be living. Vigorous women, in turn, buried their less vigorous husbands. The children suffered and were expected to suffer, within a system that decreed such exclusive relationships between parents and children, and that admitted of no substitutes. In the family systems of many other societies, where children learn to turn to one relative for solace, and to another for the mastery of a skill, the continuum of the marriage of the own parent is not so essential. Identity, security, adult backing in youth, and youthful help in old age are all assured by wider family ties. But not so in the United States. Correspondingly, our children are not prepared to trust anyone but their own parents, and as adults are not prepared to establish close and trusting ties with anyone except their own children.

Yet, more and more families are disrupted by divorce. People may expect to live much longer, and, as individuals, may undergo radical changes in social positions and social preferences. The marriage age is lower, but the amount of parental control over the choice of a mate has not increased. An unsuitable and hastily contracted marriage (agreed to by both sets of parents) because a seventeen-year-old girl is pregnant by an eighteen-year-old boy has a very poor chance of surviving. It probably will not survive long enough to provide the baby that was its ostensible justification with a permanent background for identity and security. A dismaying proportion of teen-age marriages end in divorce.

As the expectation that a marriage will last diminishes, so the fear that any given marriage may not last increases, feeding the desperation of the girl-wives (understandably seeking to retain a father for their children) and the furtive hopes of the boy-husbands (restive under such early curtailment of their own exploratory impulses). We have constructed a family system which depends upon fidelity, lifelong monogamy, and the survival of both parents. But we have never made adequate social provision for the security and identity of the children if that marriage is broken, as it so often was in the past by death or desertion, and as it so often is in the present by death or divorce. We have, in fact, as did the primitive Mundugumor, Arapesh, and Dobuan, saddled ourselves with a system that won't work.

Furthermore, the knowledge that a marriage may end in divorce creates a whole series of conditions which increase the chances of divorce. These include the fear itself, which echoes the childhood fear of the disruption of the only safety the child knows; the lack of confidence that time can heal or teach, which is obtained within indissoluble marriage; the demand that each marriage be an all-purpose marriage, satisfying every demand of each spouse, as once the marriage of the parents had to do; and the corresponding despair and disruption that comes with *any* failure in compatibility or agreement. If a marriage is viewed as a failure unless all aspects, including sex, companionship, provision of a way of life, shared recreation, and compatibility, are completely satisfactory, then the chances of its failing are very high indeed. If the correct treatment for a sense of failure is recourse to the divorce court, no matter how delayed such recourse may be, this view of marriage makes a great deal of divorce inevitable.[5]

Our present frequency of divorce has coincided with

the development of a new set of attitudes and beliefs about incest. Incest taboos are among the essential mechanisms of human society, permitting the development of children within a setting where identification and affection can be separated from sexual exploitation, and a set of categories of permitted and forbidden sex can be established.[6] Once these are established by the usually implicit but heavily charged learning of early childhood, the boy or girl is prepared to establish close relationships with others, of both a sexual and an asexual but affectional nature. The permissible sex partner, who may be one of a narrowly defined group of cousins, or any appropriately aged member of another village, or any age mate in the village who is not a relative, is sharply identified. The forbidden sex partners, a category which includes parents, aunts and uncles, brothers and sisters, nephews and nieces, and sometimes a wider group of all cousins, or all members of the clan or the community, are equally sharply distinguished. Close ties may be formed with forbidden sex partners without the intrusion of inappropriate sexuality; trust and affection, dependence and succorance, can exist independently of a sexual tie. Grown to manhood and womanhood, individuals are thus equipped to mate, and to continue strong, affectional ties with others than their own mates.

Where such incest categories are not developed, there are certain kinds of social consequences. Groups that can only absorb a non-member by establishing a sexual tie to a member, like the Kaingang of South America,[7] have a limited capacity to form wider alliances. In parts of Eastern Europe, where the father-in-law may pre-empt the daughter-in-law in his son's absence, for example, on military service, certain inevitable suspicions and antagonisms exist between fathers and sons. The complications that may result from a mother-in-law's attraction to a young son-in-law—complications that were ruled out in the case of a juvenile own son, no matter how loved—are

so ubiquitous, that mother-in-law taboos placing limitations on any social relationships between son-in-law and
mother-in-law are the commonest and most stringent
avoidance taboos in the world. The complementary taboo, between brother and sister, is also found in many
parts of the world. The stringency of this childhood
prohibition is matched by the intensity of the mating
relationship, where the mate is not the forbidden sister.
Thus, failure to choose the correct mate automatically
becomes involved with breaking the incest taboo, as has
been shown in the analyses of Eastern European Jewry
kinship relationships, where the *shiksa*—the inappropriate gentile wife—is equated in feeling with the forbidden
sister.[8] The vigorous definitions of the difference between the permitted and the forbidden sexual partner
reinforce the specificity of other relationships.

If the incest taboos are seen to make an essential contribution to the rearing of children within a situation
where their own immature emotions are respected, and
where they are at the same time prepared for both sexual
and non-sexual relationships as adults, it is then obvious
that the taboo must be extended to include all members
of the household. No matter what the size of the household, sex relations must be rigorously limited to the sets
of marital couples—parents, grandparents, married aunts
and uncles—who live within its confines. When these
rigorous limitations are maintained, the children of both
sexes can wander freely, sitting on laps, pulling beards,
and nestling their heads against comforting breasts—
neither tempting nor being tempted beyond their years.
In parts of traditional India, girls went as children to be
the protected wives of their future husbands, but this
protection of nubile young wives, was not extended to
daughters of members of the extended households who
overstayed their time within the paternal home. The
latter situation occurred in early missionary days, when
the missionaries attempted to fight "child marriages" by

keeping girls in boarding schools, but letting them go home for the holidays.

In England, until fairly recent times, the dangerous possibilities of attraction to the wife's sister, were considered so great that there was a compensatory legal rule which specifically forbade marriage with a deceased wife's sister. This device was designed to at least interrupt daydreaming and acting out during the wife's lifetime, since membership in the same household was possible after her death. In non-monogamous societies, marriage with the wife's sister is a common and often congenial type of marriage, especially in the cases where a sister may be given to complete a household into which her childless older sister is married.

Traditionally, within the Christian usages of the past, forbidden degrees of marriage have dealt more or less successfully with the problem of protecting those who live together in a single household. Stepbrotherhood and stepsisterhood are included within the impediments to marriage in the Roman Catholic Church.

However, imperceptibly and almost unremarked, the sanctions which protect members of a common household, regardless of their blood relationships, have been eroded in the United States. About all that remains today is the prohibition of sex in consanguinous relationships—a prohibition supported by the popular belief that the offspring of close relatives are defective. Stated baldly, people believe the reason that sex relationships between any close kin, father-daughter, mother-son, brother-sister, sometimes first cousins, uncle-niece and aunt-nephew, are forbidden, is simply that such unions would result in an inferior offspring—feeble-minded, deformed, handicapped in some way. This belief is a sufficient protection against incest so long as the two-generation nuclear family is the rule of residence, and the original marriage remains intact. In such households, neither aunts nor uncles are welcome as residents, cous-

ins are members of other households, and even boarders
and domestic servants are now regarded as undesirable.
The small family, united by blood ties, can thus safely
indulge in intimacy and warmth between biologically
related parents and children. It can be pointed out that
this sanction is based on a misunderstanding of the biological principles which govern the inheritance of specific genes which are more likely to appear in closely
consanguinous matings.[9] But a more serious limitation
of this sanction is that it does not provide for a household which includes a stepparent, a stepchild, stepsiblings, or adopted children.

We rear both men and women to associate certain
kinds of familiarity, in dress, bathing, and relaxation,
with carefully defined incest taboos in which the biological family and the single household are treated as
identical. We provide little protection when individuals
are asked to live in close contact within a single, closed
household, with members of the opposite sex to whom
they have no consanguinous relationships. This leads to
enormous abuses—girls are seduced by stepbrothers and
stepfathers, men are seduced by precocious stepdaugh-
ters. It also leads to a kind of corruption of the possibilities of trust and affection, confusing the children's
abilities to distinguish between mates and friends,
whether of the same age, or among those of another
generation. If the girl is below the age of consent, seduc-
tion which takes place between a stepfather and a step-
daughter, however initiated, is treated as a sex offense
against a minor rather than as incest.[10] Moreover, there
is increasing evidence of the connivance of a consanguinous member of the family in such intrigues. The
consenting minor may or may not be damaged psychologically, as she would be certain to be in a relationship
with her own father or brother, which is experienced as
incest. In fact, there is some evidence that where the
biological mother connives in a sexual relationship be-

tween a father and daughter, the daughter has not been damaged psychologically. This finding may be interpreted as a sign that there is no natural or instinctive aversion to incest. But it may also be seen as a final weakening of incest taboos in our society, as the rationale has shifted from taboos governing the relationships of persons of opposite sex and different generations in close domestic contact, to a mere precaution against defective offspring, when offspring are not in any event the purpose of such liaisons.

As the number of divorces increases, there are more and more households in which minor children live with stepparents and stepsiblings, but where the inevitable domestic familiarity and intimacy are not counterbalanced by protective, deeply felt taboos. At the very least, this situation produces confusion in the minds of growing children; the stepfather, who is seen daily but is not a taboo object, is contrasted with the biological father, who is seen occasionally and so is endowed with a deeper aura of romance. The multiplication of such situations may be expected to magnify the difficulties young people experience in forming permanent-mating relationships, as well as in forming viable relationships with older people. They may also be expected to magnify the hazards of instructor-student intrigues, of patient-doctor complications, and of employer-employee exploitation. It may even be that the emergence of the very peculiar form of sex behavior in which couples unknown to each other, arrange to meet secretly and exchange sex partners may be an expression of the kind of object confusion that has grown up in our present much-divorced, much-remarried society—a society in which, however, the ideal of the biologically related, two-generation, exclusive nuclear family is still preserved.

Another confusion in our present attitudes toward divorce and remarriage comes from our refusal to treat the coconception and production of a child as an unbreakable tie between the parents, regardless of the state of the marriage contract. In most societies, the permanency of the consanguinous tie between a child and its forbears, including the siblings of parents and grandparents, and their offspring, is taken as a matter of course. Occasionally, we still indulge in the same kind of recognition of the depth of kinship ties; the immigrant may still hope someday to meet a sibling who was born after he emigrated, and who will welcome him as a relative. People still seek for relatives in other countries. But our present divorce style often denies the tie between the child and one of the parents, and it permits the parents to deny that—through their common child—they have an irreversible, indissoluble relationship to each other. Where one parent can be declared as grievously at fault, all visitation rights or privileges of custody may be denied him or her. And custom follows law in that, in many bitter divorce battles, one parent is *de facto* denied any contact with his or her own child, and both parents are allowed and often required by custom to completely break any contact with each other.

Among the older generation, there is some feeling that any contact between divorced people somehow smacks of incest; once divorced, they have been declared by law to be sexually inaccessible to each other, and the aura of past sexual relations makes any further relationship incriminating. Lawyers may look with deep suspicion on any suggestion that one divorced spouse should ever remain overnight in the home of the other divorced spouse and his or her children. This is a reasonable precaution where there is a decree nisi to be observed, as was the case in English law until recently, but is a wholly anomalous attitude in the United States. By failing to extend the incest taboo to the stepparent, we may have displaced it upon the previous husband or wife, who now assumes the avoidance that should appropriately exist between stepparent and a stepchild of the opposite sex. On the other hand, the common practice of urging the child of remarried parents to accept the stepparent as the own parent, simply compounds the complications for the child and the stepparent when they are of opposite sex.

I have discussed three aspects of our present situation that put an undue strain on marriage and family life—all of them closely interwoven with the way in which we handle divorce and remarriage. Such analyses are fruitful only if they lead to constructive criticisms and the development and invention of new and more appropriate institutions. The conditions that need to be corrected are: the overdependence of children on the nuclear family, which leads to great demands by the children on the security their parents alone can provide, and by the parents on each other; the sanctioning of incest taboos by folk biology alone, so that the need for protection of non-consanguinous household members is not recognized; and the failure to provide some kind of viable relationship between parents who are no longer married to each other, so that there may be a continuing relationship between the child and both parents, and so that the child's identity is not shattered by divorce.

Observation of what is going on in many parts of the United States shows that there are many spontaneous attempts to deal with the first of these problems. The exclusively nuclear family is still very slightly compensated for by alliances among young married people, and by visits to relatives, especially during vacations, when time and modern transportation make such visits possible.[11] As for the inadequacy of our present-day incest taboos, this is hardly recognized as a problem. Psychiatrists continue to struggle with the psychological definitions of the incest taboo, rather than with the social conditions which create the present high incidence of steprelative sex relationships. The problem of maintaining the necessary parent-child relationships following divorce is being dealt with in a variety of ways. The organization called

Parents Without Partners is a self-conscious attempt to deal with the insecurity of children who must be reared by divorced or widowed parents. It attempts to do so by providing surrogates for the absent or alienated parent, or alternatively, by helping the parent who is only allowed occasional visitation rights in regard to his or her children. But even such measures fail to meet a basic need. What is needed here are more viable ways in which the divorced parents may share time together with their children, and provide at least brief periods when the children can feel some restoration of the identity on which they were taught to rely, and of which the divorce has robbed them.

Many young divorced women with children make a major effort to maintain closer ties with their own families, including siblings and their spouses, and nephews and nieces. Also, in many cases, they strive to maintain their children's relationships to the grandparental family of the lost father. Such attempts—unsanctioned in our present system, which permits the connecting link between the grandparents and the grandchildren to drop out completely—are often stormy and hazardous. The grandparents may jealously protect the "rights" and "privileges" which the son-father has relinquished, or of which he has been deprived. This behavior is accentuated when the daughter-in-law remarries, and a new and real father-figure for the grandchildren replaces the phantom figure of their son in the daughter-in-law's household.

We badly need to recognize a new form of marriage—a marriage between childless partners with no commitment to continuity. Such marriages should be easier to contract, should involve no automatic economic relationships, and should be capable of dissolution by mutual consent, without undue delay, cost, or supervision from the constituted organs of society. On the other hand, marriages which are parental should be placed in a different category, and have built into them once more the conception of what a marriage with children is—a life-long relationship which will end only with death. By treating every legal permission for sex relationships as, *ipso facto,* a lifelong, totally committed parental marriage, we fail to provide the necessary protection for children. At the same time, we place extraordinary burdens on young people, and encourage the use of pregnancy as a device to obtain parental consent and support for marriages which involve premature parenthood. If we could rephrase divorce as a necessary component of relationships between the sexes in a society as complex, as heterogenous, as rapidly changing, and with as long-lived a population as ours, we could then consider how to have good and appropriate divorces. As things are, we insist that the most flimsy, ill-conceived, and unsuitable mating be treated as a sanctified, lifelong choice. At the same time, we insist that every divorce, however much it is dictated by every consideration of the welfare of the children and parents, be regarded as a failure and be listed as an index of social disorder—along with suicide, homicide, narcotic addiction, alcoholism, and crime. By insisting on these views of divorce, we debar ourselves from developing new and appropriate institutions for protecting children from an unrealistic dependence upon a situation of lifelong marriage between their parents.

We also need some new kinship terms. We need a term for cograndparents which—based as it is on a biological event, the birth of a shared grandchild—will be as permanent as any other kinship term. When parents remarry, we need terms for "father's wife" and "mother's husband," to be used easily and freely by children. The word "stepmother," inappropriate in the case of a divorce, has unfortunate implications and is outmoded. The hundreds of thousands of second wives, struggling to give a good life to their husbands' children, deserve a better term. (As early as twenty years ago, American children, and American mothers, rejected the descriptions of the wicked stepmother in fairy stories.)[12] We need a term which means "my child's father who is no longer my husband," and "my child's mother who is no longer my wife." Some children, who have grown up among several sets of grandparents, resulting from remarriage after death or divorce, happily embrace them all. But possibly there should be a term for "other grandparents" which would cover "my stepsibling's grandparents" also. And we need reciprocals for all of these terms—"my husband's child," "my wife's child," "my grandchildren, by my child who is no longer married to their mother or father." No institution is fully viable unless it has verbal as well as legal concomitants. Sitters came in when the word "sitter" came in. At present, the vulgar "my ex" is all that we have to deal with the relationship which may involve twenty years and five children. We should be able to do better— and soon.

6

*Divorce Chains,
Households of Remarriage,
and Multiple Divorcers*

PAUL BOHANNAN

As the divorce rate goes up, the remarriage rate also goes up. However, records are kept in such a way as to make statistics about remarriage even less reliable than statistics about divorce itself. Mead has shown clearly in her chapter above that vast problems may occur after the remarriage of divorced parents. The simple genealogical chart below provides an even wider view of the possible range of complications (see Figure 4).

A simple household based on the first marriage of both spouses provides eight terminologically recognized relationships. They are the relationship of husband-wife; the four parental relationships of father-son, father-daughter, mother-son, mother-daughter; and the three sibling relationships of brother-brother, sister-sister, and brother-sister. Of course, the content of all these relationships changes as parents mature and children grow up. It may differ depending on the order and sex of the children, the socioeconomic level of the family, and the individual emotional and personality characteristics of family members. However, in spite of the wide variety, there is a fairly clear and simple idea of what fathers should be to daughters and what fathers should be to sons; the differences between good mothering of a son and of a daughter are known; the way brothers should treat one another, and the ways that sibling rivalry should be controlled and sibling affection expressed are held in common.

FIGURE 4

Divorce Chains and Households of Remarriage

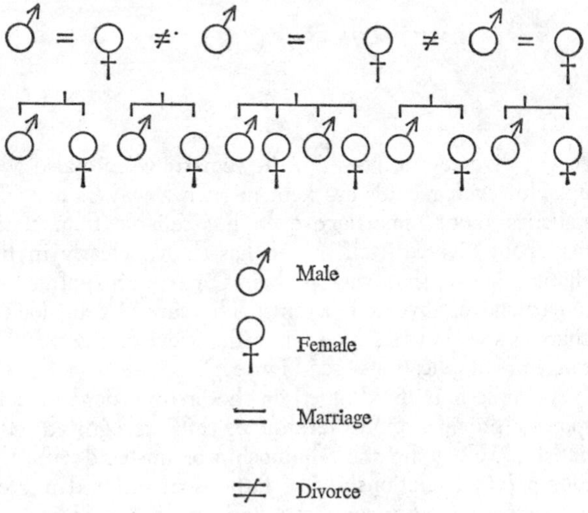

When a number of divorces and remarriages are added, however, two complications appear in this simple pattern. One is that a "chain" of relationships is formed among spouses and their ex-spouses. These "divorce chains" can be traced out along the top line of Figure 4.

The other complication ensues within the household which contains stepparents, stepsiblings and half-siblings, and the ways that members of such households behave in relation to ex-spouses and *their* families.

Divorce Chains

One of the most interesting discoveries I have made in my investigations of divorce in the United States is that pseudokinship groups are formed on the basis of links between the new spouses of ex-spouses. It is as if the ex-husband-ex-wife relationship were almost as strong as genetic relationships in the formation of such groups.

These groups first came to my attention at a very early stage of the study, while I was discussing the subject with a college friend who lives in Seattle. This man had been married, divorced, remarried, and divorced again. He was unmarried at the time of our talk, but has since remarried again. His first wife lived across the country from him, in New Jersey, with their son and with her second husband. His second wife had remarried and moved to New Orleans. He told me that when he went East, he had, of course, gone to visit his son in New Jersey. There he had met his first ex-wife's present husband (his son's stepfather). They had at first been formally polite to one another when he had picked up and returned his son for visitation. However, they found that they were congenial and that they did not threaten each other. Conversations developed and they became more friendly. His son expressed pleasure that they liked each other.

After the fourth or fifth encounter, the ex-wife and her present husband asked my friend to stay with them over a weekend so that the son could both see his father and pursue some activities he had planned with his own friends. He stayed with them, and found that he and the second husband had many business relationships in common, and that they could be of great assistance to one another in their businesses, providing good and reliable contacts from the two coasts of the continent. They ultimately collaborated on several business transactions.

The second ex-wife and the first ex-wife also were friends. On several occasions, when the woman who now lived in New Orleans came East, the two ladies met for lunch in Philadelphia. They had a lot in common, obviously, and they found they liked each other. When my friend remarried three years later, his third wife was a cousin of his first ex-wife's present husband.

I thought at the time that this story was unusual and instructive. I soon discovered, however, that although it is highly instructive, it is not unusual. I do not mean, obviously, that this is "average behavior" on the part of divorcing and remarrying people. But it is not rare—most informants can give two or three examples.

Divorce chains most often form when children are there to mediate the new relationships, but they are not a necessity. I know of an alcoholic who sometimes became brutal during his drinking bouts. His drinking problem did not become serious until several years after his first marriage. When his first wife found that she could not deal with the situation, she finally left him. She remarried—this time to a man who did not have these characteristics. The alcoholic ex-husband also remarried—this time to a more compliant wife who took her misery and unhappiness out on herself rather than on making demands for better behavior of the husband. The ex-wife and her second husband, aware of the situation, took the ex-husband's second wife to their apartment, where she stayed for about three months while she regained her health and some of her courage. They saw her through the initial stages of a divorce and into a job.

I know another case in which a man was divorced by his first wife after the birth of two children. He soon remarried and had two more children by his second wife, who had one child by her first husband. The two women met one another by chance through mutual acquaintances. After tentative beginnings, they found each other non-threatening. There may have been, at a deeper psychic level, something more in it, but the surface friendship was nevertheless real and the resulting group activity was considered by them to be useful and pleasant.

As the friendship between the two women grew, they planned outings for the entire lot of five children. The husband, at first, was uncomfortable, but when both his wife and his ex-wife were enthusiastic, when they did not give him or each other any trouble, and when he found that the children were not uncomfortable, he concurred. When he told me about this, it seemed to me that he was a little embarrassed by the situation, but he nevertheless found it effective for his children.

These divorce chains, like all American kinship groups except the nuclear family in a household, are formed spontaneously by and around individuals for specific purposes. The purposes change from one individual to the next, from one time of life to the next, from one set of kinsmen to the next. In some cases, the quasi-kinship group based on a divorce chain may perform effectively those functions traditionally assigned to an extended kinship group based on a set of descent chains.

This phenomenon has not yet been sufficiently studied, structurally or statistically or any other way. However, it is a situation that is of regular occurrence in American life—a norm for a small percentage of divorced people. Any complete study of divorce and remarriage must take it into consideration.

Households of Remarriage

Although the husband-wife relationship is broken at divorce and replaced with that of ex-husband-ex-wife, the relationship of parents to children remains intact. What divorced parents and their children do may be changed out of all recognition, but the relationship is today often not completely repudiated. There is, in the case histories and memories of doctors, lawyers, school psychologists, and teachers, a great deal of information about the relationship between divorced parents and their children, although it seems to me that there is comparatively little synthesis of all this information. The difficulty arises because the information lies so widely scattered. Each psychologist or teacher sees too few patients or students to be able to feel comfortable making generalizations. One child psychologist told me of a boy of eight who asked him for information about the parents' divorce—information the psychologist did not have. He suggested to the child that he might talk to his mother about it. The child immediately rejected this idea as impossible. After another few minutes of "playing it out," the child asked the psychologist, "Did you ever hear of child sacrifice?" In their conversation, the child went on with garbled versions of the stories of Isaac and Iphigenia—stories he had heard, in one version or another, but did not understand. The stories had in common that children were sacrificed (just how, he was not sure) in order to ensure adult happiness and the effectiveness of their endeavors.

Collection and analysis of experiences of this sort remain to be done—we know very little, in any organized way, of a child's view of divorce for all the decided opinions that divorce is bad for children.

We know a little bit more about remarriage because social scientists like Jessie Bernard and William Goode and sensitive journalists like Anne W. Simon have written about it. Here I want to examine some of the special problems in the households of remarried divorced persons.

Whereas the eight relationships of the nuclear family, which we described in the early pages of this chapter, are considered "natural" and their ideal content is well known, the remarriage of one or both of the ex-spouses creates a vast number of relationships of a new kind. In the first place, the relationship between ex-husband and ex-wife is poorly charted in American culture. When remarriage of one or both of the ex-spouses creates new husband-wife relationships, it simultaneously creates the possibility of extended affinal relationships: the two women who stand to one another in a relationship of husband's ex-wife to ex-husband's wife; another relationship of the two men who are wife's ex-husband and ex-wife's husband to one another. And if both these relationships are present, as they are at remarriage of both partners to the original marriage: the even more extended relationship of the ex-husband's wife's ex-husband to the ex-wife's husband's ex-wife.

It is not unusual for the former spouses of the two new spouses to know each other. It is complicated by relationships of stepparents and of stepsiblings and half-siblings.

The English kinship terms for stepparents and stepsiblings are singularly inadequate. In the days before the divorce rate soared and before the death rate was lowered, the term "stepmother" or "stepfather" referred to new people in the household who substituted for the "real" parents, who were dead. That is not true today in far the greatest number of cases. Rather, the stepparent is an addition, not a replacement. The difficulties are even greater.

Stepparents—especially stepmothers—have a cruel reputation throughout the world. Even when they are good and loving surrogate mothers, they suffer from this stigma, because of the emotions that are culturally associated with lack of biological connection. The childhood fantasies of what Freud called "the family romance"—a child considers that he is really the lost heir of much nobler parents than his own—are thrown into different perspective when a stepparent is present. In his book, *The Stepchild*, William Carlson Smith has shown that American men are repeatedly willing to sacrifice their children for a happy marital relationship, which means that the stepmother may not be as effectively sanctioned by her spouse in her attitude and behavior toward the children as the "real" mother would be. One has only to turn to the writings about stepparenthood in the current etiquette books to learn that the American norm is either to disregard the subject completely, or to assume that special care will be taken that no differences appear on the surface between stepparenthood and "real" parenthood. Stepparents are not "real"— and the culture so far provides no norms to tell us how they are different, or what ought to be done about them or toward them.

As Mead has demonstrated above, this situation becomes more poignant and difficult today when "stepparents" are in most instances the spouses of remarriage of the child's parents. Thus, the child has two or even more sets of parents.

Today, the stepparent is less often a substitute parent than he is an added parent. Using the vague and mildly pejorative terms of "stepmother" and "stepfather" for such persons—particularly when there are several—may prove upsetting in the child's emotional view of his world. I know several discussion groups that have been organized in California and in Illinois among the children of divorced parents. Working out terms and attitudes toward stepparents is one of the recurrent topics to which discussion returns.

Deciding what we should call stepparents is difficult in the absence of terms that differentiate them clearly from biological parents. I know a little girl of nine whose mother had married four times. She called her father, the mother's first husband, "Daddy." The other three she called Daddy-Tom, Daddy-Dick, and Daddy-Harry. Americans, as is their cultural tradition, usually utilize first names. However, using the first name may undermine a good authority relationship between stepparent and stepchild and may intensify competitiveness.

The creation of a stepchild-stepparent relationship is difficult in American culture. Most children, at the time their divorced parents remarry, are old enough to have some very pronounced ideas about remarriage in general, their parents' remarriage in particular, and their parents' choice of subsequent spouses in very great detail. In those situations in which it works at all, a relationship between the subsequent spouse and the stepchild is usually worked out before remarriage.

I know one woman who had the lack of good judgment to marry a man whose twelve-year-old daughter she had never met. Their courtship had been carried out in a foreign country while the child was with grandparents. On first meeting the little girl, she opened her arms and said, "I am your new mother." The little girl looked at her sourly and replied, "The hell you are." For this woman, even learning to say the word "stepmother" in reference to herself proved almost impossibly painful—she could never help adding that she knew that she was not cruel or sadistic.

It takes two to make a stepparent-stepchild relationship, the same as it does any other relationship. Children are often quite recalcitrant in these matters.

Doctor Mead has pointed out with great incisiveness some of the problems that can erupt when incest prohibitions are drawn to genetic relationships instead of to domestic relationships within the household. Indeed, I am convinced that the California case referred to above is a long step in the wrong direction, and that our family system will pay dearly for our continued emphasis on "blood" or genetic relationship rather than equal or greater emphasis on household relationships.

Not only does remarriage create new affinal relationships and new relationships between stepparents and stepchildren, but it obviously creates new relationships between stepbrothers and stepsisters. At the remarriage of a man and a woman, each of whom has children by prior marriages, their children become stepbrothers and stepsisters of one another. Again, the incest prohibitions and the general tone of American culture, and the axioms on which law and beliefs are based, say that these people are not "related" to one another. This means then, given our present definitions, that Americans are creating households in which more and more of the members are not kinsmen of one another. When we put with this the statistic that one child in every nine in the United States has a stepparent—the magnitude of the problem becomes apparent.

If additional children are born to the new marriage, then even greater complications ensue—there are additional relationships of half-siblings. One child may have brothers and sisters, half-brothers and half-sisters, and two or even more sets of stepbrothers and stepsisters.

The way in which the relationships of half-siblings are handled by middle-class American culture is far from clearly delineated. There is usually a significant age gap between sets of half-siblings, and it seems that there is often a relationship of studied avoidance or formality between them. Sometimes, of course, the older set of half-siblings become important parent substitutes for the younger ones. I know of no study that has focused on this problem.

Americans are struggling to create norms in all these "new" relationships; it is my own opinion that nothing short of a presidential blue-ribbon committee to consider matters, with widespread—indeed propagandistic—public relations coverage of the results can lead to new and approved patterns of family organization. The present situation approaches chaos, with each individual set of families having to work out its own destiny without any realistic guidelines.

Multiple Divorcers

All matrimonial lawyers have a few "regular clients." One lady lawyer who specializes in family matters told me about a woman for whom she had obtained five divorces—and she was not the lawyer who got this client her first one. Within a very short period after each final decree, the client calls the lawyer and says, "The most *wonderful* thing has just happened to me!" The lawyer always says, "All right, dear, bring him over." When the recently divorced client arrives with a new man—it is unquestionably a new man—he is precisely the same type as all the others: short, stocky, unkempt, shirt open at the neck, loud sports coat. As the lawyer expressed it, "Her fourth husband was a little different. He was taller, had wavy blond hair, had a necktie, and a quiet sports coat." And she added, "It took her almost six months to make *him* beat her up."

In this particular case, Marian, my lawyer informant, had tried repeatedly to get this woman into the hands of a good psychotherapist, or in some other way to educate her into recognizing the kind of mistake she kept making. Marian felt a deep responsibility for this woman, but none of her genuine efforts had been rewarded. Most matrimonial lawyers share her concern.

I know another lawyer who obtained three divorces for a prominent businessman. The businessman always picks out the same kind of mousey, mother-ridden woman, and divorces her in about three years. His lawyer is his best friend—certainly he is the friend of longest standing. The lawyer says of him, in half-pity, half-mockery, that he is his most treasured client.

We do not have any idea what proportion of the divorce rate in the United States is made up of such recidivist divorcers. Certainly the fact that one marriage in every three (or however else you want to compute this, for it depends on which figures you prefer to use) ends in divorce does not mean that one *person* in every three who marries will end up in a divorce court. The number of rate-raisers, and the ways and means by which they go about it, cannot be discerned from the present statistics, as they are now kept in any place in the United States. Even if questions were inserted into the application for a marriage license about previous marital history, there is reason to believe that many people might falsify them. It has long been known that there are considerably more women in the United States and Britain who identify themselves as widows to census takers than could possibly be true, given the other figures of the census. Although studies of the proportion of divorced persons who remarry, based on small samples, are extremely valuable, we still do not have anything but a vague notion about the national picture of divorce repeaters.

This short essay has raised more questions than it has supplied answers—that was, in fact, its purpose. It is time that Americans learned that divorce and its repercussions create problems far beyond the range of personal problems of divorcing people and their children, and that new kinds of social groups are emerging. Here we have noted that divorce chains form the fundamental links in some newly appearing quasi-kinship groups. We have noted that numbers of stepsiblings and half-siblings are creating horizontal links among families and households that are scarcely recognizable in their complexity.

Fortunately, Americans are becoming aware of problems of this sort—and they are beginning to deal with them: through special interest groups like Parents Without Partners, through discussion groups run by community mental-health organizations or psychiatric clinics, and through the studies of social scientists.

IV

Divorce Around the World

Americans make heavy going of their divorce procedures. A comparative view makes the point clearly. Doctor Rheinstein's article on Sweden is a presager of his more inclusive book on this subject. The article on the Eskimo examines divorce in a completely different context from our own, and allows us to see how very closely tied to our domestic and cultural arrangements our problems with divorce are—our problems are the very substance of our customs and our institutions. Finally, as Cohen's article on the Kanuri illustrates brilliantly, we in America do not have a high divorce rate—and, moreover, social disorganization is not a necessary concomitant of a high divorce rate. Unless, of course, we set up our institutions so that divorce creates disorganization. And that is what the American dilemma turns out to be—in order to have what we most cherish, the price we pay is the kind of divorce institutions we have now.

7

Divorce Law in Sweden

MAX RHEINSTEIN

What is the relationship between a society's laws on divorce and its actual state of marriage stability? Is it true
that a strict divorce law promotes stability of marriage
and family life? Or does immorality increase if divorce
is obtainable only with difficulty or not at all? Both propositions have been professed with equal fervor and with
an equal lack of evidence.

Of necessity, an investigation of the cause-and-effect
relation between law and life must be comparative. Are
changes in the divorce laws of a country accompanied
by changes in the incidence of marriage breakdown? Is
the incidence of marriage breakdown different in places
having different divorce laws? Of course, the observation
of differences in the rate of marriage breakdown does
not prove that they are caused by the differences in the
laws. Even incisive analysis will not yield definite proof.
But significant insights can be obtained from comparisons conducted along lines of time and place.

Such inquiries have been undertaken upon an extensive scale by the University of Chicago Comparative Law Research Center. The present article constitutes part of this enterprise.[1]

The analysis of the voluminous material has not yet been completed. But tentatively it may be stated that, among others, the following conclusions appear to be justified:

FIRST: The state of a country's marriage stability depends upon its intellectual and moral climate;

SECOND: In a highly industrialized country the incidence of marriage breakdown is greater than in a pre-industrialized country;

THIRD: The incidence of marriage breakdown tends to rise steeply while the country is in the process of industrialization; the curve tends to flatten out once the stage of full industrialization has been reached;

FOURTH: In a country which is industrialized to a considerable extent, but in which the moral and intellectual climate is either conservative or pluralistic, the divorce law of the statute book is strict, but it tends to become a dead letter. As collusive practices tend to be tolerated, authorization to remarry can be easily obtained or, if not obtainable, tends to be regarded as unnecessary for the creation of new marriage-like unions;

FIFTH: In an industrialized country with a predominantly liberal-individualistic climate of morality, the official law renders it easy to obtain a divorce and create a new home with surroundings likely to be apt for children to grow up;

SIXTH: As industrialization begins, the functions and the structure of the institutions of marriage and family undergo considerable changes, but the institutions themselves continue to constitute the basic units of society.

Sweden, together with the other Nordic countries, constitutes an example of a society whose moral and intellectual climate is predominantly liberal-individualist.[2]

1. The family is the basic cell of society. It is based upon monogamous marriage. Marriage is a relationship meant to be exclusive and to last for the joint lives of the spouses.

2. Attempts to enforce the ideal of permanency of marriage or to curb extramarital sex activity by means of law are futile.

3. The breakdown of a marriage regularly results in serious mental and economic consequences for the parties and their children. The main task of the law of divorce is that of mitigating as much as possible the damaging consequences.

4. It is not the task of the law to bar the establishment of new family homes for the parties and their children.

These are the principles of a society of liberal-individualist persuasion. They have found expression in the laws of the Scandinavian countries. The principal ground upon which a divorce, i.e. restoration to the freedom of remarriage, can be obtained, is the factual breakdown of the marriage, proved by separation of a certain period of time and the mutual consent of the parties. If the termination of the marriage tie is sought by one party alone, divorce is on general principle also obtainable without much difficulty.

Although the great majority of divorces is obtained upon the mutual consent of the parties, it is nevertheless justified to emphasize that, officially, the Sandinavian laws are based upon the principle of *Zerruettung* (deep, permanent discord) rather than that of simple agreement.

Consent is important as evidence of marital discord rather than in itself. Marriage is still regarded as being concluded for life[3]; divorce, however easily it may be obtained, is still to constitute the exception. The Scandinavian laws resemble the pre-1969 law of California where, in fact, although not in theory, a divorce could always be obtained where the parties are in agreement or where one party exhibits the serious desire to be free, but where one year had to elapse between the interlocutory and the final decree. Compared with such American jurisdictions as Nevada, Idaho, Arkansas, or even such states as Illinois, where the officially professed principle of guilt is in fact turned into that of mutual consent, the Scandinavian laws with their waiting periods are strict.

Even though the persuasion of individualism is the official rather than the hidden basis of Scandinavian divorce law, the divorce rates are considerably lower than those of the United States, where in 1968 the rate was 2.9 per 1000 population.[4] The corresponding Scandinavian figures have been as follows[5]:

TABLE 5

Annual average 1951–55:

Denmark	1.53
Finland	0.85
Iceland	0.75
Norway	0.65
Sweden	1.18

TABLE 6

Annual rates per 1000 population 1956–66:

	Denmark	Finland	Iceland	Norway	Sweden
1956	1.46	0.85	0.62	0.62	1.18
1957	1.43	0.81	0.70	0.58	1.20
1958	1.46	0.83	0.85	0.59	1.17
1959	1.42	0.83	0.88	0.62	1.17
1960	1.46	0.82	0.71	0.66	1.20
1961	1.43	0.88	0.90	0.68	1.16
1962	1.38	0.89	0.69	0.67	1.17
1963	1.27	0.92	1.07	0.67	1.20
1964	1.4[6]	0.97	0.91	0.65	1.20
1965	1.4	0.99	0.63	0.70	1.24
1966	1.36	0.99	1.03	0.69	1.24

The data on divorce can be assumed to approximate closely those of factual marriage breakdown. Once a marriage has ceased to exist in fact, Scandinavians, especially Danes and Finns, appear to be inclined to have it also terminated at law. Suits for separate maintenance[7] seem to be used almost exclusively as preliminaries to divorce. The number of Roman Catholics, to whom divorce is religious anathema, is negligible. The population almost solidly belongs, at least nominally, to the Lutheran State Church.[8]

The Scandinavian situation indicates that a divorce law clearly based upon the individualist view of life and society is compatible with the firm maintenance of the institution of marriage as the basic cell of society, even if it is accompanied by a far-reaching alleviation of traditional sex taboos.[9]

In the Scandinavian countries, especially Denmark and Sweden, the sexual revolution, which has taken place in association with modern industrialization, urbanization, female emancipation, and birth control techniques, has probably gone farther than in other parts of the once-Christian world. The change in the sex mores is a part of that general liberalization of life that has been characteristic of the countries of Henrik Ibsen, August Strindberg, Ellen Key, and Eduard Westermarck.

The starting point of the Scandinavian development was the same as that of all non-orthodox Europe: the medieval principle of indissolubility of marriage. As in other Lutheran and Reformed countries, the reinterpretation of the Gospel by the reformers brought slight inroads. Adultery and certain cases of desertion[10] were recognized as grounds entitling the innocent spouse to repudiate the guilty so as to be set free to remarry by ecclesiastical authority.

In Sweden this practice was formalized in the Ecclesiastical Ordinance of 1572, which explicitly ordered the clergy to watch over the marital lives of the people. In their sermons the pastors were assiduously to admonish the people to preserve harmony in their homes. In particular it was declared to be the churchman's duty, through individual warning and appropriate means of ecclesiastical discipline, to prevent a marriage from being broken up by discord. The rules concerning this ecclesiastical duty to deal with "quarrelsome couples," which in the long run was to have important consequences for the development of divorce, was elaborated by the Church Law of 1686. A quarrelsome couple should first be admonished by its pastor and then, if necessary, by the chapter of the diocesan cathedral. If they failed to reform, the case was to be reported to the secular authority, which should resort to imprisonment or "other appropriate punishment," meaning flogging, fine, prison, or the stock. If that would not help, the scandalous quarreling was to be stopped by forcibly separating the parties from each other for a limited period of time, during which the congregation were to pray for their reformation. Ultimate punishment, after futile public admonition from the pulpit, could be the Great Bann, which meant not only exclusion from participation in worship but social boycott in secular affairs as well, possibly leading to banishment from the realm. The same extreme punishment was to be meted out to a married man or woman who had deserted the home, driven out his spouse, or stubbornly refused to resume a peaceful marital life.

It is a far cry from such ecclesiastical coercion of marital harmony to the present law. The intervening steps reflect the growing secularization of the state and society and the concomitant transformation of the basic morals. A first step was taken in the Church Law of 1686 itself, which transferred to the secular courts the investigation of the facts in cases of application for marriage-tie termination on the grounds of adultery, flight from the realm or disappearance. The issuance of letters of divorcement remained with the cathedral chapters. But they were not to issue letters until so ordered by the secular authority.

No major change was made by Sweden's great codification of the law, Sveriges Rikes Lag of 1734, which, preceding Napoleon's codes by seventy years, constitutes the second oldest of the great codifications of European law.[11] Significantly, however, quarrelsome couples were henceforth to be punished exclusively by fine, which, it is true, could be transformed into flogging or imprisonment in the case of non-payment. The ultimate punishment of the Bann was not abolished, but became obsolete. The authorities came to prefer to drag out the case until one party might provide the other with the divorce ground of adultery or flight from the realm or seven years' disappearance, or until the matter found a natural end through one party's death. Or, and this device was to assume increasing significance, the innocent party would receive a royal dispensation freeing him from the tie of the marriage that had become a sham, and thus restore him to the freedom of remarriage.

The practice of granting freedom of remarriage by special governmental dispensation was not peculiar to Sweden. It was indeed common to all those countries which broke with Rome in the course of the Reformation. In territories of monarchical rule, the power of dispensation was exercised by, or in the name of, the monarch. In England, the grant of divorces by the King in Parliament, which meant by private act of Parliament, was the only way in which a divorce could be obtained until 1857. Until 1969 it was the only way for residents of the Canadian Province of Quebec, who could not obtain a divorce in any way other than by private act of the Parliament of the Dominion.[12] The practice long prevailing in numerous states of the United States, to have divorces granted by the legislature, also derived from the English tradition.[13]

In Denmark, Norway, and Iceland, the majority of divorces is still granted by administrative agencies in a well-established, inexpensive procedure.[14] In fact, from a theoretical point of view, no reason exists why restoration to the freedom of remarriage should not belong to the domain of the executive, at least in all those cases—and they are the overwhelming majority everywhere, including the United States—in which the parties are not in dispute at all or have been able to settle whatever dispute there may have been on child custody, alimony, or property settlement. It is the courts' function to decide controversies. The reason why courts have been charged with jurisdiction to grant freedom of remarriage is an accident of history.

In Sweden, divorce by governmental dispensation first occurred at about the same time as in England—the late seventeenth century. As in England, it long remained rare. Two to four cases constituted the annual average.

The earliest dispensations were granted in cases in which the commission of adultery had been made highly probable, but was not proved with that strict certainty the courts demand. Other early instances were cases of quarrel and dissension in which the measures of ecclesiastical discipline as well as the fine imposed by the secular authority had failed to reunite the couple. As flight from the realm was regarded as being recognized by Holy Writ as a ground for judicial divorce, the government found it appropriate to grant dispensations also in the case of a spouse being banished from the realm by way of punishment. A sentence of life imprisonment and, since the late eighteenth century, punishment for a crime involving moral turpitude were added. Following ancient tradition, spouses of lepers were occasionally granted dispensation in early times. In the fourth decade of the eighteenth century, spouses of persons found to be incurably insane were allowed to remarry when it was necessary to provide a new home for a mother and her minor children, or a new provider for a woman. As the eighteenth century progressed, dispensations were granted in other cases of hardship or special merit, such as one spouse's attempt upon the life of the other; or violence of character threatening the petitioner's life or safety; habitual abuse of intoxicating liquor; persistent refusal of marital intercourse; infectious disease; habitual wastefulness in matters of property; and, finally, such deep and lasting discord as would preclude any hope of resumption of a normal marital life.

Quite regularly the government requested a statement of opinion of the diocesan chapter before it granted a petition. The liberal attitude of these ecclesiastical authorities is remarkable. From the early eighteenth century on, liberalism was potent in Swedish theology. In the latter part of the century, ideas of rationalist natural law had come to be popular among the intelligentsia, especially the urban clergy. Governmental practice of dispensation was particularly liberal during the regency period between the assassination of King Gustavus III (1792) and the accession to the throne of Gustavus IV (1796), when the screws were tightened again. The reactionary regime was ended with the king's deposition on 13 March 1809. Bernadotte, the later King Karl Johann, was imposed as crown prince upon the new king and with the arrival of this son of the French Revolution, Swedish liberalism was revitalized. Among the demands for reform of many traditional institutions, marriage and divorce occupied a prominent place.

Upon the king's request, the Law Committee, a body of jurists, prepared the draft of a new law, that, as the accompanying report expressed it, should be based upon the idea "that marriage, as a moral union, is founded upon the mutual respect of the spouses, so that, once that mutual respect has vanished, the marriage has ceased to exist in their sentiments and in their conscience, even though there may still exist the appearance of the tie that had once been established."

This expression of individualist liberalism was approved by all four Houses of the Diet, including the House of the Clergy. But the new law that was promulgated as the Royal Edict of 27 April 1810 was a cautious document that left many doors open.

The list of grounds for judicial divorce was slightly extended by the addition of those situations in which the granting of a governmental dispensation had become customary: banishment from the realm; attempt upon the plaintiff's life; sentence to imprisonment for life; and incurable insanity that has existed for at least three years.

In a conservative vein there was added the proviso that the divorce was to be refused where the plaintiff had provoked, or participated in, the commission of the crime for which the defendant had been sentenced, or if the defendant's insanity had been caused or accelerated by the plaintiff's conduct.

For the rest, the government should remain authorized to grant dispensation for special reasons. By way of example, but without intent to bind the government, the following were stated:

Sentence of death, of loss of honor, of dishonoring punishment or of honorable detention for two years or more; wasteful management of property; alcoholism, cruel temperament; and, finally, in elaboration of earlier practice, the situation in which "the sentiments and thoughts of the spouses so manifest themselves in mutual hostility that, breaking out at every occasion, they ultimately turn into aversion and hatred."

As to that last ground of mutual aversion and hatred it was apparently expected, although it was not clearly prescribed, that the ancient procedure of admonition and fine should have remained without success. It was clearly stated, however, that the government was to examine the spouse of the petitioner and that it should obtain the report of the pastor of the parish, as well as the advisory opinion of the cathedral chapter of the diocese and of the Supreme Court of the realm.

The dispensation was a strictly personal matter. It authorized the person to whom it was granted to receive from the cathedral chapter of his diocese that letter of divorcement, which he needed if he wished a pastor of the church to perform for him a ceremony of remarriage. On general principle, no such authorization would result for the spouse of the grantee. As to him, the impediment of existing marriage continued until that marriage would find its natural end through the death of his partner. Gradually, this original theory seems to have been obscured. Remarriage of the partner became permissible first, it seems, upon the grantee's remarriage, then upon

the grantee's consent. Besides, the government could
always grant the dispensation to the petitioner's spouse,
too. In the nineteenth century such permission came to
be regarded as a matter of course. A prohibition of remarriage of the grantee's spouse had to be expressly stated in
the decree of dispensation.

The proceedings were cumbersome and time consum-
ing; they remained so even under the comparatively
liberal practice of the later nineteenth century. They
came to be commonly referred to as "the long road to
divorce," in contrast to the "short road" that was developed out of the ancient institution of judicial divorce
for desertion beyond the borders of the realm that had
figured as a ground for divorce as early as the Ecclesiastical Ordinance of 1572. Also known as Copenhagen divorce, this institution was simply a consent divorce,
disguised as divorce for misconduct and tolerated by
the courts. One spouse would take the train to some city
beyond the Swedish border, usually Copenhagen, and
would obligingly write from there that he, or she, had
left the marital home without intention to return to it.
Action for divorce upon the ground of desertion could be
started in the Swedish court on the next day, and being
uncontested, be decided quickly. Appeal would be
waived. The "deserter" could return and both parties
were free to remarry.[15]

Compared with present figures, the number of divorces was modest even in the early years of the twentieth century.[16] But it was sufficiently high to provoke
some viewing with alarm. The judicial farce of the short
road was criticized not only because, as a law inviting
migratory divorce always does, it results in advantage of
the affluent over the poor, but also because of its inherent hypocrisy. That kind of critique was bound to
be strong in Scandinavia, where literature, theology, and
philosophy unite in calling for truthfulness and sincerity
in all walks of life.

TABLE 7

	NUMBER OF DIVORCES	PERCENTAGE OF MARRIAGES TERMINATED BY DIVORCE	DIVORCES PER 1000 POPULATION
1831–40	106	0.49	
1841–50	108	0.49	
1851–60	121	0.44	0.03
1861–70	130	0.49	0.03
1871–80	193	0.63	0.04
1881–90	234	0.80	0.05
1891–1900	538	1.15	0.069
1901–10	474	1.49	0.089
1911–20	911	2.55	0.159
1921–30	1813	4.62	0.3
1931–40	2925	5.68	0.45
1941–45	4876	7.78	0.75
1946			
1947	7058	11.83	0.97
1948	6782	11.69	1.09
1949	7602	13.97	1.14
1950	7991	14.75	1.19
1951	8431		1.19
1952	8185		1.14
1953	8393		1.17
1954	8676		1.2
1957	8558		1.203
1958	8657		1.168
1959	8761		1.177
1960	8958		1.198
1961	8696		1.156
1962	8849		1.170
1963	8496		1.117
1964	9169		1.197
1965	9563		1.237
1966	10288		1.318
1967	10727		1.363
1968	11011		1.391

SOURCE: Statistisk Årsbok för Sverige. 1951. Table 49; 1955. Table 45; 1969. Table 40.

Sweden, which had long been an agrarian corner of Europe, had started upon its remarkable economic and social transformation. Industry began to grow to impressive size.[17] A laboring class appeared and organized itself into a powerful political party. The cities expanded from small towns into large centers of industry, shipping, and commerce. Women entered the institutions of higher learning and the offices of business and government. They began to demand equality with men, politically, socially, and sexually. The double morality of the nineteenth-century bourgeois came under attack. Sexual freedom that was enjoyed by men was postulated for women, too. In plays that were to stir the world, Henrik Ibsen gave expression to the new spirit. The tragedies of unhappy marriage were presented by August Strindberg in an as yet unheard-of manner of realism. The traditional taboos of sex were passionately attacked by Ellen Key.

In 1905 the new spirit found expression at the polls. The Agrarian Party which had dominated the political scene was defeated. In 1909 a new constitution was made. A total revision of the code of early eighteenth-century vintage was one of the reforms demanded. The pain felt over Norway's secession from the personal union with the Crown of Sweden (1905) came to give way to a strong feeling of Scandinavian solidarity which resulted in the establishment of a scheme of Scandinavian co-operation in legal reform.[18] In both Norway and Denmark, transformations similar to those of Sweden had generated plans to adapt to the new spirit the laws on family relations, especially the relation of husband and wife.

The revision of that part of the Swedish General Code which deals with land (Jordabalken) already had been initiated under the old political regime.[19] For the new Cabinet of the Liberals, family law was naturally chosen as the next field of reform rather than the obsolete

scheme of civil and criminal procedure, where modernization was regarded as more urgent by the conservatives.
In the family law they demanded only one change, the
abolition of the Copenhagen divorces. But a much more
comprehensive reform was demanded by the liberal element that had now assumed the leading rule in the intellectual and political life. Their most urgent demand was
female emancipation, above all abolition of the wife's
subordination to the husband in matters of family
management, education of the children, and marital
property.

As to divorce, the demand was for a clean break with
the remnants of a religious dogma that had lost its spell
even in the leading circles of the church. The demand
was for a law that would no longer favor the rich over
the poor, that would no longer expose the parties to the
"humiliating indignity" of public admonition in church,
that would instate truthfulness in the place of the hypocrisy of a feigned desertion to foreign parts. Above all,
the new divorce law should no longer aggravate the emotional and economic shock of divorce, but should rather
facilitate it for all persons concerned—spouses, children,
and even a paramour—to re-establish new, happier
homes. There should also be abolished anomalies and
hardships that had arisen in consequence of the haphazard way in which the old divorce law had grown
up, such as the lack of a possibility adequately to provide
for the needs of a spouse, especially a wife, that might
arise in consequence of the divorce. The unbending rule
of property forfeiture that accompanied judicial divorce
for adultery was to be replaced by a flexible scheme of
damages that would apply in all appropriate cases.

Reform was also demanded with respect to the rules
on the conclusion of marriage. Obsolete institutions
should go, such as the effect of a formal betrothal to
prevent the conclusion of a marriage with a third person.
Abolition was also demanded of the ancient institution

of "incomplete marriage." That counterpart to American common-law marriage had been developed by ecclesiastics as a means to reduce illegitimacy. By subsequent sexual intercourse, a promise of marriage was transformed into a marriage, which, although valid, would not have the full status and property effects of a marriage celebrated in church. In Sweden, this once general notion of medieval churchmen was preserved into the twentieth century. It was defended as being needed in view of the custom, widely followed among the peasantry, that partners to a betrothal would have sexual intercourse, but delay the ceremony of marriage until pregnancy was apparent. "Incomplete marriage" was thought to be apt to prevent a man from backing out after intercourse. It was demanded that more appropriate ways be found, generally, to improve the situation of illegitimate children without forcing anyone into an unwanted and prospectively unfortunate marriage.

High on the list of the reformers' postulates was the full equalization of secular and religious conclusion of marriage, and the removal of anomalies that had arisen in consequence of the hesitant and unsystematic way in which secular marriage had come to be admitted.[20]

The list of reformist demands was long. But they were all expressions of one and the same spirit of secular liberalism that had come to dominate the intellectuals of Scandinavia, including the theologians, as well as the growing numbers of working people united in a Social-Democratic Party, whose leadership was no less individualist in matters of life and culture than the bourgeois leaders of cultural and spiritual life. Sweden, like Denmark and Norway, had turned into a country of firmly established liberalism. All three countries were ready resolutely to reshape their laws in accordance with the new spirit. A clear insight into the key role of the family resulted in the choice of family law as the first topic to be reformed, just as family law, together with the land law, was to be the first field to be reshaped in post-World War II Japan and is now being reshaped in the countries of Africa and Asia.

The task of remaking the entire body of family law turned out to be so extensive that it was undertaken in stages rather than all at once. But so pervading has been the effect of the new spirit that in spite of this method the several parts constitute a coherent whole, a consistent legal embodiment of individualist liberalism. The community of this spirit also made it possible that in its essential parts the work could be carried on co-operatively by Sweden, Denmark, and Norway, whose scheme of uniform legislation was later on joined by Finland and Iceland shortly after these countries had obtained national independence.

The greatest urgency was felt to exist for the reform of the law on conclusion and termination of marriage. The statute dealing with these topics was enacted in Sweden in 1915, in Denmark in 1922, in Norway in 1918, in Finland in 1929, and in Iceland in 1923.

Of the later laws, the most important are those on the Incidents of the Marital Relationships, especially marital property (Sweden 1920, Denmark 1925, Norway 1927, Finland 1929, Iceland 1923) and on Illegitimate Children (Norway 1915, Sweden 1917, Finland 1922, Denmark 1908 and 1937, Iceland 1921).

The concern about human rights and individual welfare, by which these laws have been inspired, has found further expression in the comprehensive legislation on social security and public welfare through which the Scandinavian countries have established themselves as models of the welfare state. In Sweden this vast body of legislation has furthermore been enlarged by a great number of laws designed to reverse the falling trend of the birth rate by measures encouraging childbirth and favoring large families.[21] This policy has not prevented, however, the continued implementation of the liberal tradition by legislative legalization of birth control and abortion.[22]

Acts of Swedish legislation are prepared with great care. The preparation of legislative drafts of importance is usually entrusted to a permanent board of legal experts of high standing, the so-called Law Committee (Lagberedningen). That institution had long played an important role in preconstitutional days. In 1842 it had been abolished. With the awakening of reformist zeal, it was reconstituted in 1902. Among its members were Hjalmar Westring and Birger Ekeberg, jurists of the highest standing. Their draft met with high praise by the committee of four Supreme Court justices to whom, in accordance with general Swedish practice, it was submitted next. Hasselrot, the Minister of Justice by whom the draft was introduced in the Upper House of Parliament, was a conservative, but the Cabinet was as much aware as the country of the fact that it had been brought into office for the sole job of preserving the country's neutrality in the European war that had broken out in August 1914.

Hasselrot thus did not hesitate to recommend the adoption of the new provisions on divorce. They were needed, he observed, because the old law had become obsolete and inconsistent and challenged citizens to undergo, as he called it, humiliating formalities. A new law was needed that would correspond to the views that actually had come to prevail in society. "Otherwise, people might come to prefer other forms of sexual relationship to that of marriage." By this remark, reference was made to those irregular unions which were commonly called "Stockholm marriages" and which were believed to be frequent among the working-class population of the cities.

The need for both Copenhagen divorces and Stockholm marriages was to be equally eliminated by frank recognition of the futility of efforts to prevent marriage breakdown by impeding divorce. In its report the Law Committee pointed at the experience generally observed abroad and especially in Germany that the majority of couples desiring a divorce seem generally to be willing to produce the necessary "evidence."

"It is, in general, useless to try to maintain the formal tie between spouses whose inner relationship has deteriorated so thoroughly that no happy marital life can be expected any more. To require the parties to prove their discord to a court means to impose upon them hardship and discomfort. Very rarely would a judge find himself induced by such evidence to refuse the decree of separation. Dropping the requirement of such proof in cases of the parties' mutual consent simply means that their consensus is accepted as sufficient proof."

With these words the Law Committee justified the crucial provision of the draft under which a judicial separation and, upon the expiration of one year, a divorce would be pronounced whenever both parties to the marriage would agree in a statement to the court that "they have found themselves to be unable to continue their relationship."

It was on this provision that conservative opposition concentrated, but all the passionate critics within the Parliament and its ecclesiastical components could achieve was no more than a modification of the words which did not affect the substance. As it now reads, Section 1 of Chapter 11 makes it clear that the reason for the termination of the marital life is "the deep and permanent discord which has rendered the parties unable to continue their marital life," but the existence of such discord is conclusively presumed from the fact that both spouses have agreed to apply for the separation. The *Zerruettungsprinzip* is thus made to appear as the guiding policy principle, but in fact consent divorce is the legislative basis. Of a slightly more than merely rhetorical significance was the modification the opposition was able to achieve with respect to procedure. Under the draft it was not required that parties to a joint petition had previously submitted to an attempt at reconciliation. If no such attempt had been made prior to the filing of the joint petition, the draft provided that the proceedings be adjourned so as to give the parties an opportunity to see their pastor or a secular conciliator. But if they failed to avail themselves of that opportunity, the case would proceed to the decrees of separation and divorce. Upon conservative insistence, the provision was altered so as to make it a condition for the court's accepting the parties' joint petition that they would file with it a certificate of the pastor or the conciliator to the effect that an effort at conciliation had been made and failed. A motion to prescribe a second attempt at reconciliation as a necessary preliminary to transform the decree of separation into the final divorce was defeated.

Potentially, this change could be of practical significance. What it would actually amount to was to depend on how seriously the conciliators would take their tasks. In the course of events, great diversities turned out to exist in this respect, and widely diverging evaluations have been expressed.

Expert opinion seems to incline to the view that the requirement of compulsory attempt at conciliation has not resulted in hardship, but has rather helped to inhibit hasty and insufficiently considered divorces. But present opinion also tends to observe that a single attempt, made at a time when the decision jointly to approach the court has already been made, is bound to be of little effect. Marriage counseling available at any time and to be carried on by experts, if necessary over prolonged periods of time, is now regarded as more promising, provided it is not geared toward persuading parties to continue or resume marriages which are bound to be unsuccessful. An experimental scheme of marriage counseling has now been established in Stockholm and other cities.

If termination of a marriage is requested by both parties, it will be terminated, but, as we have seen, not simply because the termination has been agreed upon by the parties, but rather because the agreement is treated as conclusive evidence that the marriage is deeply and permanently disrupted. If the principle of *divorce faillite*[23] is to be carried out consistently, it must be possible to obtain the termination of a disrupted marriage upon one party's initiative, even if the other party does not join in the petition. Such a possibility is, indeed, provided.

Under Section 4, either party may obtain a divorce, i.e. the termination of the marriage tie including the immediate restoration to the freedom of remarriage, "where husband and wife have without decree of separation actually lived apart from each other on account of discord for at least three years." But if in such a case the termination of the marriage is contested by the other spouse, the court is given discretion to refuse the divorce if it deems it fit to do so "because of the petitioner's conduct or because of other special circumstances." As it has turned out, in Sweden such a refusal is almost unheard of, but in Denmark and Norway the proviso seems not to be an entirely dead letter.

No judicial discretion to refuse a unilateral petition for divorce exists where the defendant has "willfully and without just cause kept himself away from the marital relationship for two years" or more (Section 5), or "where a spouse has been absent for three years under such circumstances that it is not known whether or not he is alive" (Section 6). An immediate divorce, i.e. termination of the tie without preceding decree of separation, may furthermore be obtained upon one party's unilateral petition, where the other has exposed him to infection with venereal disease (Section 9), or where the other has been plotting against his life or has committed against him acts of severe physical cruelty (Section 10), or if

the other spouse has been sentenced to serious punishment (Section 11). If a spouse is addicted to the im-
moderate use of intoxicants, the court may grant the
other an immediate divorce "if it finds some special reason for so doing" (Section 12). An immediate divorce
may furthermore be granted to a petitioner whose spouse
has been insane for three years and there is no hope of
permanent recovery (Section 13). Of course, there is
also the old stand-by of adultery, to which there have
been added "other punishable sexual acts" (Section 8),
and the conclusion of a bigamous marriage (Section 7).
The old grounds for judicial and administrative divorce
are thus all repeated, with some additions and refine-
ments, and the elimination of desertion from the list of
grounds for the old "short road." The old possibility of
unilaterally obtaining the termination of a distasteful
marriage over the long road has been formalized and
legalized through the two-step procedure of first unilaterally obtaining a decree of separation and then, one year
later, the decree of divorce.

Under Section 2, this procedure is now available
"where one spouse is guilty of flagrant neglect of his
duty to support the other and the children, or if he otherwise ignores his duties toward them in a palpable manner, or if he is addicted to the misuse of intoxicants, or
if he is following a dissipate course of life. However, the
court may refuse to grant its decree of separation, if the
petitioner should be required to continue the relationship
in view of his own behavior or in view of other special
circumstances."

Finally, Section 2, paragraph 2 provides for the two-
step procedure upon one party's unilateral petition where
"in consequence of difference in temperament and ideas,
or of other circumstances, a deep and permanent discord
has arisen between the spouses." Here, the text provides,
however, that the court *must* refuse to grant the first step
where the petitioner "can reasonably be required to con-

tinue the marital relationship in view of his own conduct
or because of other special circumstances."

The new law has thus retained, although in a significantly modified form, the old distinction between the
short and the long roads to divorce. For the wide scope
of discretion that once rested with the administration,
firm legal rights to obtain a divorce have been substituted, although some measure of evaluation or even
discretion has been given to the courts. If the courts had
wished to do so, they might have used this power to reinforce the ancient doctrine of recrimination and to give
the defendant spouse an effective veto. But the intellectual climate of Sweden is not that of Germany of the
1950s. The dominant party is not one of Christian
Democrats but of Social Democrats, i.e. of liberal individualism in matters of personal life in general and of
sex life in particular.

Of the long statutory list of grounds for marriage
termination, one has come to be of overwhelming statistical significance, viz. that of "deep and lasting discord"
proved to exist either, conclusively, by the parties' co-
operation in petitioning for the first decree, or, in cases
of unilateral petition, by actual evidence. But such proof
is not difficult to make. In the major cities the courts
exhibit a tendency to conclude the existence of deep
and permanent discord from the mere fact of one party's
petitioning for separation, so that the courts also seem to
make little use, if any, of their power to refuse a separation, or, in the rare cases brought under Section 12
(habitual drunkenness), a divorce, because of the petitioner's own conduct or of other special circumstances.
Such at least is the opinion of Swedish experts. Decisions
of trial courts are not published and matters of divorce
are hardly ever carried up to the Supreme Court. During
the entire period from 1915 to 1955, in only one case
did the Supreme Court hold justified the judicial refusal
of a separation. The husband wished by marriage to its

mother to legitimatize an illegitimate child of his. But his petition to be separated from the wife to whom he had been married for some forty years was denied because through the divorce the wife would have lost the right after the petitioner's death to receive a widow's pension from the husband's employer. Today the divorce would in all probability be granted because under more recent legislation pension rights are no longer lost by divorce from the employee or civil servant through whom they are acquired. Under a new law, pensions may now be split between a former spouse and the spouse with whom the employee or civil servant is married at the time of his death, generally in proportion of the periods of time for which the marriages in question have existed.[24] By this elegant solution, Sweden has remedied a situation in which other countries' judges find themselves faced with the distasteful dilemma of either depriving a deserving woman of what constitutes her sole or main support in old age, or rendering impossible the regularization of an irregular union of possibly long standing and of legitimizing its offspring.

The courts are making so little use of their discretionary power because of the conviction of apparently most or all of the members of the judiciary that it is not possible for a court to obtain helpful information about imponderable aspects and matters of an intimate personal nature. Observation of life and literature seems to have convinced the judges that it is inane to search for guilt in matters of marital discord and that it is futile to attempt by governmental coercion to restore harmony among spouses who, by actually living apart from each other, have demonstrated that their marriage has come to be a failure. The individualist Swedish attitude is characterized by the absence of considerations of *praeventio generalis*. History, so it is believed, has disproved the thesis that people in marital difficulties might be induced to overcome them by the knowledge that freedom of remarriage is not easily obtainable. Examples illustrating the unreality of such a belief were contained in the Law Committee's report of 1915. The conviction that marriage breakdown is caused by factors other than easy availability of divorce, and that it cannot be prevented by a strict divorce law, seems to have come to be generally accepted.

The view just stated is confirmed by the development of divorce practice in Denmark. While the law of that country coincides with that of Sweden in most respects, a few different features have been worked into Denmark's Marriage and Divorce Law of 30 June 1922. While administrative divorce was abolished in Sweden, it has been retained as the normal procedure in Denmark. Petitions for separation and subsequent divorce are normally filed with an administrative office or with the Ministry of Justice, where all declarations and allegations of the parties are submitted in writing. If there arises a dispute of fact or law that cannot be settled by the parties, the case is transferred to a court, where an oral hearing may take place, usually in chambers.[25]

Such disputes are almost always concerned with child custody, alimony, child support, and property settlement. Even where resistance is allegedly made to the termination of the marriage, it is almost invariably a means to induce the party moving for the divorce to agree to the other party's terms on the custody and money issues. In those few cases which reach the courts, occasionally the divorce is denied either because the marriage is found not to be incurably disrupted, or because of special circumstances thought to render appropriate the maintenance of the tie of a marriage that is concededly disrupted beyond repair.[26]

Another special feature of Denmark's law is the longer duration of the period between the first and the second decree. In Sweden that interval is one year; in Denmark a year and one half, if the parties are in agreement; otherwise two and one half years.

It is regarded as probable that this difference in the laws is at least to some extent responsible for a conspicuous difference of statistical data. In Sweden the overwhelming majority of divorces are based upon the ground of deep and permanent discord. The data from Sweden are as follows: Of all marriage terminations (other than by death) the percentages of those based upon disruption were as follows[27]:

1921–25	1926–30	1931–35	1936–40	1941–45	1946–50	1951–55
89	91	92	93	89	88	89

The percentages for proceedings on the ground of adultery were:

4	3	2	2	7	9	11

In Denmark the percentages were:

disruption

62	69	66	62	50	48	51

adultery

21	21	24	31	44	48	45

While in Sweden, the percentage of adultery divorces has, although slightly rising, remained small, it has been both high and rising in Denmark. In both countries, divorce for discord has to follow the long road, which is longer in Denmark, while adultery divorce is obtainable by the short road, which in the case of an uncontested petition may be very short indeed. The data can hardly be regarded as indicating that adultery is more prevalent in Denmark than in Sweden. What they do seem to indicate is a greater readiness of Danes to resort to the short road even if it involves the admission of adultery. Perhaps this tendency is connected with the greater directness of the Danish administrative procedure. It is doubtful, however, whether the difference also indicates a lessening of the disrepute of adultery in Denmark as compared with an increasing respectability in Sweden of those irregular unions which have to wait for their regularization for the expiration of the year following the first decree.

Other differences have appeared in the statistical data. In Denmark, the divorce rate has been consistently higher than in Sweden, and in Sweden it has been higher than in Norway and Finland.[28]

In contrast to the official law of the majority of American states, in the laws of the Scandinavian countries judicial investigation of guilt has been limited to that insignificant minority of cases in which a divorce is sought neither in mutual agreement of the parties nor upon immediate admission by the defendant in proceedings commenced unilaterally. Discussion of guilt has also been reduced to a minimum in the decision of the issue of child custody. As in the United States, the dominant formula declares the best interest of the children to be decisive. Only in cases of equal fitness of both parents is the court directed to consider the comparative guilt of the parties.[29] In actual practice, little if any application seems to be made of this provision. The courts read the statute as referring to "real" guilt rather than to formal guilt in the sense of concrete acts of cruelty, adultery, or desertion. They are convinced that it is next to impossible in a case of marriage breakdown to find out by which party's guilt it was "really" caused. Like American courts, those of Sweden are thus inclined to follow the rules of thumb that custody of children of tender age be awarded to the mother and that weight should be attached to the wishes of older children.

Greater weight is ascribed to guilt in the statutory language on the problem of alimony. In deciding whether alimony should be granted to a wife and, if so, how much, the courts are ordered to consider both the wife's needs and the husband's capacity, as well as "other circumstances."[30] But then the statute adds: "However, no alimony shall be granted to the spouse who bears the principal guilt for the divorce." Again, the courts are reluctant to make use of the provision which would expose dirty linen to public view. Besides, how is a court to determine not only who is guilty in the full and real sense of the term, but *principally* guilty? Being less chivalrous than American judges, Swedish courts do not hesitate to refuse alimony to a woman able to support herself. The chances for gold diggers are minimal.

The only context in which the Swedish courts pay attention to the problem of guilt is that of damages. Under Section 24 of the statute, a spouse may be ordered to pay damages "when the decree of divorce is based upon conduct which has inflicted grave harm upon the marriage or where a previous decree of separation was based upon a serious breach of his duties toward the other spouse." By its wording, the provision eliminates the great mass of divorces obtained upon joint application. In cases of divorce for cause, however, damages are occasionally awarded to a wife if the court feels that in the property settlement she should receive more than one half of the community property fund to which she is entitled in the normal case. The provision is compatible with the general tendency to avoid painful and extended investigation into "real" guilt, because in cases of divorce for cause, guilt must be ascertained at any rate. In evaluating the Swedish law on custody, property settlement, and alimony, it is important to keep in mind that a judicial determination is made only in that minority of cases in which the parties have failed to settle their differences by their own agreement.

8

Marriage and Divorce Among the North Alaskan Eskimos

ERNEST S. BURCH, JR.

Introduction

"Do the Eskimos *really* trade wives?" This is a question that seems invariably to greet travelers returning from the Far North. Obviously, the American public is generally aware of the custom and is fascinated by it. Unfortunately, the practice has been exploited by the movies and the popular press more for its dramatic effect than for its educational value. More seriously, even the professional anthropological literature contains more fiction than fact when dealing with Eskimo "wife-trading." Consequently, social scientists as well as laymen tend to be grossly misinformed on the subject.

Recent research, however, has provided new information on numerous aspects of Eskimo* social life. Special-

* Eskimos resident in Alaska are American citizens. However, when the word American is used in this essay, it should be understood to mean "middle-class American of whatever race, color, or national origin." The point is to separate the Eskimo traditional and present-day usages from those that the readers of this book are accustomed to, and any other way of saying it eventually becomes stilted as the reader proceeds.

ists have also been re-evaluating the earlier material, and are now in a position to correct some of the errors present in the literature. Far from being the casual and promiscuous affair that it is generally pictured to have been, "wife-trading" was a very serious matter to the Eskimos. We now know that it was an integral part of their system of marriage, which also included polygamous as well as monogamous forms of union. Both "wife-trading" and polygamy, once thought to be manifestations of "anarchy," turn out to have been components of a complex but well-ordered system. In addition, it has been learned that the marriage system meshed with the other aspects of Eskimo kinship in an entirely consistent pattern. Many questions about Eskimo kinship (including marriage) remain unanswered, but the outlines of the system are now fairly clear.

The purpose of this paper is to present a general description of Eskimo marriage and divorce as we have now come to understand it, but it has been necessary to impose certain restrictions on the scope of the discussion. The first of these is with regard to the geographic area covered. The Eskimos formerly occupied a vast portion of northern North America, extending from the eastern tip of Siberia clear across the top of the continent to the east coast of Greenland. The people inhabiting this huge area were by no means as homogeneous as they are generally assumed to have been, and there were many regional variations in all aspects of social life. That such differences occurred in the realm of kinship specifically has been made quite clear by the best of the recent (and relevant) studies.[1] There do seem to be some common threads running through at least the marital customs of many Eskimo groups, but it will be difficult to know what they are with any precision until more of the research now in progress has been published. Tenable generalizations on the subject may be forthcoming in the near future, but it would be premature to attempt

them at this time. Consequently, in an effort to keep the
presentation on as firm ground as possible, the discussion will be limited to the group that has been more
thoroughly studied[2] than any of the others. This group,
the "North Alaskan Eskimos," inhabit the northern portion of Alaska between (roughly) Bering Strait and the
Canadian border.

A second limitation on the scope of the essay is based
on the difference between the "traditional," and the
"modern" or contemporary periods in North Alaska.
While the North Alaskan Eskimos were by no means
isolated from other peoples prior to the arrival of Euro-
peans, they did operate in terms of what is properly
regarded as an indigenous system of behavior. Around
the middle of the nineteenth century, however, whaling
ships began to arrive in the area in substantial numbers. The whalers were followed by traders, missionaries,
government representatives, and various others, and the
native ways of doing things began to undergo numerous
changes as a result of this contact. The process was
greatly accelerated when the United States Government
established schools and government-directed reindeer
herds in the area around the turn of the century. Since
the agents of change have been largely American, the
changes which have occurred have generally been toward the American way of doing things, and away from
the traditional Eskimo one. Since the purpose of this
paper is to describe a system that is quite different from
our own, my concern will be solely with the former
Eskimo ways of doing things rather than with the current ones, which approximate ours in many respects.

Eskimo Marriage

For purposes of scientific analysis, a "marital" relationship can be defined usefully as any relationship in

which sexual intercourse is an integral component. In our society, sexual intercourse is institutionalized *only* between husband and wife. Sexual relations between other categories of individuals do in fact occur, however, even though generally considered morally wrong. In other words, from a scientific point of view, only one of the several forms of marriage which *actually* occur in our society is of the single type *ideally* permitted. This monogamous approach of "one man-one woman" is by no means universal in human affairs, however, and numerous peoples around the world permit or even highly value marital ties of various other kinds. Eskimo societies were of the latter type, with the result that the Eskimo marriage system was more complicated than our own.

The basic building block of the North Alaskan Eskimo marriage system, the *ui-nuliaq* relationship, is illustrated in Figure 5.[3] This relationship obtained between a man and a woman who lived together and who had socially approved sexual relations. Superficially, this relationship appears identical to our own husband-wife relationship.

FIGURE 5

Simple Residential Marriage

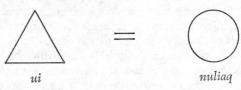

ui   nuliaq

As will become apparent later on, however, the two relationships differ in quite significant respects. In addition, where the American husband-wife relationship comprises virtually all there is to marriage in our society, at least ideally, the *ui-nuliaq* relationship was merely the keystone of a more extensive system. (In order to keep the two clearly distinguished from one another, I will use the Eskimo words when referring to their system, and the English terms when referring to ours. Other Eskimo relationships that ideally have no counterparts in our system will be referred to alternately by English and Eskimo terms.)

The establishment of the *ui-nuliaq* relationship depended on two factors, those of coresidence and socially approved sexual intercourse. In other words, all that was required for this kind of marriage was for a man and woman to live together in the same house (which was usually shared with other relatives) and have sexual intercourse. Once these two conditions had been met even for a brief period, the relationship was considered established. The Eskimos did not have any marriage ceremony and in fact, there seems to have been no ritual whatsoever associated with the founding of the *ui-nuliaq* relationship. Not only is this total lack of ceremonial embellishment unusual from a cross-cultural perspective, it was in distinct contrast to other aspects of Eskimo life. Taboos, rituals, and ceremonies of various kinds were associated with almost every daily activity and, to me, their absence here is indicative of the rather unimportant place that the *ui-nuliaq* relationship had in the ideal[4] Eskimo scheme of things.

The primary elaboration on the *ui-nuliaq* theme is illustrated in Figure 6, which represents the polygynous[5] residential marriage situation. Here we have a single man living together with two women, and having socially approved sexual relations with both of them. The *nuliaqpak* is the *nuliaq* the man acquired first, and the *nukarak* is the one he married second (regardless of the relative ages of the two women). His relationship with each followed the basic *ui-nuliaq* pattern almost com-

FIGURE 6

Polygynous Residential Marriage

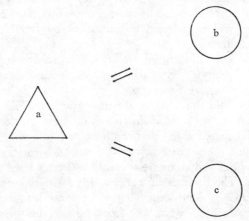

(ab) *ui-nuliaqpak*; (ac) *ui-nukarak*; (bc) *aipaq-aipaq*

pletely, at least ideally. Having the two women living together, however, resulted in the existence of still another relationship within the general marital context, namely that of "co-wives," or the *aipaq-aipaq* relationship (an analysis of which is outside the scope of this paper).

We have no exact figures on the frequency of polygynous unions in the traditional society, but there were, of course, strict demographic limitations on the possibilities. If men and women were roughly equal in number in the society,[6] either the number of polygynous unions was very low, or many men had to go unmarried. Since we know that virtually every man in the society did get married, and spent most of his adult life that way, we must conclude that polygynous marriages were fairly uncommon. They were highly acceptable, however, and numerous cases have been attested. Rather than being commonplace, they seem to have been more on the order of a luxury: something to be achieved when a man was rich enough to support more than one wife. Generally, polygynous unions involved only two women, but there are cases on record of especially wealthy men in the larger villages having three wives. One man at Point Hope was said to have had five at the time of his death.

The other primary elaboration on the *ui-nuliaq* theme, namely, the polyandrous union, is illustrated in Figure 7. In this case, there were two men involved, both of whom had approved sexual relations with one woman within the coresidential context. The woman was the *nuliaq* of both men. The man whom she married first was her *uikpak*, and the one she married second was her *nukarak*.

FIGURE 7

Polyandrous Residential Marriage

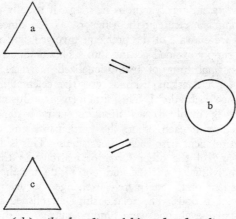

(ab) *uikpak-nuliaq*; (cb) *nukarak-nuliaq*;
(ac) *nuliaqan-nuliaqan*

The relationship between the two men was that of *nuliaqan-nuliaqan*, or "cohusbands."

The frequency of polyandrous unions in the traditional society cannot be determined with precision, but it is certain that they were extremely rare, much more so than their polygynous counterparts. Actual cases have been documented, however, and it is clear that the system had a place for such marriages if people wished to get involved in them. It seems that the scarcity of polyandrous marriages was a function of the strains that were inherent in them. On the one hand, problems resulted from the competition of the two men for the sexual relations with the one woman. On the other hand, they stemmed from the tremendous economic burden placed on one woman having to do all the butchering, sewing, and other work that being married to two hunters would entail. These tasks would of course be in addition to the duties of childbearing and child rearing that would devolve upon her. When people did align themselves in a polyandrous marriage, it usually did not last long as a result of these factors. The Eskimos themselves were aware of the problems involved, and most of them simply avoided getting into such situations.

The final form of institutionalized marriage among the North Alaskan Eskimos was the celebrated "wife-exchange" situation.[7] This arrangement, illustrated in Figure 8, involved *two ui-nuliaq* pairs becoming associated with each other, the participants engaging in sexual relations with each other's spouse. This is different from any of the other forms of marriage in that here the individuals involved did not reside together on a permanent basis, but merely exchanged sexual partners for brief periods. The relationships established through the sexual exchange were binding outside of the scope of the exchange itself however. Because of its intimate connection with the other forms of marriage, and its

FIGURE 8
Comarriage

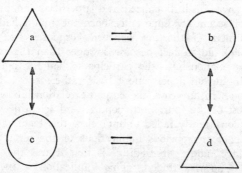

(ab) *ui-nuliaq*; (dc) *ui-nuliaq*; (ac) *uiNuzaq-nulizaq*;
(db) *uiNuzaq-nulizaq*; (ad) *nuliaqan-nuliaqan*;
(bc) *aipaq-aipaq*

general importance in Eskimo life, I shall refer to this custom as "comarriage." The older labels of "wife-trading" and "wife-exchange" have connotations which are misleading in a number of respects.

It is important to remember that while sexual relations were repeated often in most (but not all) comarriages, intercourse was really nothing more than the validating act of the union. Significantly, it had to take place only on one occasion for the relationships to be established for the lifetimes of the participants. Thus, if two couples agreed to unite in comarriage, all that was required was that each man spend a single night with the other man's wife. After that, even if the exchange was never repeated, the participants were considered to be cospouses.

In a comarriage, the relationships that were considered to be the most important were those between the two men, on the one hand, and the two women, on the other. For the co-wives (*aipaq*) and cohusbands (*nuliaqan*), comarriage meant strong bonds of friendship, mutual aid, and protection. The tie between each man and the other's *nuliaq* was institutionalized as a superficial one, and sex was of secondary importance once the union had been established. If the ties between cospouses (*uiNuzaq-nulizaq*) did in fact become stronger than the two *ui-nuliaq* relationships, the participants had the option of exchanging on a permanent basis rather than a temporary one. In any case, the cospouse relationship was the weakest of the four. Both popular and scientific writers have consistently failed to appreciate this fact.

One of the obvious implications of the terms "wife-exchange" and "wife-trading" is that it was the *nuliaq* alone who was traded.[8] This implication is incorrect, for the *ui* was exchanged just as surely as was the *nuliaq*, if not more so. Just how the exchange was effected depended on the circumstances, but, whenever possible, the wives stayed home and the husbands traded places for the night, returning home during the day. Most often, however, comarriages were established between couples who normally resided in different villages. Under such conditions, the principals might exchange sex partners whenever they happened to come together in the same place. This might occur fairly frequently if the home villages were not too far apart, but otherwise might take place only once a year or so, or perhaps even less. In some cases, they only took place once, even though the bonds thus established were permanent.

The term "wife-exchange" implies that the decision about establishing an exchange was taken solely at the discretion of the husband, but here again the popular conception is incorrect. As Heinrich has so clearly demonstrated, and as my own research has confirmed, the *ui* had absolutely no right to order his *nuliaq* around in such matters. On the contrary, the women had just as much to say about whether or not an exchange union would be established as did the men. Moreover, the women as well as the men could take the initiative in getting one started. In any case, the matter of "trading" never entered the situation.

There is little doubt that comarriage was institutionalized to a high degree among the traditional North Alaskan Eskimos. Statistics are lacking, but there is reason to believe that it was very widespread. Indeed, the majority of the adult population of the society may well have been involved in comarriage situations. Unfortunately, the extreme disfavor with which the practice was viewed by the American teachers and missionaries in the region was quickly and thoroughly impressed upon the Eskimos, with the result that nowadays it is extremely difficult to get information about it. Nonetheless, the following considerations have been established with sufficient thoroughness as to be considered facts: (1) comarriage was an integral part of the more general marriage system; (2) it involved behavioral patterns that were highly institutionalized; and (3) promiscuity had virtually nothing to do with it.

It has sometimes been alleged that part of Eskimo hospitality involved loaning a wife to a visiting male guest, and much has been made of this in the popular literature on the Eskimos. Since the distinction between "wife-trading" and "wife-lending" is a rather fine one, I would like to clarify the matter at this point. To put it briefly, the available information suggests that "wife-lending," in the sense of letting a stranger have sexual relations with one's wife, was totally non-existent among the North Alaskan Eskimos. It is well known, for example, that in the traditional society, complete strangers were invariably killed on sight[9] unless one of the following conditions was met: (1) the strangers were numerous enough to be able to protect themselves; (2) the strangers had relatives in the area to serve as their guarantors and protectors; or (3) the strangers were encountered on certain special occasions, such as a Messenger Feast (cf. Spencer, 1959: 210 ff.) or a summer trading festival when hostility of this sort was temporarily put aside. Strangers were despised and feared, and it is rather difficult to reconcile this thoroughly documented fact with the alleged practice of sexual hospitality. If a visitor had any sexual relations with a host's wife, one may be sure that the individuals were well known to each other, and that they were merely continuing a previously established relationship.

It seems that it was the American whalers and traders who in fact instituted something that might be called "wife-lending" in North Alaska. These strangers to the region took advantage of the peculiarities of the Eskimo marriage system on the one hand, and of their own wealth and power relative to that of the Eskimos on the other. In the former case, the white men pretended that they were getting into some sort of institutionalized marriage arrangement with the Eskimos, then refused to abide by the appropriate Eskimo rules of behavior. In the latter situation, the white men sometimes took Eskimo women by force, knowing that the Eskimos would not dare retaliate. In other cases (probably most frequently), the Eskimos themselves agreed on such sexual liaisons in the hope of getting some trade goods or whisky, more or less on the order of prostitution. In any case, such affairs were not native to the Eskimo way of life, but a consequence of the social breakdown which followed the arrival of rich and powerful outsiders.

Returning now to the institutionalized Eskimo marriage system, one can see that the several forms of marriage fit together rather neatly. A comparison of Figures 5 through 8 will reveal that the keystone of the system, the *ui-nuliaq* relationship, was common to all the marital arrangements. The other forms of marriage can be most easily understood simply as elaborations of this basic theme. Sexual intercourse was the common feature running through all the marriage forms, and residence was the variable. In the case of the *ui-nuliaq* type of marriage, there were two people involved, and they lived together and apart from any other spouses. In the plural forms of residential marriage, there were simply two or more members of the one sex or the other living with a single member of the opposite sex. Finally, in comarriage, the cospouses simply did not live together on a regular basis. The two additional relationships, those of cohusbands and co-wives, served to relate any members of the same sex who happened to be involved in *any* of the plural forms of marriage.

It is interesting to note that the various forms of marriage do not seem to have been mutually exclusive. An *ui-nuliaq* marriage, of course, was not only compatible with but was a prerequisite for each of the other alternatives. It is not certain, however, just how either of the plural forms of residential marriage co-ordinated with comarriage. Thus, if a man had two *nuliaqs*, just how would an exchange have been effected with another marital unit having only one man and one woman? Or how did two polygynous (or polyandrous) units establish an exchange union with each other, if they could do so at all? One can readily see that if all the logical combinations of the various basic forms of marriage could have been participated in at the same time by the same people, the real-life situations must have been quite complex. Unfortunately, the answers to the above and related questions are as yet unanswerable, although educated guesses could perhaps be made. Since all the forms of plural marriage are now either carried on in secret or are no longer practiced in North Alaska, they may remain unanswered forever. About the only thing that appears definite at this point is that a single couple could be associated through comarriage with more than one other couple at the same time.

It is instructive to consider the implications of the various forms of Eskimo marriage on subsequent generations. In the gross sense, all the offspring of *any* kind of marital arrangement were considered to be siblings to one another. Finer distinctions[10] were made as to "full," "half," "step-" and "co-" siblings, but the children were nonetheless considered to be brothers or sisters of one sort or another. This fact is significant, for in the Eskimo scheme of things, sibling relationships were extremely important, much more so than they are in the contemporary United States. Eskimo siblings were morally bound to co-operate in almost all the major activities of life, an obligation that held regardless of the form of marriage that produced or connected them.

The marital ties made at one generation level, which resulted in sibling connections at the second-generation level, produced cousin relationships at the third, and so on. The ties of kinship, once established, continued downward through the generations regardless of the form of marriage that was involved initially.[11] The same obligations and activities that were appropriate to the descendants of a simple residential marriage also held for the descendants of all the plural-marriage forms. The descendants of *any* sort of marital connection were ideally forbidden to marry one another as a result of the incest restrictions placed on relatives. This fact lends considerable support to the conclusion that each of the several forms of Eskimo marriage was really a form of marriage and not something else, for they all resulted in what was regarded as true kinship for the descendants.

Eskimo Divorce

The most fruitful application of the concept of "divorce" to the Eskimo situation is clearly in connection with the *ui-nuliaq* relationship since it was the keystone

of the entire system. In this case what is said applies
equally to the polygynous and polyandrous situations
except that only one man and one woman were normally
involved in each instance of divorce. (There was no rule
preventing a person from divorcing two spouses simultaneously; however, it just does not seem to have happened very often.) There is also a practical reason for
excluding the cospouse relationship from this discussion,
namely, a lack of relevant data. Whether or not anything
which might be usefully labeled "divorce" ever occurred
in connection with comarriage has not yet been determined as far as I know.

For all practical purposes, Eskimo divorce consisted in
the breaking of the residence tie, and the termination
of sexual relations invariably followed. Like marriage,
divorce was accomplished without ceremony. All that was
involved was one or the other spouse leaving the other,
or else making the other one go, depending on the
circumstances.[12]

If they were living with the *ui's* relatives and the
nuliaq wished to leave, she could simply walk out on
him. Ideally, at least, he could do nothing to stop her.
Likewise if they were living with his relatives and the
ui wished his *nuliaq* to leave, he had only to wait until
she was out of the house, then scatter all her belongings
outside the door. When she returned, the hint would be
obvious. If they were living with the *nuliaq's* relatives,
similar procedures in reverse would be followed. Ideally,
either spouse could take the initiative in breaking off the
residence tie, although in fact husbands had a bit more
control over such situations than did wives simply by
virtue of their superior physical strength. If a wife was
really determined, however, the husband could not stop
her from leaving him, regardless of how he felt about
the situation.[13] If both the *ui* and *nuliaq* were agreed
on a separation, an immediate result was assured.

One significant feature of Eskimo divorce was that the

breaking of the residence tie did not terminate the marital relationship. Once such a relationship had been established, it held for the lifetimes of its members, regardless of whether or not either sexual relations or coresidence were continued. What divorce did was to *deactivate* the relationship. In other words, when the residence tie was broken, the relationship was generally ignored in the course of daily life even though it was still there in theory. In the United States we sometimes have inactive relationships with relatives outside our immediate family, such as cousins, especially second cousins. We may know who our cousins are, and perhaps where they live, but we may never have any contact with them directly, even though the relationship is still there. If the members of such a relationship ever have occasion to activate it, it is a simple matter for them to do so.

In Eskimo divorce, the individuals either avoided each other altogether, or they acted as *ui* and *nuliaq*. There was nothing on the order of the "exspouse" relationship that so frequently occurs in our society, and even divorced Eskimo spouses thought of and referred to each other as *ui* and *nuliaq*. Indeed, it not infrequently happened that divorced spouses got back together again. Since the relationship had never been dissolved in the first place, re-establishment of the residence tie simply meant the reactivation of an already existing relationship. In America, if a husband and wife get divorced and then decide to get back together again, they would ideally have to go through the entire marriage procedure again, although actually they sometimes do not.

On the basis of the above considerations, it may be argued that the Eskimos did not have an institution which can appropriately be called "divorce." Indeed, Eskimo "divorce" was more like our separation than our "divorce." Properly speaking, of course, the American institution is a legal proceeding, nothing more and nothing less. In that sense it is correct to say that the Eskimos did not have "divorce." But, when you disregard the technicalities and look at situations, the two systems are not so different. The basic point is whether or not two spouses stay together or separate. It has been shown by Goode (1956: 186, 187), for example, that the greatest emotional disturbance in the American situation comes at the time of physical separation, not at the time of the legal action. Hunt (1966: 5) echoes Goode's conclusion, saying that "an emotionally genuine separation constitutes the death of a marriage, and divorce is merely its burial." On the other hand, the legal proceeding by no means necessarily terminates interaction between spouses. Indeed, Hunt[14] goes so far as to say that "divorce, though it cancels the partnership of man and wife, *never* severs their relationship entirely" [italics mine]. In short, in America, the legal matter of divorce has relatively little effect on the *de facto* aspects of the overall situation. It seems to be more of a symbol than anything else. Consequently, while the Eskimos did not have divorce in the technical sense of that term, I feel justified in maintaining that situations occur(red) in both societies, which are usefully compared under the rubric of "divorce."

It is of course impossible to know with certainty the extent of divorce among the traditional North Alaskan Eskimos, but there is reason to believe that the divorce rate (in the Eskimo sense) approached 100 per cent. That is, virtually everyone broke the residence tie with their spouse at least once, and many did so several times. What is not clear is the extent to which the initial tie was later reactivated as opposed to the frequency with which totally new spouses were acquired. Even here, however, the rate seems to have been fairly high, especially in the first years of married life.

The conditions which resulted in divorce among the Eskimos varied, of course, but some factors were clearly more significant than others. The most frequently cited source of strain in the *ui-nuliaq* relationship was infidelity on the part of one or both spouses. "Infidelity," in this case, means sexual relations outside the scope of the marriage system. Those involved in plural marriage were institutionalized, and hence did not constitute infidelity. Infidelity alone, however, did not necessarily result in divorce (although it might), but it certainly placed a strain on the *ui-nuliaq* relationships involved.

Another serious source of strain was the failure on the part of one or the other spouse to meet his or her economic obligations. In the traditional society, the family was economically self-sufficient to a high degree. It was the major locus of production, and both spouses were involved to an equal extent. The division of labor along sex lines was so complete, however, that there was virtually no overlap in the activities of the two. Consequently, when either shirked his or her responsibilities, the whole family suffered. In a society where life hovered around the subsistence level a good bit of the time, there were rather strict limits on the extent to which laziness and/or incompetence in economic pursuits could be tolerated. If a person was working hard, and his (or her) spouse was either unwilling or unable to carry her (or his) proper share of the load, it was only a matter of time before the strains in the relationship would become intolerable.

Disputes over child rearing also seem to have been a significant source of strain, although for different reasons than are usually involved in our society. When an American husband and wife argue about how to raise children, they are generally disagreeing on one of the two following points: (1) how to handle a specific incident; or (2) a general aspect of the upbringing of *all* their children. For the Eskimos on the other hand, the methods involved were pretty much agreed on, and followed traditional lines. The problems resulted from the

apparently widespread tendency for a parent to strongly
favor one child, who was usually *not* favored by the
other parent. The favored child was exempt from normal rules of behavior as far as the favoring parent was
concerned, but not from the viewpoint of the non-
favoring parent. Consequently, when one parent scolded
his or her spouse's favorite child, regardless of the reason,
the other parent would become extremely incensed, and
a quarrel would result. The depth of the emotions which
could be generated in such situations was considerable.

The above seem to have been the major sources of
strain in the *ui-nuliaq* relationship, but they were by no
means the only ones. Other sources included personality
clashes, with all that they entailed, in-law trouble,
jealousy, barrenness, and minor irritations of all kinds.
Significantly, the *ui-nuliaq* relationship was not expected
to contain any serious strains. Indeed, some things we
would scarcely regard as justification for an argument
were sufficient grounds for an Eskimo divorce. If friction
developed between spouses, separation was an acceptable
alternative at all times. Divorces also resulted from factors other than strains within a marital union, however.
For example, a person might leave a spouse to go live with
someone else who seemed more desirable even though
the first one was generally quite acceptable. Divorce
could be instituted on purely individual initiative, and
justification for such action did not have to be made to
anyone. Irresponsibility in such matters was not encouraged, however, and a person who evidenced extreme
instability in marital associations would eventually have
a difficult time obtaining a spouse.

One of the more interesting things about Eskimo divorce is the consequences that remarriage had for the
various individuals involved. A hypothetical remarriage
situation is illustrated in Figure 9, in which two couples
who were divorced then married each other's spouses. It
should be noted that remarriage rarely followed this par-

FIGURE 9

Divorce and Remarriage

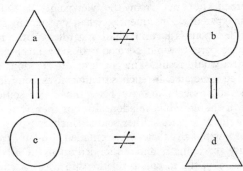

(ab) *ui-nuliaq*; (dc) *ui-nuliaq*; (ac) *ui-nuliaq*;
(db) *ui-nuliaq*; (ad) *nuliaqan-nuliaqan*;
(bc) *aipaq-aipaq*

ticular pattern because two divorced couples were not
likely to remarry on a parallel basis such as this one.
More often, an *ui* would marry someone that had no or
only distant connections with the person that his *nuliaq*
married. The resulting types of relationships would be
the same regardless of the number of individuals involved, however, hence the utility of the diagram.

Since the *ui-nuliaq* relationship, once established, held
for the lifetimes of its members, the original link between
the two marital couples in Figure 9 is not broken by
divorce; it is merely deactivated. Since everyone in the
diagram got remarried, however, two new *ui-nuliaq* pairs
were created in addition to, not in replacement of, the
original pair. The interesting thing is the relationships
that resulted for the two men and the two women involved. As Figure 8 indicates, the women stood in the

relationship of co-wives (*aipaq-aipaq*) and the two men were cohusbands (*nuliaqan-nuliaqan*). A comparison to Figures 8 and 9 will indicate that divorce and remarriage was almost identical in its formal aspects with the highly institutionalized comarriage situation. The only difference is that the relationship between cospouses (*uiNuzaq-nulizaq*) was not established in the case of divorce and remarriage, being replaced there by the residential marital relationship of *ui-nuliaq*. The similarity that Eskimo divorce and remarriage had with the basic forms of plural marriage has prompted Heinrich (1963) to label it "marriage in lesser degree," rather than as divorce.

Divorce, with the virtually universal remarriage, was for all practical purposes an integral part of the Eskimo marriage system because it resulted in the establishment of the same set of relationships as did marriage itself. Consequently, the four relationships in the system can be defined as follows: (1) the *ui-nuliaq* relationship existed between any man and woman who had *ever* had socially approved sexual relations while living together; (2) the cospouse relationship (*uiNuzaq-nulizaq*) relationship obtained between any man and woman who had had socially approved sexual relations with each other while *not* living together; (3) the cohusband (*nuliaqan-nuliaqan*) relationship held between two men who had had socially approved sexual intercourse with the same woman; (4) the co-wife (*aipaq-aipaq*) relationship obtained between two women who had had socially approved intercourse with the same man. The "had had" feature is an essential component of the above definitions because in no case did the defining criteria have to be maintained for a very long time. Likewise, a considerable length of time could elapse between the establishment of one relationship and the setting up of another. Thus, a man could enter into an *ui-nuliaq* relationship with a woman, divorce her, and marry another woman twenty years later, and the two women would still be in the co-wife relationship.

The above consequences of divorce and remarriage were of considerable importance in the traditional society. If a man and the new husband of his divorced wife had anything to do with each other at all, they were expected to behave in terms of the same highly structured relationship that obtained between the two men in an exchange-marriage arrangement. This meant that they were under obligations of mutual friendship and support. A similar situation held for the women. In short, they had the choice of avoiding each other altogether, or of getting along on very good terms indeed. The jealousy and mutual antagonism which might be expected in such situations were considered inappropriate. They did in fact occur sometimes, of course, but were considered wrong by the other members of the society. In any case, the ideal alternatives were clearly defined, as were the resulting behavior patterns once a choice had been made.

The effect that Eskimo divorce had on the children is not clear at our present state of knowledge, but was probably minimal in its negative aspects. The results varied considerably depending on the situation. If a single, very young child was involved, it was generally adopted by another family, usually relatives of one of the parents. Since the Eskimos had a well-established, highly institutionalized, and generally very satisfactory system of adoption (which cannot be gone into here), such a procedure was not upsetting to anyone. The child would not lose his ties with his real parents when taken in by someone else, it would merely gain some additional ones. When more and/or older children were involved, they usually stayed with the mother. Even while fairly young, however, Eskimo children were permitted to exercise a fair amount of individual discretion as to the person with whom they wished to live. Adolescents could pretty much make up their own minds on the subject. As was the case for marriage proper, divorce and remarriage resulted in the establishment of sibling ties for all the children of all the participants; hence there were no problems in this area either.

Property rarely caused any difficulties in Eskimo divorce because, on the whole, goods were individually owned, with fairly little overlap between the sexes. Consequently, when a divorce was effected, each person simply kept his or her own belongings. If there was any trouble at all, it usually occurred in situations where a man had been living with his wife's relatives and had helped them in some major construction effort, such as building the house in which they were living, which would entitle him to part ownership in it. Here, of course, the problem was not between the *ui* and *nuliaq*, but between the man and his *nuliaq's* relatives.[15] Its resolution depended on a number of situational factors that need not be considered here.

Discussion

It is revealing, in the analysis of divorce, to consider what the marital relationship would be like if it were functioning normally. It is also instructive in the attempt to understand any institution in one society to contrast it with the appropriate one in another. The traditional North Alaskan Eskimo *ui-nuliaq* relationship and its contemporary American counterpart, for example, differed in a number of ways. For the remainder of the paper, therefore, I am going to compare the two systems and outline their similarities and differences as I see them with respect to both marital relationships and the divorce situation. Although my primary concern here is with the Eskimos, it will sometimes be necessary to discuss our own system in some detail to bring out the contrast between the two.

One distinctive feature of the *ui-nuliaq* relationship is its similarity to what we call a "contract" relationship. Such a relationship is known in professional jargon as a "functionally specific" one. As defined by Levy,[16] this means that the various "activities or rights and obligations or performances that [were] covered by the relationship [were] precisely defined and delimited." If someone had asked a traditional Eskimo couple to list what was supposed to be involved in their relationship, they probably could have answered quickly and precisely, and then stop, having listed everything they thought relevant. If the same question were put to a contemporary American couple, however, they would probably have some difficulty in answering. They could perhaps name a few especially important things in relatively short order, but beyond that they would likely be overwhelmed by the number and variety of considerations involved.

It should be recognized, however, that the *ui-nuliaq* relationship was not functionally specific to the extent that is the case with a true contract relationship, in which both definition *and* delimitation are quite precise. In the *ui-nuliaq* case most of the considerations were relatively precisely defined, but the relationship was not precisely *delimited* to the extent that an Eskimo could state exactly where his duties vis-à-vis his spouse ended and where they began. The data suggest, however, that in both respects the Eskimos went far beyond our own husband-wife relationship, and I strongly suspect that they were relatively extreme from the viewpoint of marital relationships in any society in the world.

Of the various orientations involved in the *ui-nuliaq* relationship, sexual relations were obviously important, but the relationship was economically oriented to a degree that must be unusual for relationships in the marital category.[17] That is to say, the production of goods and services occupied an especially important place among all the activities involved in *ui-nuliaq* interaction from the Eskimos' own point of view. The *ui* was primarily a hunter, and most of his activities revolved around the chase, and the manufacture and maintenance of hunting and household implements. He was also primarily responsible for the education of his sons. The *nuliaq*, on the other hand, was responsible for the skinning and butchering of the game that her husband killed. She also had to make and maintain the family clothing, store and prepare the food, look after the small children, and educate her daughters. The duties of the spouses overlapped very little. Beyond these predominantly economically oriented activities and sexual intercourse, there was little involved in the relationship, at least ideally.

With respect to the contemporary American situation, however, the same assertions could not be made, at least with reference to the ideals of married life. While it is clear that economic considerations are very important in the relationship between husband and wife, I think it fair to say that a marriage in which they are emphasized to the same extent as was ideally the case among the Eskimos would be regarded by most Americans as one which is headed for disaster. Indeed, I would not be surprised if the American husband-wife relationship was found to be one of the most diffusely oriented marital relationships of any in the world, certainly at the opposite end of the continuum from its Eskimo counterpart.

So far, of course, I have been talking about the ideal situation with respect to the substantive definition of the relationships. Actually, however, many Eskimo marriages were relatively functionally diffuse, while many American marriages are relatively functionally specific. The interesting thing about the North Alaskan situation is that to the extent that the individuals involved in a particular *ui-nuliaq* relationship were living under favorable economic circumstances, the greater the extent to which their relationship was likely to approach the ideal of functional specificity. Couples who were living in isolated camps of perhaps one or two families were generally involved in very diffuse relationships, but the larger the settlement in which the same couples might live, the less that *ui* and *nuliaq* would have to do with each other outside of sexually and economically oriented activities. In some of the larger maritime villages, *ui* and *nuliaq* might only see one another at sporadic intervals (see below).

There was very little communication between an *ui* and his *nuliaq*, and little was expected. Furthermore, as one might suppose in a functionally specific relationship of this sort, the communication that did take place dealt largely with the practical problems of the day, and little else. Indeed, as was mentioned above, Eskimo husbands and wives were not often in one another's company.[18] The men spent their time hunting or visiting with other men, while women were either working in the house, or visiting with other women. In the larger villages and elsewhere whenever conditions permitted, the men generally spent most of their waking hours in a special building known as a *kazgi*,[19] and even ate their meals there, completely separated from their wives and young children.

In the contemporary United States, however, the situation is quite the opposite, at least ideally. Husbands and wives are expected to share experiences, ideas, secrets, and so forth, and to spend a major portion of their free time in one another's company. Not only is communication between husband and wife supposed to be frequent and informative, it is expected to be of an emotionally satisfying kind that theoretically cannot be found outside of marriage. Actually, of course, many husbands and wives interact more along the lines of their Eskimo counterparts than according to the American ideal, but, when they do, it is a sign of breakdown in the relationship. To the Eskimos, lack of communication between spouses was not only the normal state of affairs, it was regarded as the "right" one. An interesting point made by Dr. Jessie Bernard (see her chapter in this volume) is that the requirements of the American custom greatly increase the opportunities for communication at *cross-purposes*. The result is that one of the most highly institutionalized aspects of the husband-wife relationship is also one of the primary loci of strain in that relationship. The Eskimos, by minimizing communication of any kind, were able to avoid this particular problem.

Another important difference between the Eskimo and American systems is in the intensity of the emotional involvement in the marital situation. It is well known, of course, that love is considered the keystone of American marriage, and a vast folklore and literature has grown up to tell us why this must be so. Not only are American couples expected to be in love with each other, they are expected to demonstrate that affection in a variety of ways, both publicly and privately. The *ui-nuliaq* relationship, however, was much less intense than its American counterpart. Cases of romantic unions did in fact occur, but they do not seem to have been overly common. In any case, love certainly was not institutionalized as a component of the relationship. One was expected to feel affection for a spouse, but not necessarily a great deal of it. And, regardless of one's actual feelings, the demonstration of affection for one's spouse in public was regarded as being improper. It was probably minimal (although present) even in private.

Perhaps the most significant contrast of all between the two systems is in the relative strength of the appropriate relationships. In the Eskimo case, the *ui-nuliaq* relationship was ideally a very weak one (although strong ones did sometimes occur in fact). In other words, if one had to choose between the obligations to one's spouse and those to almost any kind of "blood" relative, one was expected to choose in favor of the latter in virtually

every case. In America, however, there are rather few
obligations and commitments that take precedence over
those between husband and wife. The general obligations to "God and country" are perhaps the only ones
that unequivocally come before those to one's spouse, at
least ideally. Even here, provision is made for the spouse
wherever possible (such as when married men are de-
ferred from the draft). Actually, of course, it often happens that individuals choose in favor of their job, their
golf partners, their parents, their bridge club, or whatever, over their spouse. Doing so constitutes a breakdown
of the marriage, however. Continued deferment of one's
obligations to one's spouse in favor of those to virtually
anything *but* "God and country" will frequently lead
to severe strains in the relations between husband and
wife, and perhaps to separation and divorce.

It is sometimes argued that the rising divorce rate in
the United States is a sign that the husband-wife relationship is rapidly losing its former strength. One implication of such a conclusion for the present discussion
would be that the American marital relationship is becoming more like the traditional Eskimo one, at least in
this particular respect. I think that such a conclusion is
unwarranted, however. I suspect that a thorough examination of the *actual* reasons behind the divorces in
the United States, without any regard for what is said in
court, would reveal that, on the contrary, the husband-
wife relationship is even stronger than it was in former
decades. What is happening, I suggest, is that since divorces are becoming progressively easier to come by, people are beginning to demand that their spouses live up
to the ideals of the relationship to a higher degree *in fact*
than was formerly the case, or forfeit the relationship
altogether. Easy divorce in both the Eskimo and American systems provides a means by which a person can
hold a spouse effectively responsible for his or her be-

havior. The difference lies in the kinds of behavior which are expected in the first place.

It is clear that the *ui-nuliaq* and husband-wife relationships, however similar they might appear in a diagram, occupied vastly different niches in quite different systems. It is not surprising, therefore, that divorce should have different causes and consequences in each. If it were possible to measure such things with any precision, I am sure that we would find that the *ui-nuliaq* relationship was generally subjected to fewer, and usually weaker, strains than is the case for its American counterpart. This, despite the fact that divorce was probably much more frequent among the Eskimos than in the contemporary United States. The major difference, however, lies in the fact that in America there is an overwhelming obligation to contain any and all strains which might be generated in such a relationship, whereas the Eskimos felt very little responsibility of this sort. No wonder, then, that in America[20] the divorce of mature, stable individuals is preceded by varying amounts of anguish, soul searching, sleepless nights, and so forth. It is an unhappy event for the people involved, and usually for their relatives and close friends as well. Indeed, the more one has accepted the values of our society, the more extreme the emotional strain of a divorce is likely to be. This does not mean that even the most stable person will not get divorced under the right conditions, but when he does, it is usually an extremely painful experience.

To the Eskimos, however, divorce was hardly a catastrophe. As far as economic considerations were concerned, the separated spouses could turn to relatives for temporary support. Since they usually remarried within a relatively short time,[21] divorce generally caused few difficulties in the economic sphere. Furthermore, in the case of famine or any other crisis, the full obligations of mutual support were incumbent on the individuals in-

volved regardless of how antagonistic they might be at
the time. Unfortunately, we do not know with any certainty what the psychological consequences of divorce
were in the traditional period. We do know, however,
that the individuals involved in a divorce situation were
often extremely aroused, usually in the form of anger.
The psychological impact was probably very superficial
in nature, however, certainly much less than what it
seems to be in the contemporary United States. For the
Eskimos, a rift with one's parents or siblings was an in-
finitely more traumatic experience than was a break with
one's spouse.[22]

There is also a distinct difference between the two
societies with regard to the extent to which the postdivorce situation is structured. That is, they differ with
respect to the extent to which behavioral guidelines for
divorcees are institutionalized. When an American couple gets divorced, for example, their obligations to one
another, usually with reference to the children (if any),
property, and economic support, are generally fairly carefully defined in the courts. Outside of these few, albeit
important considerations, however, the divorce situation
seems to be almost totally unstructured. The individuals
involved have to improvise their own rules of behavior.
Indeed, it is just this lack of definition which Goode[23]
cites as the major cause of the high remarriage rate
among divorced Americans. The situation is so poorly
defined, he argues, that most people find it very uncomfortable to stay in it, and they seek the only acceptable
way out, namely, remarriage.[24]

Divorced Eskimos, however, were in no such position.
On the whole, they were expected to avoid each other,
but even when confronting each other face to face they
knew how they were supposed to act. They could follow socially approved alternatives which they knew in
advance, and they did not have to make things up as
they went along. There was considerable pressure on

Eskimos to remarry, but in their case the pressure stemmed from the need to have an economic partner of the opposite sex. Lack of social definition of their status in life was never a factor.

Another difference between Eskimos and Americans is the position of the children in a divorce situation. For the Eskimos divorce was not only clearly defined with respect to any children involved, it was fully integrated with the kinship system in general. Eskimos generally had several sets of siblings, a full biological set, possibly a set or two of half-siblings, and probably one or more sets of exchange siblings. Likewise, an Eskimo was liable to have more than one set of parents, a full biological pair, perhaps an adoptive pair, and possibly one or more stepparents. Since the notion of multiple sets of siblings and parents was a feature of Eskimo kinship at its *best*, it is unlikely that the new relationships created through divorce and remarriage caused any serious problems.

In America, however, it is generally agreed that divorce produces trauma of varying degrees of severity for the children involved. Even if the degree of psychological and emotional impact of divorce on the children is not known with precision, it is clearly negative. The picture of estranged parents staying together "for the children's sake," long after their own relationship has failed, is a familiar one to all of us. The argument that the strains resulting from two such people living together might be even harder on the children than a divorce would be is beside the point, regardless of what truth it might contain in a given case.

Interestingly enough, when an American couple gets divorced, especially if there are children, the resulting situation is in some respects not unlike the one described for the Eskimos. Goode[25] and Hunt[26] have both found that divorce by no means necessarily breaks the bond between husband and wife in our society, and that often the behavior of a divorced person continues to be shaped by the attitudes of the former spouse for some time. As a minimum, certain economic obligations tie the two ex-spouses together, and if there are children involved, it is very difficult for them to avoid seeing each other on occasion. In America, the illusion is that divorce terminates interaction between spouses altogether, while in fact it is rarely the complete break we tend to think it is. In the Eskimo case, the illusion was that the divorce situation meant a continued active relationship, while in fact interaction between spouses was either greatly reduced or ceased completely.

A similar situation obtains for the other relationships involved. Say, for example, that American children of a first marriage go with the mother, as is normally the case. When she remarries, which she is likely to do, these children suddenly find themselves with two fathers, a "real" one and a "step" one. Now, if the mother has children by her second husband, they become half-siblings to the children she had by her first. If the second husband had children of his own by a previous marriage, the situation is even more complex, but rather similar to the *standard* Eskimo situation.

Likewise, if the first husband remarries and has children by his second wife, then those children are half-siblings to those he had by his first wife, and so on. To the American mind this is an extremely complicated situation, and probably a highly ambiguous one.[27] What are the relationships of the several sets of half- and step- and full-siblings to be like? How are the two husbands supposed to behave toward each other when they meet (which may be unavoidable at times)? How are the two women supposed to act toward each other? The Eskimos would have had a set of ready answers for questions like these because such situations were not only commonplace in their society even without divorce, they were highly institutionalized. Many Americans are now in situations similar to the hypothetical ones outlined above, yet they have no standards of behavior to guide them.

Superficially, at least, the traditional North Alaskan Eskimos and the contemporary Americans are rather similar with respect to the *de facto* consequences of divorce, no matter how different the two systems might be ideally. The most obvious difference is that for the Eskimos the postdivorce situation was clearly defined and institutionalized for *all* parties, whereas in the United States it is not. It is clear, however, that due to radically different conceptions of what marriage is supposed to be like in the first place, divorce has quite a different type of impact on the individuals involved. Goode (1956: 216) argues that life goes on, and that the wounds of an American divorce heal in time, as do those of a loved one's death and other life crises. There, however, lies the rub, for a wound always leaves a scar. For the Eskimos there was no wound, hence no scar. For them it was not a matter of "life going forward" in spite of it all, for there was no crisis to be overcome; life merely went on pretty much as usual, with perhaps a few temporary complications.

In conclusion, it seems apparent that divorce can never be understood except in relation to the whole of which it is a part. More specifically, divorce is non-existent apart from marriage, and neither can be understood without a consideration of their positions in the society as a whole. Eskimo society was set up in such a way that divorce was neither greatly upsetting to the principals involved nor disruptive of the community at large. Emotional and social stability depended on the operation of other relationships which, to them, were more important. This does not mean, as has sometimes been claimed, that the Eskimos were totally lacking in moral standards. On the contrary, they had very definite values—values which were strongly held. They were simply different than ours. In the final analysis, the problem seems to be largely one of emphasis. The degree to which a particular marital relationship is emphasized in a society is of crucial importance in this respect and must be taken into consideration in any analysis of divorce.

9

Brittle Marriage
as a Stable System:
The Kanuri Case

RONALD COHEN

Introduction: The Problem

A volume on divorce such as the present one should contain an examination of the theoretical possibility that divorce could become as ubiquitous as marriage, or approach such an extreme. In other words, it is legitimate to ask what would happen if all, or almost all, marriages in a society were to end in divorce. What kinds of institutions would prevent such a system from becoming a quagmire of chaotic instability for those who had to live in it? Even if such a system could exist, does it produce such tensions for those involved that the society as a whole, or at least its family system, can be looked at as a maladjusted one? All of these are important questions, and not simply theoretical ones either, for such societies do exist. Furthermore, with our own divorce frequency advancing inexorably upward, it is instructive to look at other societies that have much more divorce than we do and a much longer experience with it to see what sorts of problems may lie in wait for us if the upward trend continues.

In order to be clear about these phenomena on a comparative basis, it is important to have definitions that isolate similar behavior, no matter what the cultural context. For this purpose, I would define marriage as the socially and legally recognized union of a couple, the children of which are considered to be legitimate. Marriages can be dissolved: (a) by the death of one or both of the spouses; (b) by an annulment of the marriage in which it is proved that all conditions assumed necessary for proper and legal marriage inception are, in fact, not present; (c) by separation or desertion in which one or both of the partners to a marriage remove themselves from the socially approved, residential conditions for marriage, but the marriage is still legally valid; and (d) a divorce in which a marriage is legally recognized to have been severed and both parties are then free to remarry.

In some societies, there is such confusion over the definition of marital dissolution that it becomes difficult to tell whether the breakup was due to separation, desertion, or divorce. This occurs when there are a great many common-law unions. Such a condition is generally associated with periods of rapid social change or the inception of a plantation system as in the case of the Cameroons in Africa,[1] or of some of the areas of rapid industrialization such as South Africa. The confusion also occurs in areas of great poverty or labor migration. In many such situations, marriage unions are not just brittle, they lack legal institutionalization. In all of these cases, there is a tendency toward the development of the matrifocal family, that is to say, the only stable family group is a mother and her children; the father may, or may not, be present or may be present only for short periods. By contrast, however, I wish to examine a case where very little social change has, as yet, taken place and where divorce is a clear-cut category of its own and is equivalent legally to our Western conception of divorce. In this situation, it is also normally and traditionally a very frequent occurrence.

The Setting

The Kanuri of Bornu Province in northeastern Nigeria, according to their own traditions, have been organized as a feudal state in the Chad basin for approximately the last eight hundred to one thousand years.[2] Their language classification by Greenberg[3] and early Arabic sources supports the notion of their continuity in the region, with possible origins somewhere to the northeast of their present habitat. During its long history as an organized state, the precolonial emirate kept up continual trade and cultural contacts with the Maghreb and the Near East. The population density is approximately sixty per square mile, and there is no pressure for farmland, since it can be extended simply by clearing new bush areas farther away from the population settlements. The majority of the people are peasants who carry on three analytically separate, economic activities. These consist of: (1) farming, primarily millet and guinea corn, supplemented by maize, beans, squashes, cucumbers, and groundnuts; (2) cash cropping, mostly groundnuts; (3) a dry season, non-farming activity connected with the market. Market activities are, in turn, divided into craftwork, sales of surplus agricultural products and a complex middleman trade between markets. Except for a few full-time specialists, almost everyone does some farming. There is, however, much variation in the ratio of market activities to subsistence agriculture in each person's income.[4]

The society has a monarch, the *shehu,* in his capital city of Maiduguri, and a courtly life with titled nobles, which include the *ajia* or district heads, who live in their district capitals as subrulers of the twenty-one segments of the emirate under the *shehu*. They, in turn, have under their jurisdiction a group of contiguous village, or area, units headed by *lawan*, or village area heads. Under these latter are hamlet heads, *bulama*, in charge of small settlements of contiguous compounds. Peasants call themselves the peasants of such and such a *lawan*. Today the emirate administration departments have their personnel stationed throughout the district. Along with the district head and his chief followers, they form an urban upper class who live in the district capitals spread throughout the state.[5]

The society is stratified with status based on tribal membership, occupation, birth, age, wealth, and, lately, to some extent, on urban residence identifications. The people recognize two major class divisions: the upper, or ruling, class and the broad base of the peasant class, which is under the autocratic hegemony of the rulers. Upward mobility can be achieved by obtaining more wealth, a more highly ranked occupation, and by copying the manners, dress, and behavior of the upper class.[6]

Kanuri Marriage Inception

Kanuri girls marry for the first time at, or near, puberty, between the ages of twelve and sixteen. Girls who are well developed physically and not yet married are suspected of not being virgins. Virginity is a basic cultural norm for a girl's first marriage. Throughout a young girl's childhood, she is taught to expect an early marriage, and most women claim they had very little, or any, say in deciding when, or whom, they would first marry. Stories are told of girls who violently refused to marry the person chosen for them, and there is a customary rule that, if a young bride, or bride-to-be, runs away three times before, or just after, her first marriage, she is not required to go through with it. In practice, however, this rarely occurs after the marriage ceremony has been performed, and the vast majority of girls do comply, or are persuaded to go along with, the plans of their *luwali*, or male adult, generally the father, who has the right to dispense and negotiate the marriage arrangements.

Boys marry for the first time sometime after the age of eighteen or nineteen and often go into their late twenties before taking a first wife. As in the case of girls, it is quite common for the young boy's first marriage to be arranged and financed by his parents, or the head of the household in which he is living at the time, although many do arrange their own, and this is becoming more common today, especially in the cities.

Later marriages for both men and women are much freer as to choice, and seem to Western eyes to have practically no easily perceivable pattern of courtship. Some informants claim they knew their perspective spouse only a day or two before the marriage, others all their lives, others several years, still others not at all. In the latter case, the man usually reports that he saw the girl or woman on the street, or in someone else's compound, and sent word that he wished to marry her. Furthermore, there appears to be no relation (in over seven hundred recorded cases) between duration of previous acquaintanceship before marriage and either the rate of divorce or the duration of the marriage. On the other hand, this reported behavior masks a well-known ethnographic fact which men discuss in general, and refuse to comment on, with respect to their own marriages: this is the custom of sleeping with a divorced woman, eating her food and giving her some weekly market money, then, if the arrangement seems satisfactory, it may mature into a marriage. Again, however, even where we have been able to get quantitative information (from women only) on this practice, there seems to be no relation between any type of premarital relations and the durability of the marriage to come.

Kanuri marriages are not entered into as easily as their very high divorce rate might imply. All marriages, even the so-called marriage of charity wherein the bridewealth is waived, cost the groom, his friends, and his family a relatively large capital outlay in cash and kind. The most expensive marriage is that with a previously unmarried girl. The ceremony, itself, is more complex, as are the marriage payments; and the celebration, the drummers, the wedding foods, the number of guests, and so on—all of these are greater for first marriages than for subsequent ones. Many young men just starting out in life cannot afford such a marriage and try, instead, to marry a young divorced woman. Only later, when they are older and more well established in life, can they begin to think of the luxury and prestige of a virgin bride. Many girls, therefore, marry men who are thirty to fifty years older than themselves because only these can afford such a marriage.

Whenever a Kanuri man decides to get married, he assesses the marriage in a number of ways. First, as implied above, there is his own position in society. If he has wealth, then the proper thing to do is to spend it. Thus, marriage expenses are basically a function of the groom's socioeconomic status. Secondly, there is the previous marital status of the woman. How many times has she been married before and how durable were these unions? (Some men claimed that they did not consider this to be important; others considered it as a factor in estimating the desirability of a marriage.) The major distinction, however, is between marriage with a virgin girl as compared with marriage to a divorced woman. There are also subtle shades that often play a part. Thus, girls in their teens who have had one or two divorces are called by a special term (*njim suri*) which means that such girls have seen the man's sleeping hut, but really still know

very little about the skills of adult womanhood. They are
thus still amenable to training and are considered more
valuable than older women. In general, bridewealth
goes up as a man grows older and decreases as a woman
advances in age until, finally, at about the age of forty-
five to fifty, a woman is not considered marriageable.
Thus, the sexes have inverse paths through life—men increase their capacities and abilities as measured by bridewealth payments, while women decline, sharply, after
the first marriage and, gradually but steadily, through
each successive union. Thirdly, in general, rural marriages require less bridewealth, urban ones, more. This
reflects the generally higher income of the city people and
is thus an aspect of socioeconomic status. Other factors
that enter in are the prestige of the two families, the bar-
gaining abilities of the groom's representatives as against
the party representing the girl, and personal qualities of
the girl—her beauty, cooking abilities, proven fertility as
a child bearer, and her reputation as a docile and obedient wife.

The Conditions of Marriage

The most important general conditions of a Kanuri
marriage are: (a) its seclusiveness for women, (b) its
polygynous nature, and (c) the ideology and practice of
male dominance. The Kanuri have been Muslim for
many centuries. There is, thus, incorporated into their
ideas of the female role the general conception of Muslim seclusion of the wife. It is thus mandatory for a
young bride, after a first marriage, to remain within her
husband's household for one year and leave it for only
the most necessary family ceremonies such as the funeral
of a close relative. Divorced women remain in this condition for one week after marriage. In general, all Kanuri
men prefer their wives to remain inside the compound

as much as possible. They do, however, separate two cultural categories: *kulle,* or seclusion, and *kulle-ba,* non-seclusion, and all women know before marriage whether a prospective husband considers the coming union to be *kulle* or not. In general, most urban marriages are *kulle* while most rural ones are not. This reflects the need of the rural husband for the contribution his wife makes to farm labor and to water carrying—chores that, of necessity, take her out of the household. In practice, many women in *kulle* do manage to get out to visit friends or relatives, to have their hair done, or to go to local ceremonies. Conversely, rural women are expected to stay at home when not doing chores that demand their presence outside the compound. Constant neglect of this expectation may lead to suspicion of adultery or to loss of face for the husband in the community, especially if the wife is young. Thus, seclusion/non-seclusion is more a matter of degree than of mutually exclusive categories. That it is a matter of major importance, however, is reflected in the reasons men have given for their divorce history. Time and again male informants have said, "She went out of the house too much," or, "I came back from the market (or the farm), and she was not in the house"—and so he divorced her. One informant in the city saw his wife (in *kulle*) go out of the front door to buy some cosmetics from a street vender. He walked over and divorced her on the spot.

Kanuri marriage is polygynous; and, in rather general, statistical terms, one out of every two men has more than one wife. A few have three, and even fewer have four, but two is quite common. This means that almost all Kanuri women can look forward to having a co-wife at some time in their marital careers, and children can look forward to having some form of relationship to their mother's co-wife, or co-wives, and possibly to half-siblings. There are strict rules governing the polygynous situation, and they are, for the most part, practiced. During the inception of a new marriage, a husband should give a present wife half of the gifts given to the new incoming wife. Some variability is allowed for. In a few, quite rare cases, the husband and wife agree that he is spending so much on the new marriage that he should give the present incumbent only a token gift. Failure to obtain such an agreement, or to provide the necessary gift, leads to trouble, fights, accusations, refusal to co-operate by the wife, and the situation ends with a separation or divorce.

Relations between a husband and his wives are governed by a strict rule for taking turns. Each wife occupies the role of a sole spouse from sunset one day to the end of the next day. She brings her husband his evening meal, sleeps in his room, and prepares his morning meal and any other meals he and his male friends may eat during the day. Not to take such a turn is tantamount to asking for a divorce. There is no rule governing the taking of turns for sexual intercourse, but a wise husband, even when he may favor one of his wives in this regard, rations his favors so that none may claim total neglect. Market money, clothes, permission to visit outside the house are all governed by the same general rule of equal benefits, although, in a few cases, we have recorded families in which the husband dealt out market money and other gifts to a senior wife who, in turn, distributed these to the other wives. When questioned, many wives commented they did not like this practice.

In a few instances, we have recorded cases of multiple residence in which men, usually traders, have households in several towns and a single wife in each. These men have business activities in several places and have, therefore, set up separate households in each place. There is nothing illegitimate about such a variant to polygyny, and it functions to prevent co-wife interaction. The system is an old one and dates back to the time of the trans-Saharan trade, although it is, also, adaptable to modern conditions; thus, a truck driver of my acquaintance has a household in Maiduguri with one wife and another in Fort Lamy, one hundred and forty miles away.

The relations of co-wives are generally quite formal and reserved. The wife who has been in the household the longest is considered to be the senior woman, or *gumsu*. She takes an authoritative role in planning the cooking for festivals; she walks in front of the single file of women of the household; and she often transmits instructions from the household head to the rest of the wives. The Kanuri believe, and the statistical data on marriage duration bears it out, that to have one or two wives is much easier than to have three or four. In the case of two wives, it is believed that they can learn to get along and share the husband. However, with three, one wife always fights with the other two. With four, it is believed that conflict would be lessened as compared with three, but factionalism may still develop. Husbands also worry lest co-wives might "gang up" on them. Although this is not common, it does happen, and the result is either capitulation by the husband to demands made by the wife group, or a group divorce in which he sends all of them away at once.

In one of the projective tests we administered, there is a picture card which depicts two Kanuri women who are in a compound. Most of the seventy-five male respondents remarked that these were two women, one of whom was visiting the other, and the two friends seemed quite happy. Age differences were not often remarked on and, if they were, they were interpreted to indicate mother/ daughter interactions. Almost without exception, the card was seen by men as a peaceful, serene, and friendly interaction between two women. Our seventy-five female respondents, on the other hand, almost invariably saw the two women as co-wives—one, the older, the other, younger. They elaborated by saying that the older one seemed unhappy because the younger one was more attractive to the husband. To the women, the picture immediately suggested the co-wife situation with its attendant jealousies, competition, and conflict.

There are strict patterns of avoidance of in-laws among the Kanuri, and they affect young wives most severely. Since many households are patrilocal, the girl has a good chance of living in, or near, the household of her husband's patrilineal male relatives. This is restrictive, for the young bride must be constantly on the alert to avoid open conversations with her in-laws, especially her father-in-law. It is also considered shameful for a young man to discuss his marriage with his own parents, especially his father. Thus, when a young man marries a second wife, he often moves out of his parent's household so that he may have greater privacy and any conflict in his marriage, or between his wives, will not be openly heard by his parents.

The household is also set up so that each wife has her own sleeping hut and cooking area in the living section of the compound. This privacy is maintained so that women may, if they wish, live semiseparately from one another in the compound. However, the hub of compound life, even though women live for the most part together and away from men, is still the husband. If the husband respects and honors a senior wife and gives her not only her due but that little extra intimacy and confidence that goes along with her longer association, then, on the surface at least, the household runs smoothly. On the other hand, even a hint that the husband favors a younger wife brings serious tensions and jealousies into play that very often end in a divorce.

The third condition of Kanuri marriage, besides seclusion of women and polygyny, is that of the cultural rules and expectations of male dominance. Islamic prescriptions are clear on this point, "Man stands superior to woman in that God hath preferred the one over the other. . . ."[7]

The Kanuri believe it is a good thing for a woman to obey her husband, bad, to disobey. Indeed, a husband may, if he likes, punish his wife, especially if she is young. Thus, a district head ruled against the complainants in a case in which the husband had been accused by his wife's patrikin of beating her. The district head stated that the girl had been disobedient, and it was a husband's right to punish such acts.

In terms of everyday activities within the household, women cook, draw water for the household, and help on the farm, if they are not in seclusion. They raise garden crops in the compound, thresh, pound and grind grain, sweep and clean the compound, tend the young children, keep chickens and ducks, and engage in petty trade, usually of a retail nature. Some women specialize in creating the elaborate Kanuri women's coiffure. Others make pots, while still others make baskets, and a few are professional entertainers who work with male drummers and what are locally called "praise singers." Generally, however, these specialized activities are not common, and most women have no occupation besides that of being a housewife and, alternately, a divorced woman. The major tasks, then, are cooking and preparing food, helping on the farm, and raising children. In all these jobs, the younger girls help out and are under the authority of the older women who organize this work within the compound.

Men engage in politics, farm, dye, build, work metals, tan animal hides, work leather, buy, sell, and slaughter cattle and small livestock, tailor, embroider, make hats and musical instruments, trade, weave mats, and work as laborers. They are also religious specialists, barbers, carpenters, mechanics, clerks, civil servants, and hold a host of newly introduced jobs of European origin; and they are the tax payers. It is no exaggeration to say that the economy is controlled almost totally by men. The household head dispenses all incoming cash and kind that result from craft or farm work, although a woman may keep, and do with as she pleases, the proceeds of her small garden inside the compound. The household head deals out the weekly money to his wives for petty market purchases and makes all major purchases of food and clothing on his own. He also pays for ceremonies, transportation, and most of the gift-giving engaged in by himself and others in the household. Except for the sale of cooked food, pottery production, and female hairdressing, men control all income-producing work of any kind in the entire society.

Many cultural expectations of interaction also emphasize the male dominance. Thus, if a man and his wife are traveling together, he walks ahead, she, behind. If there is a horse or a donkey or a camel, he rides, she walks (unless she is pregnant). Men and women eat separately; the wife serves the husband first, then she eats. During intercourse, the Kanuri believe that gonorrhea will result if a man takes a sexual position under (interpreted as inferior to) the woman. In an inheritance, other claims being equal, a woman gets half as much as a man. Thus, in a host of ways, the culture points up the superiority of the male and the subordinate and inferior position of the woman.

Divorce

The Kanuri value marital stability and even perform a little ritual at the marriage to symbolize the desire of everyone that this particular marriage should be a lasting one. On the other hand, they think the idea of limiting divorce, making it difficult to obtain, or banning it entirely would be unthinkable. To them, marriage entails the possibility of divorce, and any move to limit divorce would create an intolerable situation in which marriages that should be ended would have to persist.

Such an idea they find uncivilized, or barbaric. As I have already mentioned, the divorce rate is very high. In six different interview sites (two urban; two in rural villages; and two in small hamlets), we found that the rate varied from 68 per cent to 99 per cent. That is to say, between 68 and 99 per cent of all Kanuri marriages (not counting those still extant) end in divorce rather than death, separation, desertion, or annulment. Of these types of dissolution, only death is significant—there are practically no dissolutions which result from separation, desertion, and annulment, although all of these do occur on very rare occasions (less than 1 per cent of all cases). Most divorces occur within the first four years of marriage, and after that time the duration-specific rate falls off "sharply," although it is still there. What this means in statistical terms is that 45 to 55 per cent of all Kanuri marriages end in divorce by the end of the fourth year of marriage.

The procedures connected with divorce are very simple. The man says, "I divorce you," in front of witnesses, and the marriage is dissolved. He may also send a letter, if the woman is living elsewhere. No registration of the divorce is necessary, no adjudication, nor indeed is there anything required whatsoever. Kanuri men do not speak divorce pronouncements three times, as is often done in Islamic countries, because they believe that a man may remarry the same woman, and this cannot be accomplished if he has pronounced the divorce statement for the third time. This means that they believe, at least formally, that a person may remarry the same wife twice and divorce her three times; a third marriage with the same person is impossible.

The legal possibility exists that a woman can initiate a divorce, even though the husband is unwilling to grant it. Often this involves a court case in order to adjudicate the settlement. Divorces initiated by women are called by a special term (*fida*). This refers to the settlement the

wife must pay to the husband in order to obtain her freedom. No goods are exchanged or payments made in the
case of a male-initiated divorce.

In the case of desertions, the remaining spouse takes
the matter to the courts. The court investigates the
whereabouts of the runaway spouse. If the latter can be
found, he or she is contacted. If the runaway is a woman,
she is told to return (if the husband wants her), and her
lover is fined. If the runaway is a man, he is asked either
to send for the wife who complained or to divorce her so
that she may be free to remarry. When a runaway spouse
cannot be found or contacted, the court pronounces a
divorce, and the person is able to remarry within the
rules governing this activity.

Annulments are very uncommon. They refer primarily
to physical defects of the spouse, which defects were not
known about before the marriage. One man living
in a rural area had his family in the city arrange a marriage. After all the arrangements were made, the girl
arrived, but she had a withered arm. He sent her away
immediately because he had not agreed to such a union
and should have been informed beforehand of her dis-
ability. In another case, the young husband proved
impotent. If such a condition continues for ninety days
after the wedding night, the marriage is annulled by the
courts. Although I have recorded only a few actual cases
of annulments over such impotence, there are many
stories of this same condition's having led to an annulment; during interviews in which women report on marital history, they refer to a man's sexual inadequacy as a
reason for divorce.

Remarriage is legally possible for the man at any time
after divorce. Women, however, must remain unmarried
and chaste for ninety days after a divorce pronouncement. If a woman is caught having an affair during this
period, it is considered to be adultery, and the adulterer
pays the appropriate fine to the ex-husband. If the couple

are reunited during this period, it is not necessary to remarry, but, formally speaking, if the ninety-day period passes, then a marriage must be performed if the couple are reconciled to one another. In practice, however, this rule is more flexible, and couples do reunite without a marriage even when the ninety-day period is over, unless another marriage has intervened. The ninety-day period (*tabari*) is designed to test whether the woman is pregnant. If any sign of pregnancy occurs during the *tabari*, the child is considered to belong to the ex-husband. In practice, this rule, too, is often made flexible. One inform- ant reported he had married a woman one month after her *tabari* was completed. She became pregnant during their first month of marriage, i.e., five months after her divorce. The ex-husband took the couple to court and claimed the child as his own. The court ruled that the child was a *banji* (an embryo in the womb that delays being born beyond nine months), and the woman and the child were returned to the former husband.

Although it is difficult to describe a "typical" divorce because there are so many, and so many reasons are given for them, it is possible, at a rather high level of gener- alization, to describe the course of an ordinary divorce case. It starts with a marital conflict that is initiated more often than not by the wife. She then angers the husband enough, or entreats him, or orders him, to di- vorce her; he complies, and, in that event, she moves out to return to the house of her *luwali* (the male person who arranged the marriage). Sometimes the wife runs away to the *luwali* and sends word that she wants a di- vorce pronouncement to be given to a messenger. In both cases, friends of the spouses approach the husband and the *luwali,* or the woman herself in some cases, in an attempt to arbitrate a reinstatement of the marriage. In about half the cases of such separations, some form of reconciliation is achieved; in others, the husband divorces

her; and a small minority end up in court and are ad-
judicated either by political leaders or Muslim judges.

The Reasons for Divorce

The reasons why divorce occurs so frequently among
the Kanuri can be described under three categories: (1)
the reasons given by the people themselves; (2) the statistical correlates of high- and low-divorce rates; and (3)
a theoretical synthesis which attempts to explain the extreme brittleness of these marriages as well as the variations to be found within the society.

1. REASONS GIVEN BY PEOPLE THEMSELVES: In general, the majority of informants blamed the other spouse
when reporting why a particular divorce occurred. Although the data have not been completely analyzed, our
results so far indicate that men mainly cited insubordination of the wife as the most common reason for divorce.
Examples are: "She went out when I told her not to";
"She refused to cook for my friends"; "She was not
respectful." They also referred to a lack of women's skills:
"She cooked badly"; or "She was dirty." Men also referred
to abnormal behavior: "She was an adulteress"; "She was
'proud in the hut' [refused to have sexual relations with
her husband]"; "She was a thief"; "She was a Lesbian."
They frequently mentioned co-wife jealousy and conflict as the reason why a divorce was necessary.

Women referred to their image of an inadequate male
role. Examples are: references to lack of sufficient economic support by the husband with respect to food, clothing, shelter, or references to sexual impotence, weakness,
or lack of skill. Women also mentioned co-wife jealousy
within a framework of resentment and often accompanied this reference by a statement such as, "He
married a new wife and didn't want me around any
more," or "He wanted to marry a new wife and told me

to leave." Women, more often than men, also mentioned their obligations to their own kin and the husband's blocking a visit or attendance at a family ceremony. Women also mentioned in-law problems more often than men as causes of their divorces.

From a rural population of secondary-school boys and girls (aged fourteen to twenty-five), we have obtained (through essays) a sample of reasons for divorce that correspond very closely with those reported by people concerning their own divorces. However, unlike respondents reporting on their own divorces, the students agreed much more with one another, and there were many fewer sex differences, even though, on other material (an essay on "My Future Marriage"), there were sharp and widely varied distinctions between the sexes. For this reason, and because the students seemed quite interested in the essays on reasons for divorce, we believe that the students (without having the problem of revealing their own personal involvement in a particular divorce) honestly tried to assess the reasons why divorces occur in their own society. Table 8 shows the results of this study. It should be noted that several of these responses are the reverse of statements given by informants who discuss their own personal divorces. No man ever mentioned marital sexual inadequacy in discussing his own divorce, yet, among our students, almost all of this particular response came from men rather than women (No. 14 in Table 8). More importantly, in the essays, students recognized that inadequate husbandlike behavior (No. 2) and lack of maintenance by the husband (No. 4) are major reasons for divorces, while men rarely, if ever, mentioned these reasons as important among the causes of their own divorces. Again, in the essays, boys referred to the parents of both husbands and wives (No. 7) as interfering and causing divorces, but, in reporting on their own divorces, men and women complained of interference only from their in-laws, not

TABLE 8: DIVORCE ESSAYS

Reasons for Divorce from Secondary-School Boys and Girls*

Variable	Women Respondents	Women Responses	Men Respondents	Men Responses	Totals Respondents	Totals Responses
1. Female Insubordination	191	431	283	556	474	987
2. Inadequate Male Role	198	416	279	529	477	945
3. Inadequate Female Role	163	313	214	353	377	666
4. Lack of Maintenance by Male	93	132	137	198	230	330
5. Western Education or Culture as a Cause	85	140	124	159	209	299
6. Co-wife Relations	93	141	88	145	181	286
7. Parents as a Cause	59	80	129	196	188	276
8. Abnormal Female Role	75	101	93	108	168	209
9. Abnormal Male Role	57	73	74	87	131	160
10. Religious or Ethnic Reason	32	40	61	77	93	117
11. Illness or Deformity	49	56	46	52	95	108
12. Ease of Marriage or Divorce	41	59	19	21	60	80
13. Barren Women	24	25	24	24	48	49
14. Male Sexual Inadequacy	7	7	36	38	43	45

* Measured in terms of number of responses given and number of respondents who made such comments. See Appendix for definitions of categories. Variables have been ordered in terms of the number of total responses given for each variable. Content analysis of the divorce essays was carried out by Mrs. Inez Oberteuffer, research assistant, and checked independently by the author.

from their own parents. In general, then, women's behavior is seen as a more important cause of divorce than men's. Lack of proper wifely behavior (Nos. 1, 3, 6, 8, and 13) is responsible for the largest single category of responses in the table.

If we look at it another way and calculate which sex breaks the most rules for which people could be taken to court, we get 386 for men and 479 for women. Thus, the secondary-school students believed that men break legally binding rules concerning marriage less often than women. However, this result is an artifact of the coding, since there are many more marital activities for which women can be prosecuted than men, and there is, therefore, a greater chance that such rules will be broken by women. In other words, women break more of the legal rules because there are so many more that pertain to wifely behavior as compared with that of the husband.

2. The Statistical Correlates of High and Low Divorce Rates: Although a complete analysis of our data has not been carried out, a number of factors have been clearly identified to be related statistically to variance in divorce rate. These are: (a) socioeconomic status of a husband, which is positively correlated to the rate of divorce; (b) bridewealth, which is positively correlated to the divorce rate (this is an aspect of a; (c) rural or urban status, urban being higher and rural being lower in rate; (d) fertility of the wife, which is negatively related to the divorce rate; and (e) age of the man, which is negatively related to the rate. We have also measured, among other things, the upward mobility of the husband, kin involvement in own kin group for each partner to the marriage, the size of the household, the nature of the husband's occupation, the nature of the co-wife situation per marriage and divorce, the length and nature of acquaintanceship before marriage, the nature of decent relationships between spouses (where applicable), the socioeconomic status of husband's and wife's kin groups,

the previous marital history of each spouse, and the marital and divorce record of the spouse's parents. So far, in the analysis, none of these variables show any systematic relation to the divorce rate, although a more refined analysis may turn up more relations than those identified above.

3. A THEORETICAL SYNTHESIS WHICH EXPLAINS KANURI DIVORCE: Kanuri divorce is easy—as easy, comparatively, as the breakup of a Western courtship relation or an engagement—indeed, easier, as I shall show, since breaking up a Western courtship requires both a pronouncement and an emotional break, while the Kanuri divorce requires only the former, and very little of the latter results from the breakup. The Kanuri pronouncement is, however, primarily a male prerogative—a woman must pay for the privilege, which is often impossible. This means that the divorce is structured: (a) to promote passivity on the part of wives because they have little access to the means of support or (b) to create a revolt by the women who simply refuse to act as if they do not have access to divorces or (c) to impel the women quietly to manipulate their husbands into pronouncing a divorce. The first alternative of passivity (a) occurs, but not often. The second approach—of revolt (b)—occurs quite frequently. The classic and most common example in our records is the wife who clutches a husband's robe, tears it, screams insults, and yells for the neighbors. The wife then says she will not stop the disturbance until the husband pronounces a divorce, and he generally complies. The third approach—quiet manipulation (c)—for example, is taken by the wife who simply refuses to carry on. She may refuse to cook for him, or his friends, or refuse him sexual intercourse, or refuse to work on his farm, or she may simply run away to her *luwali* and send word that he must divorce her. Some women cook badly or, in many other ways, do not meet the wifely role expectations. The man must then choose either to tolerate

this or divorce the wife. The fact that Bornu has a very high rate of divorce and has had one for a very long time, at least as far back as records and informants' memories can go, means that there is very little fear of divorce. It is just as normal an outcome of marriage as any other— indeed, more so, since most marriages end in divorce. Again the fact that the status of divorced women (*zowers*) is common and normal means that both sexes have nothing to fear, no court procedures, no alimony, and no arguments over little children who are under the father's control before the divorce and remain so after the breakup. Thus, the very mundane quality of divorces ensures that there will be more of them. Although the Kanuri may sometimes say divorce is "a bad thing," they laugh at, and disapprove of, other systems which inhibit divorces, such as the Western one. To them, a marriage should be easily ended; not to do so would create animosity and difficulties in that aspect of their lives in which they have always demanded great flexibility, that of interpersonal relations.

The ideology of male dominance can be subverted, but it angers men; yet women constantly try. In rural areas, men need wives as their prime source of labor. Women know this and use it as best they can. In extreme cases, it can lead to a henpecked husband. Usually, it leads to divorce. Men in rural areas, however know that women are scarce, and sometimes rural men wait until they can actually replace a wife before divorcing the one they have. Others lose their tempers, or their wife demands a divorce, and the labor on the man's farm is depleted. The result is that, when rural men calculate crop increases or decreases, they always mention a recent marriage or divorce as the determining factor in their estimates of agricultural productivity.

In the cities, incomes are generally higher. Women are much more available, and men, especially wealthy ones, can afford to marry many times if their demands for the ideals of female submissiveness are not met. Even so, rich or poor men need women to cook for them. If they do not have wives, then this must be done by other women or their concubines or female relatives. If not, a man eats at the household of a relative or friend and thereby incurs an obligation. By having wives to cook for others, a man turns his own household into a place where people may come for his hospitality and largesse. This means that he is successful; it means he can create clients and obligations and enter the role of the successful mature man. Thus, men are dependent upon their wives to fulfill their masculine roles in society. This, too, gives women some leverage, and they use it.

Men seem to have an ideology of marital maturation that applies less to the very rich but, to some extent, to everyone. As a man approaches the age of thirty-five to forty, he should, say the Kanuri, settle down and not quarrel in public. He should stop having extramarital affairs—or at least having them openly—and he should be more tolerant of his wives. Certainly, divorce does slow down noticeably at this period, and marriage durations get noticeably longer.

The Kanuri also want children very much. Many women are barren. Thus, a woman who has shown she can have children is always favored and tolerated more than others. Furthermore, if the children are young, there is a tendency for the men to say that the mother and her children should be kept together. This depresses the rates more for Kanuri women, but, it should be stressed, even fertility only slows down Kanuri divorce rates. Most fertile women divorce, and the family is consequently broken up.

Another factor in stimulating divorce is the attractiveness of the divorced status to the married woman and/or the attractiveness of a lover or a potential next husband. A Kanuri wife knows that, in her divorced status, she is a free woman. She can entertain lovers, visit with relatives, and no man has a right to order her about. In the city, many of these women rent rooms and must take lovers in order to raise the necessary cash. However, the lack of restraint of the divorced status and the excitement it offers is always there as a stimulant to any marital conflict. Furthermore, adultery is rife in Bornu. The degree of its practice is difficult to tell, but suspicion by both sexes in a marriage is common. Most Kanuri men, married or not, have affairs, usually with divorced women. This is formally adultery, but almost everyone accepts it. Indeed, in one case, a married man called in witnesses to see that he had brought a *divorced* woman home for the night during his wife's absence. He did this to show he was not having relations with a married woman. For married women, however, extramarital affairs are serious offenses. On the other hand, as one woman said to me, "You can have almost any woman you want in Bornu, just send her gifts secretly and promise her more." Indeed, there is a special term for a go-between (*serser*) who acts for men in inveigling a married woman into an extramarital affair, often with the promise of a forthcoming marriage after she has caused a divorce within her present union.

Added to this factor of sexual variety and widespread adultery is the value placed by men on youth. The best wife is a young one, the best bride is a virgin. Youth is beautiful, strong, sexually active, and more attractive, while age is the reverse. Furthermore, men claim that a virgin girl is one you control yourself, "You are the only master she knows." However, as I have pointed out elsewhere,[8] the very young girl is not attractive sexually, but socially; indeed, the semipublic consummation ceremony of a virgin is a moment of great anxiety to the men who must, on such occasions, display their sexual prowess to the community. They suffer this ceremony because:

Kanuri social life is a constant search for fruitful social contact in which one man is the superior and the other a subordinate to him. Between the sexes, the culture defines women as inferior in rank to men. Thus, the place universally available to all men for the achievement of subordinates is the family and the household, and the ideal female subordinate is a young girl, one who has not yet been divorced, that is, rejected her subordination to her husband, and one whom the husband can train to become properly obedient to his own personal wishes. Thus, marriage to a previously unmarried girl symbolizes what every man wants, not sexually, but socially; unblemished and complete obedience from docile subordinants who receive material benefits in return for subordination. Seen in this light, the marriage with young girls then becomes more understandable, for it represents some of the most profoundly important values in the society.[9]

This means that simply because of the attractions of youth, a man may divorce an older wife in order to obtain or keep a younger one. Kanuri women know this, and, as we have seen, they complained about it when they explained why their divorces occurred.

Finally, there is the very nature of the husband/wife relationship itself. Kanuri husbands and wives are, for the most part, very formal, distant, and reserved with one another. They avoid speaking to each other in public, avoid the use of each other's names, never eat together, and, in hundreds of little ways, avoid close or intimate contact. In scores of the essays on "My Future Marriage," this was a quality that the girls criticized and which they said they hoped would change radically in the future.

The very few exceptions to this generalization are startling when observed at close range. I have known only three cases of long-term marriage in which I was closely associated with the household. In all three cases, the wife had been in the house over twenty-five years;

the husband was a rich, powerful, political leader, and the wife had obtained great power in the household and the community because of her husband's position. In all three cases, the husbands had high divorce records which reached to over ten for each of them, as well as a number of female slaves who had come and gone over the years. These senior, long-term wives were all, in their way, magnificent diplomats, extremely intelligent, and totally devoted to their husbands' interests. Over the years, they had maneuvered themselves into what really amounted to a Kanuri male role—that of a chief subordinate, or *wakil*. Indeed, one of them *is* called by this title which is used by the people of the ward as a nickname. Such cases also involve a problem in that other wives who come into such a marriage have little chance of competing for an equal status in the household. A problem develops in which a stable, long-term marriage, which involves an intimate and trusted wife, is associated with the turnover of others who come, stay for a short while, and are then divorced.

In general, however, compared with Western forms of marriage, Kanuri marriage involves relatively little emotional involvement. Kanuri men and women speak of ex-spouses, either divorced or dead, in matter-of-fact tones, and they pity and censure others who become emotionally involved. Stories are told, however, especially of men, who have gone out of control because of their desire for a woman. Other men censure such behavior and explain their own feelings by saying that there are many women available—why become upset over not getting, or keeping, any particular one? The only area in which men and women *do* seem to become emotionally disturbed is when they are counting the loss of children, and, among the men, it is only noticeable when the informant is telling of many births in which there has been no live issue that has survived. In other words, the Kanuri are, in general, not tied emotionally to marriage; to break the relationship does not produce observ-able, psychic costs. This is true even though the loss is great. One informant smiled as he told us how he had divorced a very good wife by mistake. She was fertile, obedient, a good cook, even beautiful, but was falsely accused by the co-wife of causing trouble in the house-hold. The mistake eventually brought on difficulties with the co-wife who remained, and she, too, was divorced not long afterward. "There are other women," the in-formant said, which implied that it was not that serious a mistake and could be remedied without too much trouble.

The Effects of the System

The effects of Kanuri marriage and divorce ramify into its social and political structure, into the nature of sex and kinship roles, the personality development of its people, and its age-grading system. The basic unit of Kanuri social and political organization is the household, and, as I have pointed out,[10] these units are linked to-gether through their male heads into settlements whose leading household head is linked to larger political group-ings right up the political hierarchy to the head of the royal household—the Emir of Bornu. Each household is a political unit within itself under its household head who must administer it as a polity among others. Family life takes place within the household; the family organiza-tion is extremely brittle because of the high divorce rate that produces a constant turnover of women in the house-hold. This tends to emphasize the importance of the household and its central place in the social and political structure of society. It means, as well, that when a Ka-nuri thinks of his "home," he thinks of the household he was raised in—not the family—for, in general, the family breaks up in a few years. Put in Bohannan's terms, the household is a basic, "back-up" institution, while the family is, in most instances, transitory.[11]

This also means that almost all Kanuri children have "lost" a mother through divorce. They still retain knowledge of her whereabouts, the children and their mother visit one another, possibly, but she is in another household, sometimes another town. This means that the children are often raised by one of their father's other wives. The Kanuri term for such a person, in polite conversation, is *ya,* or mother, but the term of reference (deemed an insult if used to her face) is *ya chintu* (far, or distant, or far-removed mother). Young men have told me bitter stories of having been mistreated by these women, and there is a sense of emotional loss that was felt when their mothers were divorced. As a means of alleviating this problem, a number of fathers give young children, especially girls, to a female sibling, in other words, to a sister of the father. She, it is believed, would treat the children more kindly, especially if she is barren, because they belong to her brother, that is to say, they are her agnatic kin, not simply "children of my rival," which is how a wife describes her husband's children by a previous marriage. Thus, there is a feeling toward the father's other wives akin to our own folklore figure of the "wicked stepmother," and, toward the father's sister, the culture promotes the image of the rather kindly aunt who looks after the interests of her brother's child even against its own father. In a kinship structure that has many cognatic qualities, this tends to emphasize the role of the father's sister as compared to other female roles in the kinship system. She plays an important part in the *rites de passage* of both boys and girls, and, in the royal court of Bornu, it is significant that she is one of the three female relatives of the monarch, besides his mother and senior wife, who has a noble title and who, originally, administered her own fiefs. As the *magara,* the monarch's sister was, traditionally, considered to be the formal head of all divorced women of the kingdom. One of the primary functions of this organization was to offer hospitality to strangers who came to town or to a section of the city. These women were organized under a local head woman, also called a *magara,* to feed the strangers and administer to their comforts during their stay in the settlement. Again, there is an association of the king's sister with tender womanly concern for those who lack such care. It should be remembered that the king is spoken of as the "father of us all," and, therefore, his sister is the "father's sister of us all." In other words, a high divorce rate and a constant breakup of the family has tended to create a maternal image of the father's sister who is a stable female in the agnatic group to whom the child must cleave since the father keeps the children after a divorce. This seems to have ramified out into the culture as a whole and made this particular kinship role more important than many other female positions in the Kanuri social structure.

The "trauma" of mother loss must, however, have its functional contributions to the social system as a whole. Kanuri social, economic, and political structure provides opportunities for those who can move easily and readily from one set of allegiances to another. As I have pointed out elsewhere,[12] clientage is one of the most important institutions in the society; clientage demands that a person bargain with his loyalty and obedience (defined in terms of the behavior norms applicable to the father-son relationship) in order to obtain an advantageous position for himself. Furthermore, in the warlike quality of Bornu's history, it is constantly stressed that a man can lose close relatives or friends in the violence of war, raiding, and even the tyranny of those who should have been protecting those dependent upon them. Thus, it has always been, and still is, an advantage to be able to switch one's allegiances easily and quickly. We may, in fact, be developing today a similar system in modern

America—but we come from a tradition that honors Damon and Pythias, not Machiavelli.

High divorce among the Kanuri, plus their custom of living in a number of compounds during childhood, may very well produce personality structures among adults in which emotional development, or affect toward others, is either suppressed or developed to a very low degree. I have hypothesized, therefore, that a loss of mother (plus the movement from household to household that characterizes Kanuri childhood) is adaptive to the Kanuri social structure in that it produces personalities that have comparatively low levels of interpersonal affect. This also helps, of course, to perpetuate high divorce by maintaining low affect between husbands and wives. In the modern Western world, low levels of interpersonal affect and high amounts of social-spatial mobility have become a necessary part of industrial society, but Americans are socialized into family situations that involve intimate and deeply affective relationships. Thus, we agonize over the growth of alienation and feel guilty about "dropping" our friends. However, what this present research among the Kanuri seems to suggest is that alienation may not be a universal correlate of industrialization because alienation itself may be dependent upon certain types of family structures and on early socialization experiences, which are characteristic of stable, low-divorce systems. Only in these systems does the young child develop strong emotional attachments to stable, parent figures. Where this is absent, the emotional development may be either suppressed or inhibited in its development.

Two other interrelated effects are produced by high divorce in Kanuri society. First, there is the problem of the aged women. Kanuri women pass out of marriageable status at the time of menopause. They then take on the status of old women and are looked after by sons or brothers or, in a few cases, by well-to-do ex-husbands.

Men expect that, later in life, they will take care of their mothers and feel a strong obligation to do so.

This prospect of a mother's returning eventually to her son's house has other chain-reaction effects that feed back into family life. As already noted, young Kanuri brides experience the presence of a mother-in-law in their husband's household. This adds to the number and kinds of relationships in her married life and is one of the more onerous relationships because of the strict patterns of respect and avoidance that she must practice toward her mother-in-law. It also, however, affects the relationship between co-wives. If more than one co-wife has produced children, there is a great interest by each wife in the inheritance potential of her own offspring, and this obviously becomes more intense as the fruits of inheritance are proportionately greater. One thing that affects everyone is the fact that one among a group of half brothers will take over the father's position as household head, and that particular person's mother, among the co-wives of today, will become the oldest and most respected senior woman of the compound organization. In one case, admittedly an extreme one because slavery is involved, a slave woman gave birth to the only male heir of a wealthy chief. His senior wife was barren, and he had not performed a marriage ceremony with the slave that would thereby have freed her. Ultimately, the son, who is a freeman because his father is free, will take over his father's compound and important political office. When that happens, the boy's mother will become the senior woman of the household she now serves as a slave, while its present senior woman will go elsewhere. The boy's mother knows this, as does everyone else. Yet the mother is, at present, of slave status, which is very much beneath that of the full, free wife. The result is a tense and uneasy relationship between the senior wife and the slave woman, who, in general, avoid one another, although the wife has the right to demand the obedience and service of a female slave of the household. At the very top of the society, each royal wife knows that, if her son can become Emir of Bornu, then she will gain the title (and, originally, a set of fiefs) of a Queen Mother. Co-wives traditionally plotted and intrigued with major political groupings in the state over the royal succession. They sent secret messages to a son on a military campaign if they thought the present Emir was fatally ill so that their son could be in the royal capital at the time of succession. In general, then, the practice of the son's looking after his mother can intensify tension and conflict between co-wives who must look to their own future status as old and unmarriageable women or as women whose sons have successfully taken a major share of the patrilineage inheritance.

Secondly, perhaps the most dynamic quality of the system is the basic dissatisfaction that it produces among women. As we have noted, a woman's bridewealth declines throughout her lifetime. In other words, her worth on a quantitative index of self-worth declines as she matures. I would suggest that this factor, plus the strong norms of male dominance in the culture, produce a sense of constant frustration for women, and they retaliate by attempting to subvert male dominance whenever possible. This continually angers men and tends to perpetuate the high divorce rate. Women also retaliate by elaborating sexuality and rating men as more or less successful at sexual skill. In their turn, men are anxious about sex and manifest this through the use of magico-religious techniques which are designed to increase their skill and their potency in the sexual act, which, in itself, is probably a more culturally elaborated performance than in our own society, and thus the sexual act makes greater demands on men.

In such a social structure, women are constantly prone to accept change. In the traditional system, this means trying out a divorced woman's freer role. In contemporary Bornu, however, it means an attraction to Western marriage, lower divorce, equal status for women, and a more positive attitude toward modern solutions to problems as compared with men of the same age and educational background.[13]

The "lesson" of Kanuri society is, in the end, a traditional, anthropological one. Very high divorce rates involve adaptations in the social and political structure, the sex and kinship roles, the personality structure, and the age-grade system of the society as a whole. Only in such a way can a high divorce rate be incorporated as a stable part of a stable society. Even so, there are tensions, as well as adaptations, which result. If our own divorce rate is changing upward, we must prepare for widely ramifying effects in the society as a whole. I do not claim that they would be the same as the ones described here, but I am certain they will be profound and affect, in the end, the nature of the entire society and of the individuals who compose it.

APPENDIX: Definitions of Variables for Table 8

1. FEMALE INSUBORDINATION: a direct or assumed denial or thwarting of the husband's authority. Examples: She doesn't obey her husband; she refuses the sexual advances of her husband; she leaves him and refuses to return; she refuses to cook for him.
2. INADEQUATE MALE ROLE: inadequate fulfillment of the cultural expectations of a husband's role (not counting maintenance, see No. 4 below). Examples: He treats his wife cruelly; he divorces for no reason; he listens to gossip about his wife; he makes promises before the marriage that are not kept.
3. INADEQUATE FEMALE ROLE: the same as for the male. Examples: She doesn't cook on time; she is careless; she is lazy; she is selfish; she never stays home; she doesn't welcome his friends.

4. LACK OF MAINTENANCE BY THE MALE: a direct or implied abdication of the responsibility of caring for, or being responsible for, his family. Examples: He is too lazy to work and care for his family; he doesn't keep the house in good repair; he divorces the wife so he can supply his own needs; he expects the wife to support the household with her own money.

5. WESTERN EDUCATION OR CULTURE AS A CAUSE: a specific reference to Western education or to a norm or value of Western society not present in Kanuri society which produces a conflict that leads to divorce. Examples: Women are cheap because most of them are uneducated; there is no law against divorce; girls today want to be modern; an illiterate woman can't cook modern foods.

6. CO-WIFE RELATIONS: specific references either to polygyny or interwife relations as a cause of divorce. Examples: He loves wives unequally; he has four wives, sees another and wants her, therefore, divorces one in his house; having three wives means trouble; polygyny causes divorce; child brides have trouble with older wives.

7. PARENTS AS A CAUSE: a specific reference to the parents of either husband or wife as a reason for divorce. Examples: He pays more attention to her parents than to her; he doesn't appreciate how good her parents are; a boy's (girl's) parents force them to marry someone they do not want; divorce is caused by bad home training.

8. ABNORMAL FEMALE ROLE: a specific reference to an extreme attitude or activity on the part of a wife that causes divorce. Examples: She becomes unreasonably jealous; she tries to poison the stepchildren; she practices magic; she is a thief; she sells the gifts her husband gives her.

9. ABNORMAL MALE ROLE: the same as for the female. Examples: He is a thief; he is a sorcerer; he wants to live alone; he sells his wife to someone else; he always prefers divorced women to wives.

10. RELIGIOUS OR ETHNIC REASON: a specific mention of ethnicity or religion as a cause of divorce. Examples: Muslims have rules about marriage and divorce; some tribes (people) are stupid; Northern Nigerians are quick tempered; people forget religion; Nigerians think it is good to divorce.

11. ILLNESS OR DEFORMITY: a specific reference to illness or deformity as a cause of divorce. Examples: Men divorce sick wives; women divorce lepers or madmen; the wife brings a disease to the household.

12. EASE OF MARRIAGE OR DIVORCE: a specific reference to the customs and rules concerning marriage and divorce as a cause of divorce. Examples: It is too easy to marry (divorce); the bride price is low so men can buy wives cheaply; women are too accessible here so couples do not have to solve their problems.

13. BARREN WOMEN: the wife's infertility is a reason for divorce.

14. MALE SEXUAL INADEQUACY: a specific reference to the husband's sexual inadequacy as a reason for divorce. Examples: He is sexually inadequate; he is not a whole man.

V

Reform

Social scientists are often asked, "If you know so much about it, why don't you do something?" These articles are an outline of some of the things that have to be done, and the basis for making these statements. How they are to be done is more difficult. It will take citizens' committees, lawyers' committees, divorcees' action groups, and many others to arrive at the new solutions. But the problems to be solved can be stated quite clearly. The answers are tougher, because people must realize that they have to change some of their ways of living to find an answer—when the present situation results in the present situation, as it were, the only way to change it is to change it.

10

A Family Court:
The California Proposal

HERMA HILL KAY

The Family Court, the Juvenile Court, and the
Boundary of the Legal

The idea of a family court has been discussed for many years. Such a court, it is said, should have integrated jurisdiction over all legal problems that involve the members of a family; be presided over by a specialist judge assisted by a professional staff trained in the behavioral sciences; and employ its special resources and those of the community to intervene therapeutically in the lives of the people who come before it.[1]

In the United States, the idea of a family court was apparently stimulated by the optimism resulting from the success of the juvenile court movement in establishing specialized courts to deal with neglected and delinquent children. Thus, a leading American proponent of the family court, Judge Paul Alexander of Toledo, in one of his earliest articles, could say:

> We suggest handling our unhappy and delinquent spouses much as we handle our delinquent children. Of-

ten their behavior is not unlike that of a delinquent child, and for much the same reasons. We would take them out of the quasi-criminal divorce court and deal with them and their problems in a modern family court. When the marriage gets sick there is a cause. This cause manifests itself in the behavior, or misbehavior, of one or both spouses. Instead of determining whether a spouse has misbehaved and then "punishing" him by rewarding the aggrieved spouse with a divorce decree, we would follow the general pattern of the juvenile court and endeavor to diagnose and treat, to discover the fundamental cause, then bring to bear all available resources to remove or rectify it.[2]

The first flush of pride in the juvenile court has given way in the United States to serious reappraisals. Indeed, it is now generally conceded that the juvenile court has failed to achieve its goals. The Supreme Court's opinion in *In re Gault*[3] (1967) has compelled an observance in delinquency proceedings of the child's constitutional rights to representation by counsel, notice, confrontation, and cross-examination of witnesses, and the privilege against self incrimination.

Since the original family court idea was largely copied from the juvenile court model, it becomes necessary for modern advocates of the family court to re-examine their proposal in order to discover whether the common aspects of the two schemes are among those that have contributed to the present dissatisfaction with the juvenile court and, if so, whether these defects can be remedied or avoided.

A preliminary question, raised by some opponents of the family court, must first be mentioned: Is a court the proper institution for settling family problems? The question arises because a basic assumption common to both juvenile and family courts is that their daily work is not limited to the decision of legal questions. Issues of parental fitness and child custody, for example, often present complex questions of the analysis and prediction of human behavior that cannot be resolved by the simple application of a legal formula. And the neglect and delinquency of children and the disintegration of a family appear to involve a degree of emotional stress not normally encountered in litigation involving real property, corporations, or contracts.

Moreover, it is assumed that the unique resources of a court, namely the presence of a lawyer-judge, the right to use compulsory process to secure the attendance of parties and witnesses and to enforce judgments, and the tradition of deciding individual cases according to rules of law are inadequate to deal with such non-legal problems.

One may ask why a court should attempt to act in these areas, if it is so ill-suited to the task. The juvenile court has as part of its duty the protection of society against the seriously destructive acts of minors; insofar as incarceration is used for this purpose, the Constitution requires the use of court-administered legal standards such as due process for the protection of the defendant. Similarly, the use of a court to decide divorce cases may be justified in part by the need to decide such primarily legal issues as the identification and division of marital property and the assessment of support as well as the need to enforce judgments concerning these matters. Further, a court is necessary to protect the parties and their children by orders for temporary custody and support during the divorce proceedings. Again, the supervision and enforcement of custody orders during the minority of children would appear to be a proper judicial function. Finally, courts are subject to well-established techniques of review under standards set by constitutional provisions, legislatures, or higher courts, and such review guards the parties against basic unfairness.

In view of these advantages, it appears more appropriate to provide courts with non-legal techniques and personnel than to supply legal authority to non-judicial agencies—even those better equipped to deal with the primarily emotional and psychological problems of family dissolution.

Having decided to use a court of law to deal with non-legal matters, however, one must next consider how the courts can best be equipped to enable them to work productively in a new dimension. To respond to this need, juvenile and family courts proponents have traditionally relied upon three techniques: (1) a specialist-judge to direct the court; (2) a professional staff to gather information as well as diagnose and sometimes actually treat the emotional difficulties of the court's clientele; (3) the substitution of a therapeutic environment for the law's traditional adversary procedures.

Juvenile court experience with each of these three ideas has led to serious criticism. If care is not taken, each may predictably lead to trouble for the family court. As the President's Task Force on Juvenile Delinquency has pointed out, the "mature and sophisticated judge, wise and well-versed in law and the science of human behavior"[4] has been conspicuous by his absence in juvenile courts throughout the land. It is no secret that juvenile and domestic assignments go to junior judges in many urban courts and that even a six-months stint in the job is more than many judges would like. Yet, no existing family court plan has failed to include a proposal for a judge who can be trained to cope with the sensitive and demanding problems of disintegrating families and who will stay with the assignment long enough to become an expert.

Providing a court with a professional staff raises difficult problems of recruitment. It has been argued that there are probably not enough trained social workers, let alone psychologists and psychiatrists, to meet the demand that would be created by widespread establishment of family courts. Nor, it is said, is a public agency likely to be able to offer the necessary pay scale, permanence in employment, and opportunities for research and professional advancement offered by competing private agencies. Further, it has been argued that, even if enough highly trained, sensitive, and dedicated staff members could be found to man the family courts, the knowledge of human psychology has not yet matured sufficiently to enable it to give reasonable assurance that diagnosis and treatment will lead to prediction and cure in a majority of cases. Finally, it is said that the authoritarian atmosphere which inevitably accompanies courts is not a proper setting for what will be, essentially, a family service agency.

Many of these objections have been given bitter point by the juvenile court experience. Nevertheless, the idea of a professional staff is central to most family court plans.

The creation of a therapeutic atmosphere in the juvenile court was thought to require an informal procedure marked by the removal of lawyers, relaxed observance of the technical rules of evidence, and a firm decision that the constitutional rights of adults charged with criminal acts did not apply to the assertedly noncriminal proceedings of the juvenile court. Nearly all of these decisions were set aside by the United States Supreme Court's opinion in the now-famous *Gault* case, which demonstrated the essential wrongheadedness of attempting to help children by depriving them of the safeguards guaranteed to adults. As Mr. Justice Fortas' opinion notes, in delinquency matters the substitution of unbridled discretion and the concept of *parens patria* for the specific protections of the Constitution too often produced arbitrariness rather than "careful, compassionate, individualized treatment."[5]

Further, it has been suggested that the juvenile court's very effort to treat the offender rather than the offense was not understood by the offenders themselves who may

have felt more threatened by the court's attempt to intervene in their lives for rehabilitative purposes than they
would have if its aim had simply been to punish them
for misconduct.

What, then, can be expected of the family court's effort
to ignore marital misconduct in order to rehabilitate the
faltering married lives of persons who come before it?
Rheinstein has suggested that even if the court's professional staff can be expected to discover, in every case, the
"true" cause of marital discord, the state should not be
given the power to attempt the transformation through
psychiatry of the personality structure of an individual
"simply because he has failed to make a success out of
marriage with some other individual."[6]

Enough has perhaps been said about the juvenile court
experience to indicate some of the hard questions that
require a response from advocates of the family court.
Here I shall consider, in light of these problems, a particular family court proposal, that of the California Governor's Commission on the Family. There are, however,
two striking, overall differences between the California
family court plan and the juvenile court that should be
considered before examining the details. Both seriously
affect any evaluation of whether any family court can be
expected to escape the dilemmas of its predecessor.

The juvenile court contained within its very structure
a conflict between coercion and confidentiality so basic
that the system was ultimately unable to survive its disruptive effects. The therapeutic ideal, as it was formulated for the juvenile court, meant the virtual elimination of lawyers from the court's proceedings. The
probation officer was thus cast in the inconsistent roles of
prosecutor and helper: his duty was both to establish the
court's jurisdiction over the minor by proving his neglect
or delinquency, and to gain the minor's confidence afterward in order to make the court's treatment plan ef-

fective. The use, in larger courts, of a special "court officer" to present cases—a person who did not himself attempt to work with the children—only barely disguised the conflict. Calling upon the juvenile court judge to protect the minor by acting as his "parent" served only to confuse the situation further. The reintroduction of lawyers to the juvenile court, first by statutory reform in some states and now in all states by virtue of the *Gault* decision, has brought this conflict into the open.

The proposed California family court does not handicap its professional staff by a similar conflict of interests. The California plan does not place the caseworker in the unhappy position of gathering information from a party to be used against him. It does not provide for compulsory counseling. It is careful to protect voluntary conciliation counseling with the safeguard of absolute confidentiality. Reports made to the court will be submitted to the attorneys for both parties for approval before they are given to the judge. By these and other devices to be discussed more fully below, the professional staff and the persons before the court are protected against the conflicting loyalties and compulsory atmosphere that so greatly hindered the effective work of the juvenile court. Nor should there be a mass exodus of lawyers from the family court. Rather, the proposed system hopefully will free the attorney from his present role as an amateur family therapist and allow him to devote himself to the legal aspects of family dissolution such as the division of property, the establishment and enforcement of support, and the protection of children.

The second major difference lies in the degree to which the California proposal rests upon reform of the substantive law of divorce. The juvenile court proponents established an institution and a procedure for dealing with child neglect, dependency, and delinquency, but they did not question the use of violation of the criminal law as one basis for the court's jurisdiction. The court was to treat the offender, not the offense; indeed, the offense was unimportant except as an identifier of the child who needed the court's services. The point is that, while the juvenile court movement produced no critical review of the criminal law as it applied to children, the California proposal begins with the conviction that establishment of a family court without an accompanying thoroughgoing revision of the substantive law of divorce would be a useless gesture. Since the two concepts are thus intentionally made interdependent, I shall begin by examining existing divorce law and procedure.

The Present Divorce Law: Matrimonial Offense and the Adversary System

The development of the American law of divorce is well known[7] and will be mentioned here only to set the family court proposal in historical context. The Anglo-American history begins with the exclusive jurisdiction of ecclesiastical courts in England over matrimonial actions. These courts granted two kinds of "divorce": divorce *a mensa et thoro,* which merely authorized the separation of the parties, and divorce *a vinculo,* which declared that the marriage had never legally existed. Divorce, in the modern sense of a judicial decree dissolving a valid marriage and allowing one or both partners to remarry during the life of the other, did not exist in England until 1857, although Parliament sometimes permitted individuals to remarry following an ecclesiastical separation.

Although a few legislative divorces were granted in the United States, most American legislatures very early enacted general statutes granting the courts jurisdiction to dissolve marriages only on specified grounds. In many states, these grounds consisted of the old ecclesiastical grounds for separation, uncritically carried over and made to serve as grounds for absolute divorce. The state's interest in marital stability, thus delegated to the courts, was to be guarded by the judge's diligence in requiring that evidence clearly established the ground relied on for a divorce, that the defendant had no valid defense to the plaintiff's suit, and that the parties had not conspired to put on a false case. Divorce was thus cast in the traditional common-law model of an adversary procedure: plaintiff's success depended on proving defendant's fault; both parties, assumed to be at odds and dealing at arm's length, were expected to bring forth all the relevant facts about their marriage and its disintegration to be assessed by the judge in reaching his decision.

In addition to the statutory grounds for divorce (which assume that a wrongful act has been committed by one party to the marriage after the marriage has been formed), the law recognizes annulment. Annulment, like divorce, gives the parties the right to remarry; unlike divorce, however, it is granted because of an impediment that existed at the time the marriage was contracted and that made the marriage "voidable." The law gives certain-named persons the right to establish the invalidity of the marriage. If the marriage is not challenged by the persons having authority to object to it within a prescribed period of time, the marriage is valid for all purposes. If the marriage is annulled, however, in strict legal theory it never existed at all.

California's basic divorce law was established by its first civil code in 1872. The code provided six grounds for divorce: adultery, extreme cruelty (defined as "the wrongful infliction of grievous bodily injury, or grievous mental suffering, upon the other by one party to the marriage"), willful desertion, willful neglect, habitual intemperance, and conviction of a felony. Other provisions of the 1872 code, establishing "connivance, collusion, condonation, or lapse of time" as defenses to divorce, attempted to ensure that the spouses would not obtain divorces based on marital wrongdoing that resulted from acts consented to by both parties, acts that had not in fact occurred or acts that had occurred but that had been forgiven or that had occurred an "unreasonably" long time before the divorce petition was filed. In addition, the defense to divorce known as "recrimination" was generally understood to prevent divorce if each spouse had been guilty of marital wrongdoing sufficient to give the other a complaint for divorce so that neither spouse was innocent of marital wrongdoing. This result was proper, according to one of the English cases, in order that "the parties may live together, and find sources of mutual forgiveness in the humiliation of mutual guilt."[8]

In California, annulments may be obtained (1) by the parents or guardians of a minor boy under twenty-one or girl under eighteen who marries without their consent, or by the underaged minor; (2) by either party to a bigamous marriage performed by at least one party in good faith or by the former spouse; (3) by a person (called the "injured party") married to a person of unsound mind, or by the relatives or guardian of the person of unsound mind; (4) by a person whose consent to the marriage was procured by fraud; (5) by a person whose consent was obtained by force; or (6) by a person whose spouse is physically incapable of marital intercourse.

In the case of annulments based on fraud, the marriage may not be annulled if the defrauded party, with knowledge of all the facts constituting the fraud, freely cohabits with the other party as husband and wife. Similarly, marriage based on force may be ratified by cohabitation. And the code provides that if the party of unsound mind "comes to reason," or the underaged spouse attains the age of legal consent, they, too, may ratify the marriage by freely cohabiting with their spouse.

The statutory theory of divorce and annulment in California in 1872 was that, if the contract of marriage was undertaken freely and without impediment so that it could not be annulled, the contract was binding on both parties until such time as one of them, himself innocent of marital wrongdoing, perfected against the other a cause for divorce based on the other's fault. Once the cause for divorce had been proven and the defendant had failed to establish an adequate defense to the action, the plaintiff was not only released from his own marital obligations to the defendant but also was entitled to a dissolution of the marriage in partial legal compensation for his suffering.

This traditional approach to divorce is commonly referred to as the "matrimonial offense" or "fault" theory. The law's adherence to the fault theory has been severely criticized. The notion that a plaintiff who has avoided the commission of acts that technically constitute formal grounds for divorce is "innocent," ignores the realities of marital behavior. Obviously, then, it provides an unsound basis for legal policymaking. Psychiatrists say that the law's insistence on fault and adversary techniques in family litigation aggravates the already conflicted interpersonal situation of the spouses and may have undesirable repercussions for their children.[9]

Wadlington[10] has pointed out that the present divorce law assumes either that marriages break down only because of specific acts recognized as grounds for divorce, or else that dissolution should be made available only for marriages that have suffered such acts. The first assumption, he argues, is factually incorrect and the second rests on long-discarded social attitudes. He concludes that reformers must persuade legislators not only that marriages break down for reasons other than the wrongful act of one party, but also that the interests of society can best be served by allowing the termination in law of any marriage that has ceased to exist in fact simply because it has ended.

The "marriage breakdown theory" has already been recognized in California. Two recent events have sharply modified the traditional fault concept by establishing alongside it the opposing, and in my view incompatible, theory of marriage breakdown. In 1941 a seventh ground for divorce was added to the code. Called "incurable insanity," it provided that a divorce might be granted to a person upon proof that his spouse had been incurably insane for a continuous period of three years immediately preceding the filing of the divorce action; had been confined for those three years in or under the jurisdiction of a mental institution; and was, in the opinion of a member of the medical staff of the institution, incurably insane. Divorces thus granted were not based on the deliberate misconduct of the defendant, but on the impossibility of a functioning marriage.

Then, in 1952, in the *DeBurgh* case,[11] the Supreme Court of California interpreted the recrimination statute as permitting divorces to be granted to *both* parties if the trial court, after considering the prospect of a reconciliation between the parties, the effect of the marital conflict upon the parties and upon third persons (including the children), and the comparative guilt of the spouses, decided that the legitimate objects of matrimony had been destroyed. In such a case, the defendant's right to divorce would not be "in bar of" the plaintiff's right to divorce, and divorces could thus be granted to both parties.

The *DeBurgh* case was a landmark in California law. The opinion, written by (now Chief) Justice Traynor, firmly established the principle of marriage breakdown as the basis of divorce. Professor Armstrong said of the case that "no single decision has done more for the integrity of the bar, the preservation of the sound morals of the community, and the wholesome functioning of the equity powers inherent in our courts."[12]

Since the *DeBurgh* decision in 1952, California divorce law has existed in an uneasy state of ambivalence and inconsistency. If a plaintiff, for example, establishes that the defendant has committed a single act of adultery and no defense is offered, he is absolutely entitled to a divorce based on defendant's matrimonial offense. But if defendant establishes that plaintiff has also committed adultery, or has been guilty of other marital wrongs sufficient to create a cause for divorce, the court is required to decide, before granting the divorce, whether the marriage has in fact broken down.

By its insistence on a more detailed analysis of the actual state of the family, the breakdown principle as enunciated in the *DeBurgh* case thus protects society's interest in preserving marriage more effectively than the matrimonial offense principle.

There is no doubt that the matrimonial offense principle lent itself to abuse by spouses who are agreed on getting a divorce. Figures released by the California Bureau of Vital Statistics covering the year 1966 indicate that 95 per cent of all complaints for divorce (95,538 total) and separate maintenance (4224 total) filed during that year were based on the ground of extreme cruelty. During the same calendar year, 60,467 interlocutory decrees of divorce were granted,[13] and the California Judicial Council estimates that 61,957 interlocutory decrees of divorce and separate maintenance were heard on the uncontested calendar. Although the Judicial Council figures relate to cases filed in earlier years as well as some cases filed in 1966, the number of divorces that are uncontested is a significant proportion of the total divorce complaints filed.

The Report of the Governor's Commission on the Family reproduces "a typical example of the melancholy and perfunctory litany of uncontested divorce" on the grounds of extreme cruelty:[14]

ATTORNEY: Q: Mrs. X, have you resided in the State of California for more than one year and in this county for more than ninety days prior to the commencement of this proceeding?

PLAINTIFF: A: Yes.

Q: And during your marriage with Mr. X, has he on many occasions been cold and indifferent to you?

A: Yes.

Q: And as a result of this conduct on the part of your husband, have you become seriously ill, nervous and upset?

A: Yes.

Q: And was this conduct on the part of your husband in any manner caused by anything you have done?

A: No.

(Where a Conciliation Court is maintained)

Q: And have you done everything in your power to preserve this marriage, but without success?

A: Yes.

(Optional)

Q: And during the marriage, you at all times did your best to be a good wife to Mr. X?

A: Yes. . . .

(Following the questions relating to child custody and alimony, if appropriate, the remaining questions are addressed to the corroborating witness)

Q: Mrs. Y, you have known Mrs. X, the plaintiff herein, for —— years?

A: I have.

Q: And you have heard the testimony she has given here this morning?

A: I have.

Q: And to your personal knowledge, is all of that testimony true?

A: Yes, it is.

ATTORNEY
TO JUDGE: Anything further, Your Honor?

JUDGE TO
ATTORNEY: No, that will be sufficient. Plaintiff is granted a divorce on the ground of defendant's extreme cruelty . . .

The California situation thus illustrates the wide gulf that exists between theory and practice in the divorce area.[15]

It is significant that the drive to reform divorce law originated in California with lawyers who handle divorce cases. The pressure to find an accommodation between felt needs and unyielding laws has fallen most heavily upon the professionals whose craftsmanship is essential to produce the desired result. Nor can it be supposed that judges are unaware of the reality thinly concealed behind the masks of the courtroom players. An uncontested divorce which takes more than fifteen minutes of the court's time is rare indeed, and the average case occupies no more than ten minutes. The plaintiff and his or her witness have been rehearsed in their parts by the attorney. Sometimes the rehearsal becomes almost too letter-perfect: Virtue reports of the form favored in Chicago that "the number of cruel spouses in Chicago, both male and female, who strike their marriage partners in the face exactly twice, without provocation, leaving visible marks, is remarkable."[16]

The uncontested divorce, then, is intended to beguile neither its participants nor its specialized audience. It seems clear that the matrimonial offense theory of divorce does not accomplish its primary end of guarding society's interest in preserving marriage by preventing divorce except upon clearly established statutory grounds. Rather, the existence of a well-established legal charade with a script written by divorce lawyers and acted out by the parties to permit the judge to achieve a result permissible by the letter of the law but forbidden by its spirit suggests that the law's present response to the divorce problem has been strongly influenced by unarticulated and imperfectly understood human impulses.

The California Proposal: Marriage Breakdown and the Family Court

Once the conclusion is reached that the matrimonial offense approach to divorce should be modified, several alternatives present themselves. One possibility, which has already been acted on by a number of states, is to add a non-fault ground of divorce—usually voluntary separation for a specified number of years, but sometimes incompatibility as well—to the existing grounds based on fault. A second possibility, the one proposed for California and by the Mortimer Commission in England,[17] is that of abolishing the matrimonial offense doctrine altogether and substituting in its place breakdown of the marriage as the sole basis for divorce. A third suggestion would add to existing grounds a provision for divorce by mutual consent. A fourth proposal put forth in Canada, prior to the enactment of its new statute, was to combine the breakdown approach with voluntary separation as the sole ground, allowing divorce following a two-year separation if the parties show that the marriage is not likely to be resumed through cohabitation.

During the summer of 1966 the report of the Mortimer Commission, a group appointed by the Archbishop of Canterbury to review the divorce law of England, was published. The report, called *Putting Asunder: A Divorce Law for Contemporary Society,* strongly urged the adoption of marriage breakdown as the sole basis for divorce. The California Commission, in reaching the same conclusion, closely followed Chief Justice Traynor's opinion in *DeBurgh.* He emphasized in that case that "when a marriage has failed and the family has ceased to be a unit, the purposes of family life are no longer served and divorce will be permitted."[18] The two studies thus share a common understanding that the essential notion of marriage breakdown is that one party to the marriage is unwilling to continue the relationship so that family life is no longer possible.

Critics have argued that adoption of the breakdown standard will undermine marriage by making divorce too easily obtainable, thus causing an increase in the divorce rate. These arguments usually fail to grasp the distinction between the divorce rate and the marriage breakdown rate. As Rheinstein has painstakingly pointed out, the critical figure is not the number of divorces granted, but the number of marriages that fail; otherwise, marriage stability would be statistically perfect in all societies (such as Italy, Spain, or Brazil) that do not allow legal divorces. Moreover, as the *DeBurgh* case suggests, when the marriage has ceased to exist, public policy is not served by attempts to lower the divorce rate by denying divorces. The marriage breakdown proposal is an attempt to encourage spouses to concentrate on the realities of their relationship rather than on the legal fictions of present divorce law.

Both the Mortimer Commission and the California proposal rejected the compromise of adding marriage breakdown to the familiar list of fault-based grounds. Both found the two theories inconsistent; if a divorce is to be granted because of breakdown, proof of fault is simply irrelevant. If, on the other hand, proof of an unjustified and unforgiven wrong act is sufficient to terminate the marriage in law, inquiry into whether the marriage has ended in fact is unnecessary. The two approaches cut in different directions; seeking opposite goals, each relies on different facts.

The aim of those who would make the breakdown approach the exclusive means of divorce is twofold: (1) to allow society to express effectively its interest in the stability of marriages by attempting to discover, in every divorce case, whether or not the marriage has irreparably broken down; and (2) to rescue the administration of justice in the divorce area from the perjury and legal fictions presently required by courtroom practice under the fault system.

The forced cohabitation of such incompatible partners as the breakdown theory and the fault theory in the same statute might corrupt the new law rather than purify the old one.

It may, however, be argued that even the exclusive use of the breakdown standard will not eliminate fault and guilt as controlling factors in divorce proceedings because courts will continue to inquire into the parties' marital misconduct to establish whether the marriage has broken down. This argument fails to distinguish between the indirect relevance of marital conduct to divorce in a true marriage breakdown system and its central importance in a matrimonial offense system. Perhaps the distinction can be clarified by considering the effect accorded by each of the two systems to an act of adultery committed by a husband. Under a matrimonial offense system, a wife who proves that her husband has committed adultery is absolutely entitled to a divorce if he has no defense, whether or not the marriage has broken down. In a marriage breakdown system, on the other hand, the husband's adultery is relevant as a symptom which indicates that the marriage may be in danger of breaking down. Taken alone, however, adultery is not a sufficient reason for terminating the marriage. When a judge inquires into an act of adultery under a true marriage breakdown system, he does so in order to discover whether the marriage has been damaged so greatly that it cannot be continued. If, after his investigation, he concludes that the marriage has in fact broken down, he may indicate that the act of adultery both resulted from the actual breakdown and in its turn caused an even greater emotional separation between the spouses. If his investigation has been thorough and careful, however, he will not normally conclude that a single act of adultery is the sole cause for the divorce. Thus, although marital conduct will remain relevant to divorces based on breakdown, it is not accurate to say that the breakdown standard does not eliminate fault as a controlling factor in divorce law.

Drafting a statute to embody the breakdown principle presents many problems: What standard is to be used to decide whether a marriage has broken down? Who will decide whether the standard has been met in a particular case? What will be the result if the parties think their marriage has broken down, but the court disagrees? Should dissolution be permitted if the party pressing for divorce is one who has himself committed what would have been a matrimonial offense under the old law? Should divorce be permitted against the will of a spouse who has not been guilty of technical fault under the old law? Should divorce be allowed upon mutual consent of the spouses even if breakdown cannot be legally established? These and other problems will be discussed in the context of the California plan.

Unlike that of the Mortimer Commission, the California proposal closely integrates the establishment of the breakdown principle with a comprehensive plan for marriage and divorce counseling to be made available through the family court in co-operation with private and community facilities. The proposed formulation of the standard for dissolution, which closely follows the California Supreme Court's language in the *DeBurgh* case, is as follows:

> At the hearing, an order shall be made by the court dissolving the marriage if the court, after having read and considered the counselor's report and any other evidence presented by the parties, makes a finding that the legitimate objects of matrimony have been destroyed and that there is no reasonable likelihood that the marriage can be saved. The court's order dissolving the marriage shall be effective when made.[19]

The suggested procedure begins with a neutral petition— "In re the marriage of John and Mary Smith," rather than "*Smith* v. *Smith*"—requesting the family court to inquire into the continuance of the marriage. No specific acts or grounds are to be alleged. Temporary orders safeguarding the personal and property rights of the parties and providing for custody and support during the proceedings will be available. Within five days after the petition has been filed, the clerk of the court must fix a date for an initial interview between the parties and a counselor in order that they may "begin to explore together the desirability of continuing the marriage." Attendance at one interview is mandatory, and is made a condition of the petitioner's continuing the proceeding; the parties may be required to attend this session together, in the discretion of the chief counselor. Provision is made for situations where the defendant is unavailable or beyond the court's jurisdiction. If the defendant is within the court's jurisdiction, but willfully fails to appear, his failure can be punished by contempt, but will not defeat the court's power to terminate the marriage.

The California proposal does not provide for mandatory attempts at reconciliation. Neither does it require marriage counseling, as that term is commonly understood. The sole function of the mandatory initial interviews is to discover the current situation in order to help the parties see their own situation clearly and to make available to them such of the court's services as they may choose. Its purpose is diagnostic and exploratory rather than curative. Thus, the interview may disclose that the petitioner is a woman who has been abandoned by her husband for many years. She may not know where he is, or even whether he is alive. Reconciliation counseling would obviously be unnecessary. Again, parties may have attempted reconciliation themselves with the help of a private therapist. If such efforts have proved unavailing, the parties may not want further marriage counseling from the court. In the more usual case, however, the parties may not have sought any professional help and they may be confused, ambivalent, and emotionally distraught. The counselor may be able to help them look at their situation constructively. Even if the parties and the counselor agree during the initial interview that the marriage has irreparably broken down, the understanding gained from having worked out the problem together may lessen hostility and bitterness that might otherwise be expressed in the form of legalistic and retaliatory arguments over division of property, alimony, or the custody of children.

The period during which the initial interviews may be held expires thirty days after the filing of the petition of inquiry. At that time, the counselor who has been working with the parties must inform the court whether the parties have decided to become reconciled, to undertake voluntary marriage counseling for the purpose of attempting a reconciliation, or to proceed with their petition with a view to the possible dissolution of the marriage. Each of these three possible decisions has different ramifications. If a reconciliation has been effected, the

petition will be dismissed. If the parties desire reconciliation counseling, sixty days are allowed for them to meet
either with the court's professional staff or a community
agency or private therapist. The draft statute expressly
provides that all communications made by either party to
any counselor during the period of reconciliation counseling, whether or not the counselor is a member of the
court's staff, will be absolutely privileged.[20] This legal
protection of the confidential relationship between therapist and client seems necessary in order to help create a
favorable opportunity for the development of rapport
between the spouses and their counselors.

If the parties have decided not to undertake reconciliation counseling, or if they have done so and decided not
to reconcile, the commission's recommendations suggest
that divorce counseling (rather than marriage counseling) should be made available to them. That is, the parties may undertake further consultation with the court's
professional staff for the purpose of working out the
best adjustment possible of the social and psychological
circumstances attendant upon the dissolution of their
marriage. Couples who have tried reconciliation counseling, but have decided not to reconcile, may already
have gained important insights into new problems likely
to confront them after their marriage is dissolved. Experience reported from courts specializing in reconciliation counseling indicates that couples who did not repair
their marriages were nevertheless able to work together
with less hostility to plan their future and that of their
children after counseling.[21]

One important function of divorce counseling is to
help the separating partners understand that divorce is a
beginning as well as an end. Bohannan and Huckleberry have reminded us that divorce begins as a specialized relationship between the former spouses and their
children, relatives, and friends and often grows to include the second (or third or fourth) spouses and *their*

children as well.[22] We are told that one out of every nine children in America is a stepchild[23]; although many stepchildren have lost one parent through death rather than divorce, the problem of preparing children for the divorce and possible remarriage of their parents is a serious one that deserves attention from the family court.[24]

Divorce counseling has a second, equally vital function: that of helping the spouses gain insight into the reasons for their marriage failure so that they may be better able to avoid repetition of the disastrous pattern in their next relationship. A great deal has been written by psychiatrists about the unconscious impulses and motivations that control the choice of a marriage partner.[25] If a marriage is one between two people in conflict with themselves, only the reduction of such conflict will result in any real hope of a permanent solution.[26] The family court, even if it were manned exclusively by trained psychotherapists, could not hope to undertake long-term treatment of the kind necessary to achieve this task. The most that can be expected in such cases is that the individual might begin to see the nature of his internalized conflicts and to accept a reference to a private therapist. Such extensive treatment by its very nature can be undertaken only as a voluntary matter.

Fortunately, however, not all cases of marriage failure require medical treatment. Professional caseworkers, under the direction of experienced supervisors and in consultation with psychiatrists as anticipated by the California proposal, can be expected to work productively with many families.[27]

Paradoxically, divorce counseling can become one of the most effective forms of marriage counseling. Although it may be difficult to persuade two persons who are eager to marry that they should delay their plans to take a second look at their chances of success in the marriage, it should be relatively easy to demonstrate to two people whose marriage has just failed the value of attempting to gain the self-awareness necessary to avoid another mistake. Although great care must be taken to avoid coercion, affording the opportunity for voluntary re-examination of past marriages seems to be a realistic and desirable way of expressing the state's interest in the stability of future marriages. Moreover, when the matter is viewed in this way it becomes clear that eligibility for the counseling service should not be limited to divorcing couples who have children, for the childless couple left without help may soon become involved in two unhappy marriages *with* children.

After the period allotted for divorce counseling, and no later than one hundred and twenty days after the initial interview, the counselor must submit a report to the court setting forth his recommendation as to the continuance of the marriage. He is required to consult with counsel for both parties prior to preparing his report and copies of it will be furnished to counsel or to the parties. This report and all other records of the family court are confidential and will not be available to the general public. If a custody investigation has been ordered by the court, that report will also be prepared and submitted ten days prior to the hearing. As we have seen, the court must decide at the hearing whether the legitimate objects of matrimony have been destroyed. The counselor's report, the petitioner's testimony and any other evidence the parties may produce will be before the court.

If the parties and the counselor have agreed that the marriage has in fact broken down, the judge may make a like finding and enter his order dissolving the marriage. If, however, the judge finds that the marriage has not broken down, he may continue the proceedings for ninety days "during which time the parties may, if they so desire, pursue further the possibility of continuing the marriage." The purpose of this provision is to allow the parties, with knowledge that the court believes their marriage can be saved, to make a final attempt at reconciliation. The help of the court's professional staff will be available to them if desired. The intent appears clear, however, that no attempted reconciliation is required. If the parties do not choose to try again, they may simply wait for the ninety-day period to elapse.

At the end of the ninety-day period, the draft provides for a second hearing. If at that time the decision of one or both parties is that the marriage should be terminated, "the court shall enter its order, effective when made, dissolving the marriage." Thus, if the parties have been unable to agree on a reconciliation and it is clear that the marriage has ceased to exist in fact, the court is directed to terminate it in law as well. This provision is an effective guard against the objection[28] that the breakdown principle allows a judge who dislikes divorce to require the perpetuation of hopeless marriages under the guise of finding reconciliations to be possible in all cases.

The California Commission's solution is in sharp contrast to the proposal of the Mortimer group which concluded that in cases where an "innocent" spouse objected to being divorced and where the petitioner "had not only been patently responsible for ending the common life but had blatantly flouted the obligations of marriage and treated the other party abominably," society's interest in dissolving empty legal ties would be outbalanced by other considerations, and the court should refuse the divorce, even though breakdown was established, since to grant it would be "contrary to the public interest in justice and in protecting the institution of marriage."[29] Although one may sympathize with the churchmen's dilemma, it is difficult to see how refusing a divorce even in their case protects the institution of marriage. Their solution is an obvious attempt to warn by example other potential petitioners who contemplate similar reprehensible conduct that freedom from marriage bonds cannot be purchased in this manner; yet it appears doubtful that the fruits of such warnings, if heeded, will be more stable unions. The very fact that a petitioner is prepared to go so far to achieve a legal termination of his marriage indicates that the marriage has already broken down; indeed, the Mortimer Commission conceded that breakdown could be established in such a case. Their proposal on this point, then, is simply a decision, however reluctantly reached, to use continuation of marriage as a punishment for outrageous behavior. As Justice Traynor made clear in the *DeBurgh* case, California's public policy is just the opposite: rather than a protection of marriage, its use as a device for punishment is a degradation of marriage and a frustration of its purposes.

The Mortimer Commission also concluded that divorce should not be granted against the wishes of an "innocent" spouse even when breakdown is proved, unless the court is satisfied that the provisions concerning that spouse's property, maintenance and pension rights are equitable.[30] The problem is a serious one. Planning in this area must frankly recognize that the economic position of women in the United States is not, despite years of effort and the provisions against sex-based discrimination in employment contained in the Civil Rights Act of 1964, equal to that of men.[31] Present California law ties the division of community and quasi-community property to the grounds for divorce: if the decree is rendered on the grounds of willful desertion, willful neglect, habitual intemperance, or conviction of a felony, the community and quasi-community property must be divided equally; but if the grounds are extreme cruelty, adultery, or incurable insanity, the court must divide the property unequally.[32] Continuing its effort to reduce the importance of matrimonial offense as a basis for divorce, the commission recommended that, except where the economic circumstances of the parties require an unequal division, the community and quasi-community property be divided equally in all cases.

Although this recommendation can be expected to work equitably where the parties have accumulated enough property during the marriage to provide for both of them after the divorce, it will not solve cases in which the accumulation is inadequate. In such situations, alimony remains the only practical means of providing adequate maintenance for the divorced wife who is unable to support herself. In making its order for the support of a party, the commission directs the court to consider the circumstances of the parties, including the duration of the marriage. The standard for ordering support will thus remain the need of one party and the ability of the other to pay. Alimony can be awarded to both parties under the commission's proposal.

It cannot be assumed, however, that alimony alone can provide for the economic consequences of divorce. For one thing, alimony is generally not sufficient to support the wife adequately. Even when alimony is granted, there exists an enormous practical problem of enforcing its payment. Generally speaking, existing enforcement procedures are not utilized adequately in many states. The commission recommends that the family court be allowed to require that the district attorney appear on behalf of a spouse and children to enforce alimony and child support orders in any case in which an order for alimony had been made to a spouse having custody of minor children and an order of child support had also been made for the children. This proposal would broaden existing law which permits the court to direct that the district attorney appear on behalf of minor children to enforce child support orders. In my view, the court should also be allowed to direct the district attorney to enforce support orders for women who do not have minor children living in the home.

Having so consistently taken the firm position that

marriage breakdown should be the only basis for divorce, the commission recommended abolishing the present law of annulment and substituting the marriage breakdown theory there as well. Stating its conviction that no essential difference between annulment and divorce exists, the commission pointed out that if the parties continue the marriage with knowledge of the impediment, the marriage has not broken down. If, however, an annulment is sought, the underlying reason for doing so is that the marriage has broken down and that issue should be tried directly just as in any other dissolution proceeding. As we have noted, present California law permits third parties to commence annulment proceedings in some cases. The commission would continue this provision only in the case of parents who may seek annulment of the marriage of their under-aged children, but it also would allow the spouses to invoke the counseling aid of the professional staff of the family court if they wished to continue their marriage against parental opposition.

Under present law, a party who has established a cause of action for divorce may request separate maintenance rather than divorce. The logic of the commission's position on marriage breakdown might seem to compel the abolition of legal separation, which permits the parties to live apart but continues the marriage bond. There are, however, some couples who desire to remain legally married in order to retain benefits such as social security and yet do not wish to live together. The commission saw no reason to forbid this result nor yet to require that it be achieved only by voluntary separation. The draft therefore provides that the court may order a legal separation if the parties jointly request it rather than a dissolution of the marriage.

Apart from its emphasis on divorce counseling directed at reducing hostility between the parties that might otherwise erupt in legalistic battles over the children, the commission took at least two other steps in modifying the

present law and procedure of child custody. One inno-
vation, that of permitting the court to appoint an attorney
to act as guardian ad litem for a child if good cause appear therefore, was taken over from the Wisconsin law.
Although the Wisconsin experience with guardians ad
litem has been favorable, my own view is that the intro-
duction of a third attorney to represent the children will
be less useful in the California family court. The marriage breakdown theory and divorce counseling in California hopefully will reduce the parties' hostility and
bitterness so that they can see themselves as parents who
must co-operate in planning the future of their children
in a sensible way. Wisconsin, however, still operates under the full rigors of the fault theory and the adversary
system; in this situation the children may well need the
protection of an independent advocate.

A second, more important, recommendation affecting
children attempted to steer a middle course between the
"dominant parental right" theory of present California
law (which requires a finding of parental unfitness before custody can be awarded to a non-parent) and the
"best interests of the child" theory.[33] The draft proposes
that in awarding custody the court should be guided by
two considerations:

(1) Custody shall be awarded to either parent accord-
     ing to the best interests of the child.
(2) Although preference in an award of custody shall
     be given first to either parent, and second, to the
     person or persons in whose home the child has
     been living in a stable and wholesome environ-
     ment, the court may award custody to persons other
     than the father or mother or the *de facto* custodian
     if it finds that such award is required to serve the
     best interests of the child.

This provision received more severe criticism than any
other part of the draft statute when legislative hearings

were held on the bill. Objections were raised that the measure reposes unlimited discretion in judges to find that the best interests of children requires their placement with outsiders even if their parents are fit, and that such discretion is likely to be abused. Much of this criticism was stimulated by the Iowa Supreme Court's unfortunate opinion in *Painter* v. *Bannister*,[34] granting custody of a seven-year-old boy to his middle-class, mid-Western "stable" grandparents rather than to his "bohemian" California father. It cannot be doubted that this opinion has had a great impact in California and that it has given rise to many doubts about the "best interests" standard.[35] In an effort to meet this criticism, the present bill might be amended to make clear that before custody may be given to non-parents, the preference favoring parents must be overcome by a showing that the child's needs cannot be adequately met in the parental home. Such an amendment would avoid the requirement of present law that a negative finding of parental unfitness be made before the child can be given to outsiders, while still maintaining the original draft's affirmative emphasis on the child's needs.

A Comparison: The New Family Court and the Old Juvenile Court

In evaluating the California family court proposal in the light of the juvenile court experience, one sees immediately that several institutional similarities exist between the two courts. Thus, the California plan retains the concept of the specialist-judge and his professional staff. The dependence upon the judge as the critical factor in the court's operation that was so central to the early juvenile courts, however, is lessened by the California proposal's attempt to give the professional staff a more influential role in determining the court's administration than the probation staff of the juvenile court commonly enjoys. Although the family court judge has authority to select his staff, the quality of the staff is protected by the high degree of professional training required of its members, the opportunities for consultation with outside specialists, and the commission's specific recommendation that the employment standards of the National Association of Social Workers be followed. The problem of attracting a high-caliber staff is a real one unless sufficient funds can be found to provide adequate salaries. One possibility is to begin the court's staff on a small scale by limiting its caseload to divorces involving children or to employ group counseling where absolute confidentiality is not required.

The California plan ultimately depends for its success on the family court to therapeutic principles. This notion must be justified if it is to be adopted as the policy of the state. No one denies that the state is legitimately interested in fostering the continued existence of the family, for, as Parsons[36] has noted, the family is the functioning social unit which provides the primary basis of psychological and emotional security for the normal adult and acts as the primary agency for the socialization of children. The real question is whether the large-scale commitment to the therapeutic approach recommended by family court advocates will be justified in terms of increased family stability.

In their imaginative discussion of this problem,[37] Foote, Levy, and Sander have implied that it is just as false and misleading for a therapeutically oriented generation to believe that individual failure causes our high marriage breakdown rate as it was for a religiously oriented generation to believe that the root cause was a personal immorality. Both approaches, the authors suggest, emphasize false issues and thus prevent serious consideration of the basic problems of family life in modern society. Family court proponents do not contend, however, that persons who get divorced have failed in their marriages because they are sick and that if only they could be cured, stable marriages would result. Rather, the suggestion is that the "basic problems of family life in modern society" can be approached constructively through the normal individual's deeper understanding of himself and his increased awareness of how he presents himself to others within the context of his marriage. No one suggests that a divorce court is the only or even the best place to acquire such understanding and awareness. For many, however, it may be the only place available at the critical time; and for them, it will hopefully become a convenient place to begin.

The California plan ultimately depends for its success on creating a comfortable working relationship among judges, lawyers, the court's professional staff, family members, and the general community so as to permit the family court to work with families in a non-adversary and constructive fashion. As we have seen, the success of the juvenile court depended in part on the same possibility; too often that possibility did not materialize, perhaps because too many hopes were staked on the critical leadership of the judge. Some progress has no doubt been made since the time when it was thought that half an hour's exposure to a wise and kindly judge could change the life pattern of a misguided child. Basing one's hopes for the success of a family court on notions of "saving marriages" through an hour's contact with a marriage counselor, however, appears similarly unrealistic. If the family court is to become truly non-judgmental and oriented toward helping each family discover what is in its own best interests, rather than simply prescribing the same cure for all families, "saving marriages" cannot be the court's primary goal. There must be a frank recognition that "some marriages are not worth saving and should be terminated for the welfare of all concerned."[38] Nor should this recognition be limited to

couples without children, for research in California has
indicated that couples who are in constant conflict should
divorce for the sake of their children instead of remaining
together for the sake of the children.[39]

The court's objective, when it is petitioned to inquire
into the continuance of a marriage, must be to discover
the facts; when the facts lead to the conclusion that the
marriage should be dissolved, the court must be prepared
to act accordingly. Only in this way will the court's professional staff be free to work honestly with each couple,
rather than feeling compelled to produce statistical "reconciliations" to justify the court's existence. And, if, after a full opportunity for reconsideration, one party refuses to continue the marriage at the final hearing, the
court will be able to grant a dissolution, knowing that it
has done what it could for the marriage and hoping that
any future marriages entered into by the divorcing parties will have a better chance for success because of its
efforts.

Limits of the Current Reform: The California
Family Law Act and the English Divorce
Reform Bill

The intense public interest and discussion stimulated
by the reports of the Mortimer Commission and the California Governor's Commission on the Family produced
legislative action both in England and California in
1969. The English bill was apparently the result of a
compromise between the commission and the bar: the
lawyers insisted upon a bill that would allow proof of
marriage breakdown by reference to the more familiar
concepts of fault and separation. The result is a law that
provides in section one for irretrievable breakdown as the
sole ground for divorce and then requires in section two
that irretrievable breakdown be proven by showing one

of the following facts: that respondent has committed adultery and petitioner finds it "intolerable" to live with respondent; that respondent has "behaved in such a way that the petitioner cannot reasonably be expected to live with the respondent"; that respondent has deserted petitioner for at least two years immediately prior to the petition and that respondent does not object to the divorce; or that the parties have lived apart for five years, regardless of whether respondent objects to the divorce. The English version of marriage breakdown, only slightly caricatured, thus comes down to mean adultery, mental cruelty, desertion, and separation for a period of time.

The new California law was also a product of compromise, but its marriage dissolution provisions seem closer to the original recommendations of the Governor's Commission than those of the English bill are to the proposals of the Mortimer Commission. The California legislature succeeded in abolishing "divorce" entirely, substituting in its place the "dissolution of marriage." All the traditional, fault-oriented grounds for divorce were abolished and irremediable breakdown was established as the common basis for marriage dissolution.[40] Irremediable breakdown will be proven by a showing that "irreconcilable differences" (defined as "those grounds which are determined by the court to be substantial reasons for not continuing the marriage and which make it appear that the marriage should be dissolved"[41]) exist between the parties. The California law, unlike the British one, does not refer expressly to the old grounds for divorce. The continued use of the word "grounds" in the definition of irreconcilable differences seems unfortunate, however, since it calls to mind traditional notions of fault and thus may lead some attorneys and judges to approach the new law as though "irreconcilable differences" were merely a new name for "mental cruelty." The legislature attempted to lessen this temptation by providing that evidence of specific acts of misconduct are inadmissible in marriage dissolution cases, but the value of this safeguard is seriously undermined by the exception that allows such evidence to be used if the court determines it necessary to establish the existence of irreconcilable differences.[42] It seems clear that in all contested cases the petitioner's attorney will be required to have such evidence available. Since many uncontested cases at least start out being contested ones, the new law may not alter substantially the practice in attorney's offices regardless of how much it alters procedure in the courtroom.

The procedure established by the new law for the dissolution hearing adopts the neutral petition, but departs from the proposals of the Governor's Commission at a critical point. If the judge believes that a reasonable possibility of reconciliation exists, so that the marriage has not broken down irremediably, he is instructed not to deny the dissolution but instead to continue the proceedings for not more than thirty days.[43] The purpose of a period of postponement in the commission's view was to allow the parties to explore the possibility of reconciliation in the knowledge that the court believed it to be a viable alternative to termination of the marriage. If, at the end of the period, one party moved to have the marriage dissolved, the court's prediction that reconciliation was possible would be shown to have been unrealistic and the court could then conclude that the breakdown was irremediable. Since the commission accepted the policy of the *DeBurgh* case that the state has no interest in the legal preservation of marriages that have ended in fact, the commission recommended that the court be required, in such circumstances, to recognize the reality of the situation by granting a legal termination of the marriage.[44] The legislature, however, was apparently unable to recognize frankly the social undesirability of permitting a court to continue a legal relationship after the human relationship on which it was based has ended. Accordingly, the new law permits the court to refuse to terminate the marriage after the period of postponement even if one party—or presumably even if both parties—moves for termination.

Irremediable breakdown is not, however, the sole basis for marriage dissolution under the new law. Despite testimony that its retention was unnecessary in light of the breadth of the general breakdown standard, the legislature continued in existence the non-fault ground of incurable insanity. Of the 95,538 complaints for divorce filed in California in 1966, the last year for which published figures are available, thirty-three (less than 0.1 per cent) were filed on the ground of incurable insanity.[45] If petitions for marriage dissolution on this basis continue to occupy such a small proportion of the total, irremediable breakdown will be, for all practical purposes, the only basis for marriage dissolution in California.

The legislature accepted only in part the commission's proposals regarding property division and child custody. The commission's principle of equal division of the community property except where economic circumstances require an unequal division was modified by the legislative concept of an offset for "deliberate misappropriation": The court may reduce one party's share of the community property by any sum it finds that party to have deliberately misappropriated from the community.[46] The new law provides no definition of deliberate misappropriation, and its meaning will have to be worked out by the courts on a case-by-case basis. A broad construction of the phrase could effectively limit the husband's power to manage and control the community property, while a narrower interpretation would merely provide a small measure of protection against fraudulent dealing.

The child custody provisions of the new law continue in effect the general preference for parents over nonparents and the specific preference for mothers over fathers if the child is very young.[47] The result of the com-

mission's efforts to soften the harsh requirement of
existing law that parental unfitness must be established
before a child can be awarded to a non-parent over a parent's objection is a statement in the new law that, before
making such an award, the court must find not only that
the award to a non-parent is required to serve the best
interests of the child, but also that parental custody would
be "detrimental" to the child.[48] The shading of difference between proving that a parent is unfit to have custody of his child and that parental custody would be
detrimental to the child is a fine one indeed. To the extent that the new law is interpreted to emphasize the
quality of the relationship between parent and child
rather than the personal weaknesses of the parent, it will
be a change for the better. Unfortunately, the legislature
seems to have worked at cross purposes with itself on this
matter: it specifically excluded child custody cases from
its general prohibition against the use of evidence of
specific acts of misconduct in dissolution proceedings.[49]
This exception may encourage some attorneys and
judges to continue their former practice of deciding what
is best for a child by showing how "immoral" his parents
are. It is to be hoped that the admonition of recent, well-
considered cases decided under the juvenile court act
that adultery alone does not make a home unfit for children[50] will not be lost on those who interpret the new
law.

In my view, the most serious shortcoming of the new
law is its failure to enact the commission's family court
proposal. The reasons for legislative rejection of the family court were apparently varied and complex. Some,
who see the proliferation of specialized courts as
harmful to a unified system of judicial administration,
were opposed to following the precedent of the juvenile
and probate courts by establishing yet another specialized
family court. Some were unwilling to pay the cost in-

volved in hiring the professional staff required to serve the divorcing population. Others, who misunderstood the intent of the commission's proposal, insisted that they opposed the family court because they opposed mandatory counseling—even though no mandatory counseling was actually proposed. The immediate result of this defeat is that, since the new act became effective on January 1, 1970, professional counseling has been available to those seeking dissolution of their marriages as part of the court's services only in the dozen or so counties that have voluntarily established courts of conciliation. Since many of these courts presently limit their resources to marriage counseling in an attempt to produce reconciliations, one of the commission's most imaginative ideas—that of divorce counseling—is lost. Hopefully, the courts of conciliation will begin to offer divorce counseling on a voluntary basis so that some experience can be gained with this new idea.

The action of the 1969 legislature may not, however, be a final defeat of the family court proposal in California. The new act gives the Judicial Council power to provide by rule of court for practice under its provisions.[51] These rules, which are currently being developed, not only could suggest additional criteria to be used by a presiding judge in assigning judges to hear family matters, but also could effect some modest consolidation of family cases on the calendars of these judges. Members of the legislature who are dissatisfied with the new law's failure to deal adequately with the matter of counseling have indicated their intention to raise the question again, perhaps in the 1970 session. In the meantime, a new study[52] of existing family courts in the United States has produced valuable information that will be useful in structuring a new proposal. The 1969 act may ultimately be seen as only the first of many progressive steps toward a sensible and humane family law.

Conclusion

As this brief description of its principal features has attempted to make clear, the California proposal seeks to remove matrimonial offense as the basis for divorce, property division, and alimony; to diminish parental rights as the sole touchstone of child custody; and to substitute a factual inquiry into marriage breakdown as the basis for divorce, economic circumstances as the criteria for property and support issues, and the best interests of the child plus a parental preference as the standard for child custody decisions. Some progress toward these goals was achieved by the Family Law Act of 1969, but much remains to be done.

I do not imagine that it will surprise the reader to learn that I continue to favor the family court proposal. Its future in California and elsewhere, however, is far from clear. The help of all persons concerned with the family is needed so that the law may ultimately find its way to the adoption of principles that favor honesty over perjury, a concern for the individual over legal fictions, and a commitment to understand and deal fairly with the realities of family interaction rather than to pursue an artificial search for fault and an unproductive assignment of blame.

11

Some Thoughts on Divorce Reform

PAUL BOHANNAN

The authors of this book have put forward a number of ideas that might be summed up: What we "ought" to do about divorce depends not merely on our notion of divorce, but even more on what we think marriage "ought" to be. A divorce does not end everything about a marriage. It severs the legal contract between the husband and wife—but leaves a moral and emotional "contract" between ex-husband and ex-wife. It shatters the household that was based on the marriage. But it definitely does *not* break the kinship network that the children of the marriage create merely by their existence.

What a Divorce Ends and How

Spouses do not simply cease to be associated at divorce; they become ex-husbands and ex-wives. Your wife cannot become your non-wife (as all the girls you never married might be considered); rather she becomes your ex-wife.

Although it may not involve seeing her or doing anything to maintain a relationship, nevertheless the basis for a relationship and the history of a relationship are still there. It was DiMaggio who made the funeral arrangements for Marilyn Monroe. Your ex-wife or ex-husband may cease to be your responsibility in a legal sense—but in some attenuated sense or other, no matter how completely you have accomplished the psychic divorce, you choose autonomously to take a new kind of responsibility.

Divorce also shatters the household. This may be devastating if there are young children involved. It is the isolation of American and European households from stable and long-term association with the kinsmen of the spouses that leads to many of the sharpest problems at the time of divorce. Americans have a word for this shattered household—they need it. It is a "broken home." The single-parent household is understaffed, and hence the division of labor is altered. Our do-it-yourself world assumes both an adult male and an adult female in the household. When one or the other is not there, but children are, a harrowing lack of services results.

There is also a lack of role models for everyone in the household. The absence of father at home (no matter how present father is in every other sense) leads to a different structuring of a child's world. A good and workable relationship can be built, but it is not the same relationship. In many societies of the world, the married couple moves in with the husband's parents—and that, of course, may include all his brothers and their wives and his grandfather and his wife or wives. In these extended households, a divorce makes less difference. If the child goes with his mother at her divorce, he enters another large household—either her father's household, or that of her new husband. If he stays with his father, there are many adult females in the compound who are "mothering" their children, including him. He is not uniquely dependent on his very own father or mother in order to have a good idea of what fathers or mothers do.

Divorce, therefore, shatters the alliance between husband and wife—which can be rebuilt into a thinner compact between ex-husband and ex-wife. It breaks the household and so thrusts the family members into a condition in which the economic system of our society does not provide adequate services. It also disrupts the larger community in which the divorce occurs, but does not "break" it the same way it does the household. There is, in the community of friends nothing analogous to the kinship system which must be repaired and maintained at the time of divorce. Americans join and leave groups and communities—and divorce is just another time for regrouping, no matter how painful an experience it may be when one is undergoing the process.

What a Divorce Does Not End

Divorce never sunders a kinship relationship. And once a child is born, his parents are kinsmen to one another. Westerners have for centuries thought of kinship in terms of "blood." This idea, under the pressure of modern science, has given way to the more correct expression in terms of genes, but has not changed in essence. Many other peoples of the world, however, trace kinship through descendants as well as through ancestors. Thus, through the mixture of their genes in a child, a man and woman become kinsmen—and all of their kinsmen become kinsmen of one another.

The most important thing that a divorce cannot cancel is the kinship. Moreover, if a ritual was performed at the time of marriage, no civil divorce can set it aside (although a church may choose to honor the divorce as tantamount to breaking the ritual, others do not).

Divorce does not break clean. There is always a residue to be dealt with.

What a Divorce Begins

Just as a wedding institutes a marriage, a decree institutes a divorce. The things about a marriage that a divorce decree does not end provide the basic content of the institution of divorce. Divorce is a social institution as much as marriage is. And it has a purpose, residual though it may be: the divorce must achieve the unfinished tasks of the broken family. Children must still be loved and educated; household tasks must still be done.

Divorce may be, for the participants, just as difficult an institution as the family it replaces. Although there is less pressure on divorcees today, and although divorced women are not unusual or unfairly treated (at least because of their divorces) in the labor market, there is still no public image of the way a divorce ought to be run. The divorce (like the marriage) devolves on the stability and organizing sense of the people concerned—everyone else is likely to stand back. After the searing experience of legal divorce, this new relationship will not be easy.

There is, moreover, no built-in sanction except the courts for ex-husbands and ex-wives to apply to one another. The parent-child relationships, backed by court orders when necessary, keep it together. Courts take a vast amount of time trying to make ex-husbands pay alimony and divorced fathers carry out obligations of support.

Thus, one of the areas in which we are weakest and in which a lot of social ingenuity must be put is into the contractual aspects of divorce. Our present system occupies judges, social workers, lawyers to an end for which a simpler solution would be cheaper and more comfortable. I do not know what that solution is, but we must search for one.

Divorce also begins a housing problem. The living arrangements that divorced persons must make all tend to be considered inadequate by them, unless they are single individuals with no dependents. Here are some of the solutions—most of them considered haphazard by the people who live in them.

THE BACHELOR HOUSEHOLD. Bachelor apartments, for men or women, are part of the American scene and do not provide much difficulty. Therefore, the ex-spouse without the children passes into this category: "single householders." American culture provides adequate services to single householders.

THE MOTHER-CENTERED HOUSEHOLD. Just as a bachelor household can be called "individual centered" and the ordinary "normal" home can be called "couple centered," so the household of a divorced woman or widow is a mother-centered home. (Widows, however, do not run into the full range of complications.) We have seen that American tradition and economy are geared either to the individual-centered or the couple-centered households. The mother-centered household, on the other hand, has difficulty in carrying out the routine tasks of living, especially when children are young, because services are not provided except at the most exorbitant prices. Who does the man's job is always a problem; for children, there is a single source of both authority and affection—what we might call a direct current instead of an alternating current.

Obviously, there is a tendency in mother-centered households to search for a second adult. Several interesting forms have resulted.

THE BAR-BELL HOUSEHOLD. One not unusual form of household results from the compound of the mother-centered household with the bachelor household of the divorced husband/father. The bar-bell is composed of a house on one end, the apartment on the other, joined by an automobile. I know several instances in which reduction of interaction between spouses more or less cured

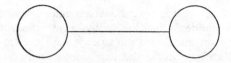

their problems, so that they have been able to live for some years in these compound households. The ex-husband (and this form of household may of course occur without divorce) comes back to do some of the chores around the house—I have found no instance in which the ex-wife ever does any chores in the bachelor-household unit, but we have already seen that such services are available.

The bar-bell household offers maximum opportunity for a rapprochement between ex-spouses. I know instances in which the ex-husband sometimes eats with the mother-centered family and may ultimately come to spend two or three nights a week there, sleeping with his ex-wife.

This kind of household results when spouses are not ready to give up their associations with one another, but have never learned to live within the confines of a single house. Theirs is a tenuous solution, and this kind of arrangement is brittle, but it seems to occur with some regularity.

THE ODD-COUPLE HOUSEHOLD. Two men, one or both of them divorced, may try to move into a single apartment in order to save money. As Neil Simon's play, *The Odd Couple,* reported vividly, they react to one another just as they reacted to their spouses. This play is about roles, more or less independent of sex—some households (and therefore some marriages) fall apart because the close interconnection between people in a household is unbearable. Anyone who is not capable of close intimacy has trouble in an American household—it doesn't matter who the other people are.

THE INVERSE ODD-COUPLE HOUSEHOLD. Sometimes

two divorced women, both with custody, form a household. One takes care of the children of both, while the other works. Sometimes both women work, trying to dovetail their hours so that one of them is always home. They thus form a sort of dark image of the normal household. Sanctions are difficult—those based on love and kinship are seldom there, and hence one must fall back again on the weaker links of respect and good will: and the threat that if this household should break up, there is no ready substitute that provides any services at all. Not surprisingly, such households are full of tensions; they seem to be short-lived.

SIBLING HOUSEHOLDS. Sometimes brother and sister, one or both with children from a broken marriage, live together in what they consider to be imitation of a normal household. Such households are usually full of tension, and there may be a great deal of guilt if there is unconscious sexual attraction between the siblings (and I venture that there often is). I have found no households made up of two sisters or of two brothers, but do not see why they should not exist. I have found one uncle-niece household that tried to imitate normal household patterns.

GRANDFAMILY HOUSEHOLDS. Many divorced women take their children back to their own parents to form a three-generation household. I have known many who tried, few who were happy with the arrangement. The greatest difficulty is to be found in conflict for the woman between her daughter role and her mother role. Public opinion is also hostile: Her return may be interpreted (perhaps correctly) as her being "tied to the apron strings." American values say very specifically that "you can't go home again."

Occasionally men are offered a place by their parents, and a few accept. My information on this type is limited —perhaps because such men do not join organizations, but I believe this is because of the rarity of the arrangement.

All these types of household have one thing in common: They show individual adaptation to an overall social situation that is poorly defined and morally unsolved. Every person in such a group feels that he has to make compromises in order to get along.

It makes little difference whether the mother-centered family is isolated in a mother-centered household or whether it is grafted onto some other form of household, the division of labor is at odds with that of the majority group. Husbands return to mow the lawn; children learn to iron shirts at a "tender" age; women become more or less adequate plumbers. And perhaps most important of all, they all resent it.

The Kinship Aspects of Divorce

Although divorce does not alter the relations in the kinship system, it necessarily has a great effect on the way they are carried out. The relationship between one parent and the children ceases to be any business of the other parent. If you are a man, it is now none of your business what their mother—your ex-wife—does with the children so long as she does not expose them to situations that the court (not you, the court) would consider physically or morally dangerous, and as long as you get your visitation rights. That is true even when the parents have joint legal custody.

Similarly, a divorced woman cannot control what her ex-husband does with the children when they go for vacations or visitations with their father. She cannot make issues about where they will or will not go, what he will or will not teach them to do, what influences he will or will not expose them to. Unless the court decides that what he does has a morally disruptive influence on the children, there is nothing she can do about it. It is "officially" none of her business. After divorce, being wife and mother no longer "go together," because a man is no longer husband to the mother of his children.

Both parents have, of course, some say in the education of their children, and in some of their life decisions, but unless the ex-wife communicates about it with the ex-husband, and unless he is willing to discuss matters with her, such rights are difficult or impossible to enforce.

The difficulty shows up in many ways: the children either no longer want to stay with the mother, or they do not want ever to go with father at all, even for an afternoon. They may be grouchy and cranky, and perhaps physically ill. After such a visitation, their mother may try to stop all visitations. The father sees this as an infringement of his rights (which it is, unless she has done it with the consent of the court), and therefore uses the only weapon he has in the divorce institution—he stops child-support payments. The mother then has to go through legal channels to make him pay. It is difficult not to use the children as means of communication in all this—especially if direct communication leads to bitterness and recriminations.

The ideal of the mother image does not change on divorce. But the activities and practices of the mother must change. The responsibilities which the cultural tradition puts on a father do not change—but the means of meeting or compromising these responsibilities certainly do. The relationship among brothers and sisters may be altered—it may become more or less intense, either for good or ill.

The kinship aspects of divorce are even further complicated when remarriages ensue. Remarriage does not change divorce structurally, but only complicates it further. If marriage is not easy, divorce may be no easier. And divorce and remarriage may become almost impos-

sibly complicated. Unless, of course, we laugh and turn
it into farce—*Divorce, American Style*.

The Natural History of Divorce

Distinctions and ideas pointed up in various chapters
of this book allow us to create a chart of the problem
areas of divorce. Some are adequately dealt with, others
are dealt with badly, and some not at all. Just as some
of the characteristics are accreted during courtship,
others assumed at the wedding, and still others accreted
during the marriage, so some of the aspects of divorce
begin with erosion during marriage, some are canceled
at the time of the decree, some more or less solved by
the institution of divorce and some are "leftovers" and
not solved at all.

During courtship, the couple participate in what I
have elsewhere called an adventure in intimacy,[1] as a
part of which they work out an agreement to seek a
major proportion of their companionship in one another,
and to intertwine their lives in an emotional interde-
pendency—what might better be called "interautonomy."
Although both spouses can be independent if they like
or if they are pushed to the point that they have to do
so, they prefer to depend upon one another materially
and emotionally. They therefore make a pact, in part
presumed by the culture, in other part overtly stated. Although companionship and emotional interautonomy are
subject to tremendous change and to ebb and flow during the course of a normal marriage, the foundations
are usually in place before the wedding.

At the time of the wedding, a legal relationship between the spouses is cemented. This means, among other
things, that in the eyes of the state and of its various
communities, these two people have entered into the civil
status of married people. They lose the legal right to

marry again until the extant marriage is canceled, either by death or by divorce: They acquire some specific legal rights in each other.

The wedding establishes rights to form a financial unit composed of husband and wife. Many states in the United States create of this unit a property-owning corporation; all states regard financial co-operation as a requirement on the parties. In the ideal case, the husband is expected to support the wife, and the wife is expected to spend her portion of the husband's income (as well as any income of her own) wisely and judiciously.

Still at the wedding, the basis for a domestic union is recognized. The husband and wife now have claims on each other that a household will be established, and that together they will form a team to provide for the needs of one another and of their children. A choice must also be made by the spouses as to where the new household will be located. Most of the American states have laws stating that the husband has the ultimate right and duty to decide where the couple, and eventual family, shall live. The wedding also indicates community approval of sexual cohabitation.

In the course of the marriage, new characteristics are added. One of these characteristics can be called "coupleness." Coupleness is different from the emotional interautonomy that continues to grow throughout a successful marriage. Whereas emotional interautonomy is related to the psychic welfare of the two individuals and to their personal and private relationship with one another, "coupleness" is the way in which they function together as a unit, vis-à-vis third parties and the outside world. Many of us know of couples who function socially as a unit long after emotional interautonomy has been abandoned. These are the people who have experienced emotional divorce but have not proceeded through the rest of the stations.

With the birth of children, of course, the husband and

TABLE 9   Areas of Divorce Reform

1. The Emotional Divorce   4. The Coparental Divorce
2. The Legal Divorce   5. The Community Divorce
3. The Financial Divorce   6. The Psychic Divorce

	Companionship and Emotional Interautonomy	Legal Relationship	Financial Cooperation	Sex Rights	Coparents	"Coupleness"	Child Support	Domestic Rights	Community Choice	
Inadequately Institutionalized for Divorced	6 *	-- *	--------		*		-- *	*	⟩*	Areas of interaction between ex-spouses which are inadequately resolved by divorce. These are areas in which divorce reform is needed.
Institution of Divorce			3		4					
Canceled or Solved at Decree		2							5	
Eroded during Marriage	1									
Accreted during Marriage										
Assumed at Wedding										
Accreted during Courtship										

CONTRACT
KINSHIP and HOUSEHOLD

wife take on obligations to children as well as kinship obligations to one another. Child support—both financial and emotional—is taken as a matter of course to be the responsibility of both parents.

Only two of these many aspects of marriage are un-equivocally dissolved at the time of divorce. The legal relationship of spouses ends, and both are remarriage-able. The law also says quite unequivocally that their legitimate sexual rights in one another are canceled. By indirection, the domestic rights are also canceled.

Though domestic rights may be "canceled" by a decree, domestic problems are not solved by it. The decree ac-complishes only what we have called the legal divorce.

The institution of divorce is left with those problems the decree failed to solve. The institution of divorce in-volves a new form of financial co-operation between the ex-partners. Financial co-operation may be settled once and for all at the time of the decree, but if there are children, this financial co-operation is subject to recon-sideration by the court. Child support remains the re-sponsibility of both parents, but now their responsibilities are spelled out in somewhat greater detail—and there-fore there are more loopholes. The normative sort of child support known in the course of the marriage is no longer enough to ensure the support of the children. The activities and expectations of coparents are greatly dif-ferent in divorce from what they were during marriage.

Most divorcees change communities at the time of the decree, as they changed communities at the time of the wedding. Choice of community is now open to each, although the court may circumscribe the right of the parents to remove children from a specific state.

We are left with the residue—those aspects and factors of the marriage that have not been solved either by the decree or by the institution of divorce. The spiritual task of developing autonomy again; working out satisfactory emotional and training relationships with the children;

creation of adequate domestic groups so that physical and emotional security of adults and children is assured; the community into which divorced people move.

Divorce Reform

In discussing divorce reform, we must distinguish things we do badly and want to improve from things we do not do at all.

ASPECTS OF DIVORCE TO BE IMPROVED. The two main areas which we now deal with, but which could be improved, are the legal sphere and the psychological sphere. In Chapter 1 Doctor Bernard has described the legal reforms that are being worked out by the Commission on Uniform State Laws, to make breakdown of the marriage replace the old idea of grounds and the adversary procedure. England adopted such a basis for divorce in 1969. California was only a few months behind. There seems today to be general agreement in a major part of the population that (without "approving" of divorce) we should have less painful ways of canceling those marriages that cannot be saved. The family court proposal for California, outlined by Herma Kay above, is one of the most cogent of the movements in America. Here the "dissolution of the marriage" (rather than "divorce") would be heard by a court as a motion "in the interests of the John Doe family" rather than as *"Mary Doe v. John Doe."*

We are also living in the midst of a growing set of programs to establish and improve mental health facilities. Some of them are turning to the problems of divorced people and their children.

Both the legal and the psychiatric professions have turned their attention to the problem. It is not primarily in the decree-granting that we are hung up—it is in the institution of divorce that follows on a decree. There

less can be done because improvement demands fundamental social and cultural change. There is difficulty in
financial co-operation of ex-spouses that is vastly wasteful of legal activities and the time and effort of highly
trained people. And what we have is only a clumsy institution, involving the court as it does—clumsy when it
works at all.

Aspects of Divorce Reform in Which We Must Start from Scratch

We must look to the residues on the chart—areas in
which we do nothing. Americans badly need some kind
of community campaign for understanding the problems that regaining emotional autonomy involve, for creating for divorced persons a positive role with a moral
dimension, for creating a morality about the rights and
obligations of divorced coparents that depends less fully
on the courts for its sanctions and therefore is more likely
to work.

Perhaps most important of all, we have to provide,
hopefully through the private sector, the services required by households of divorce. If the private sector
cannot do it, then government must. Both the psychic
and the economic costs of running a single-parent household today are ruinous. Finally, we must deal with
amending and improving the community life of divorced
persons. There must be *something* besides Parents Without Partners to fill the gap between dating bars and soli-
tude.

We have not even mentioned here the problems of remarriage, and of the new kinds of extended families,
which Doctor Mead's chapter has gone into.

The Shield of Ignorance

The most discouraging factor for an investigator of divorce is the realization that large numbers of people, even divorced people, do not want to know anything about it. Yet, their number is, I think, dwindling. The first thing we must do to establish knowledge is to question the trite proverblike homilies: (1) Marriages should be saved. (2) When a marriage "dies," its shell is "insincere," "hypocritical," or, what seems to be worst of all, "cynical." (3) Easy divorce may lead to casual marriage and the demise of the family. (4) Difficult divorce may lead to unhappy and destructive marriages and the demise of the family. (5) Divorce is bad for children. Anybody who likes can add others—propositions that keep us from thinking; statements that block explanations because they masquerade as explanations.

Is DIVORCE BAD FOR CHILDREN? This is a silly question. Is polio bad for children? Of course divorce is bad for children—but living in the clogged atmosphere of emotional divorce may be worse than living in the cleared and knowledgeable atmosphere that can come with the completion of the six stations. Children need antidotes, not protection.

Although pediatricians, teachers, and psychiatrists have great funds of knowledge about the subject, little has been organized and published about the attitudes and ideas of the children themselves. The only "shocking" discovery of my study of divorce is the large number of divorced people who never give children any explanations, let alone adequate ones. "You can't kid kids —they know what is happening" is the refrain. The first half of the statement is undeniable—but the second half does not follow from it and is false. They know *something* is happening but, unless they are told, they seldom know what.

EASY AND DIFFICULT DIVORCE. I have never known a divorced person who got his divorce for silly or flimsy reasons. The grounds may have been trumped up and absurd—but the reasons were not. Ease and difficulty have little to do with grounds. Rather they have to do with the emotional tension and legal procedures that accompany divorce. Easing the grounds always follows wholesale dishonesty in using the grounds that were previously available—it is the law catching up with the community.

Although it is weakening, there is still an American penchant for resisting knowledge by claiming that it is inimical to good feelings. The homilies we have cited are old-fashioned. As Jessie Bernard said in the first chapter of this book: it is no news that new ideas are dominating the sexual, family, marriage, and divorce practices in this country. That being the case, we had better discover the new questions: How do we make the necessities of a full life available to people who happen to have failed at one of our favorite institutions? Moralize if we must—but we can no longer stop there. What is called for is massive community ingenuity. And the leaders in it will be—must be—intelligent and hard-working divorced people whose pain at their own situation has been turned to righteous wrath that society could make straightening out your life so difficult.

NOTES

1. A study, by Fred Plog and Paul Bohannan (NIMH Grant No. MHO6551), of articles indexed under "Divorce" and "Alimony" in *The Reader's Guide to Periodical Literature,* 1900–1965, reported an overall secular decline in number of such articles but with cyclical fluctuations (Figure 2). Notable for our purposes here was the decline in number of articles dealing with religious attitudes toward divorce, and divorce as a social evil. Interesting and relevant also was the increase in articles dealing with postdivorce problems and children of divorce. The implication is that the public had become reconciled to the existence of divorce and was now mainly concerned with ways of meeting it rather than bewailing it as a social problem.

2. The Reverend W. Nemser of Fairfax (Virginia) Unitarian Church has gone so far in structuring divorce as to work out a religious ceremony—"rite of passage"—to mark the end of a marriage. He was enraged at the attitudes which viewed the divorced as "cowards, miscreants, failures, godless, lecherous, immoral, and scrofulous." He would like to restore respect to those who find divorce a necessary step.

3. Vernier, Chester G. and Frank, L. A. *American Family Laws.* Stanford University Press, 1938, p. 5. In 1938, a poll by the *Ladies' Home Journal* reported that 82 per cent of the women who responded disapproved of alimony if there were no children and the woman could support herself (Pringle, Henry F. *Ladies' Home Journal,* February 1938). When David Susskind interviewed a trio of divorced women on his television pro-

gram in the winter of 1967, the audience expressed its disapproval of their acceptance of alimony.

4. Nye, F. Ivan and Hoffman, Lois W. *The Employed Mother in America*. Rand McNally, 1963, p. 8.

5. U. S. Census of Population, 1960, *Employment Status and Work Experience*, p. 25. In the 35 to 44 age bracket, 80.9 per cent were in the labor force. Among white women, the proportion was 66.8 per cent.

6. U. S. Census of Population, 1960, *Marital Status*, p. 97.

7. U. S. Department of Health, Education, and Welfare, Public Health Service, *Divorce Statistics, 1966* (January 6, 1969); *Divorce Statistics Analysis*, United States, Government Printing Office, 1963.

8. Ibid.

9. How a divorced man can be a good father without at the same time being the child's mother's husband is an extremely difficult problem. Elliott Liebow has made a perceptive analysis of the situation in the case of street-corner Negro men (*Tally's Corner*, Chapter 3, Little, Brown, 1966).

10. Nye and Hoffman, op. cit., pp. 3, 6.

11. Women's Bureau, *1969 Handbook on Women Workers* (United States Department of Labor, 1969), p. 41.

12. On the basis of a very small set of data—104 employed mothers and 82 mother-substitutes—one study concluded that "the employed mothers were fairly successful in finding and keeping the kind of mother-substitute they wanted, and . . . the treatment of the children was not radically different from that which they would have received from their mothers, had they not been working" (Ibid., p. 189). Employers, it was reported, felt no obligations in this area (Ibid., Chapter 26).

13. U. S. Census of Population, 1960, *Persons by Family Characteristics*, p. 7.

14. Parents Without Partners has 17,500 members in 160 local chapters and about 7,000,000 children are in-

volved. The organization publishes a magazine; it holds
annual conventions.

15. Goode, W. J. *World Revolution and Family Patterns.*
    Free Press, 1963, p. 84. Women seemed to be more ac-
    cepting than men; in the *Ladies' Home Journal* poll re-
    ferred to above, 69 per cent of the women "believed in"
    divorce, although they were no more liberal than the
    laws then actually in effect so far as acceptable grounds
    were concerned.
16. Tumin, Melvin. "The Functionalist Approach to Social
    Problems." *Social Problems,* Spring, 1965, p. 383.
17. Ibid., pp. 383–84.
18. Ibid., p. 384.
19. Ibid., p. 386. For further discussion of the defense of
    adultery see Bernard, Jessie. "Infidelity: Moral or So-
    cial Issue?" *Science and Psychoanalysis,* Vol. 16, 1970.
20. Tumin, Melvin. Loc. cit., p. 387.
21. See, for example, Despert, J. Louise. *Children of Di-
    vorce.* Delphic Books, 1962. None of the research con-
    cludes, of course, that children in broken homes do not
    suffer more than those in nonconflicted unbroken
    homes.
22. Bergler, Edmund. *Divorce Won't Help.* Harper, 1948.
23. Terman, L. M. and Wallin, Paul. "The Validity of
    Marriage Prediction and Marital Adjustment Tests."
    American Sociological Review, 14 (August 1949), pp.
    503–4.
24. Bernard, Jessie. *Remarriage, A Study of Marriage.* Dry-
    den Press, 1956, pp. 83–85.
25. Ibid., Chapter 3.
26. Ibid., pp. 108–13.
27. Neither the personality-oriented nor the team-oriented
    approach to the "causes" of divorce is, of course, com-
    plete. The "causes" of divorce also include, in addition
    to current ideologies and values (Goode, 1963, Chapter
    1), all the factors associated with the assimilation of di-
    vorce. Interesting in this connection is a study of di-

vorce in the Soviet Union which gave as major causes: hasty marriages, crowded housing conditions, meddlesome in-laws, and drunkenness.

28. The process by which the friendly divorce became acceptable, even respectable, in the highest social classes can be traced in the works of Edith Wharton and Emily Post. For this class, divorce was assimilated in the second decade of this century. Edith Wharton pinpointed the precise generation in which it occurred in her short story "Autre Temps." In this story a woman who had lost her position in society when she divorced her husband returns to this country for the remarriage of her own divorced daughter. She finds that women were no longer *déclassée* if they had been divorced. She was herself still rejected; but everyone accepted her daughter. The old disapproval of divorce and the punitive attitude toward those who dissolved their marriages had all but disappeared. Thus in early editions of Emily Post's book on etiquette, "according to the rules of etiquette, as codified by Emily Post, divorced persons were supposed to meet socially as non-speaking strangers, the underlying theory being . . . that the divorce would not have been sought in the first place if the grievance of one of the parties had not been irreparable and unforgivable. But as divorces became more common, particularly with the advent and spread of 'friendly divorces,' this rule became difficult to enforce. In some social circles it would have meant that an awkwardly large number of people, including the friends of divorced persons, would find themselves in embarrassing situations. The old rule was therefore changed by consensus and later formulated by Mrs. Post. Now it is quite proper for divorced persons to meet as friends" (Bernard, Jessie. *American Family Behavior*, pp. 210–11). So many highly thought of men and women had resorted to divorce—millions of people voted for a divorced man for the presidency in 1952—that wide-

spread condemnation would belie the facts. The apotheosis, if not a burlesque, on the concept of the friendly divorce was that of Frank Sinatra. According to press reports, he continued to retain a warm, intimate, post-divorce relationship with his first wife and children along with a number of remarriages and attachments to other women. His daughter, for her part, understandably noted that divorce could be fun. An older concept was represented by Marlene Dietrich who remained married to her first husband from first to last, reflecting an old European attitude toward the formal inviolability of the marital bond which did not, however, interfere with public friendships with other men. Evelyn, M. "Idol Remembered." *Esquire Magazine,* 64 (July 1965), pp. 84–85.

29. Nimkoff, M. F. "Contributions to a Therapeutic Solution to the Divorce Problem: Sociology," paper in Conference on Divorce, The Law School, University of Chicago, 9, 1952, pp. 55–62.

30. Levy, Robert. *Uniform Marriage and Divorce Legislation: A Preliminary Analysis,* prepared for the Special Committee on Divorce of the National Conference of Commissioners on Uniform State Laws (mimeographed, no date).

31. Kinsey, Alfred C.; Pomeroy, Wardell B.; and Martin, Clyde E. *Sexual Behavior in the Human Male.* Saunders, 1948, pp. 585–86.

32. Public Health Service, National Center for Health Statistics, *Divorce Statistics Analysis 1963,* Series 21, No. 13, October 1967, Table 7, p. 49.

33. Kinsey, 1948, op. cit., p. 412. The authors explain the exception in terms of too small a sample size. In any event, the divorce rate is lower in the more highly educated segment of the population.

34. Kinsey, Alfred C.; Pomeroy, Wardell B.; Martin, Clyde E.; and Gebhard, Paul. *Sexual Behavior in the Human Female.* Saunders, 1953, p. 442.

35. Ibid., p. 434.
36. Ibid.
37. Ibid., pp. 434–35.
38. Cuber, John F. and Harroff, Peggy B. *Sex and the Significant Americans*. Penguin Books, 1966.
39. See Bernard, Jessie. "Infidelity, A Moral or Social Issue?" *Science and Psychoanalysis*, Vol. 16, 1970.
40. ". . . decrees are obtained on the ground that is least unpleasant to claim and easiest to establish in legal proceedings." U. S. Department of Health, Education, and Welfare, Public Health Service, op. cit., p. 28.
41. Kinsey and his associates are more tentative in their discussion of extramarital relations than in discussion of other "outlets." They conclude that "it is probably safe to suggest that about half of all the married males have intercourse with women other than their wives, at some time while they are married" (Kinsey, 1953, op. cit., p. 585); such relations tend to occur early in the marriage of lower-class men; later, in higher-class levels (p. 587).
42. Public Health Service, National Center for Health Statistics, *Divorce Statistics Analysis 1963*, Series 21, No. 13, October 1967, Table 7, p. 49.
43. Bernard, Jessie. "The Adjustments of Married Mates," in *Handbook of Marriage and the Family*. Harold Christensen, ed., Rand McNally, 1964, pp. 675–739; Lee Rainwater. "Some Aspects of Lower-Class Sexual Behavior." *Journal of Social Issues* 22, April 1966, pp. 96–108.
44. Komarovsky, Mirra. *Blue-Collar Marriage*. Random House, 1966. The parallel or segregated pattern may be said to constitute, in effect, a kind of institutionalized quasi-divorced status. The interests of the two partners are certainly not divorced; but there might well be a divorce-type situation so far as the personalities of the spouses are concerned.
45. Bernard, Jessie. *American Family Behavior*. Harper, 1942, p. 18.

46. Jacobson, Paul H. *American Marriage and Divorce*. Rinehart, 1959.

47. In North Carolina, over 90 per cent use this ground; in Louisiana, about two-thirds (Ibid., p. 125).

48. Goode, W. J. *After Divorce*. Free Press, 1956, pp. 133, 136, 140–41, 150. Among urban couples, desertion may be an acceptable substitute for voluntary separation. In the 1880s, desertion was alleged in almost half (40 per cent) of all divorces; at mid-century, fewer than half that many (18 per cent) were using this ground (Jacobson, op. cit., p. 124). Jacobson explains this drop by the younger age at divorce; the longer a marriage lasts, the longer the time a spouse has in which to desert. But the same could be said of any grounds for divorce.

49. Sumner, William Graham. *Folkways*. Ginn & Co., 1906.

50. The concept of a divorce rate is by no means unequivocal. One measure uses total population as the basis; another uses the total number of marriages; still another uses the ratio between marriages and divorces in a given year. They do not always coincide (Bernard, 1964, op. cit., p. 721).

51. National Center for Health Statistics, *Monthly Vital Statistics Report*, March 12, 1969.

52. Christensen, Harold T. and Barber, Kenneth E. "Interfaith versus Intrafaith Marriage in Indiana." *Journal of Marriage and the Family*, 29 August 1967, pp. 461–69.

53. If they were willing to picket for the right to freedom under Clark Kerr, they would not hesitate to picket for the same right under anyone else.

54. Kinsey, 1948, op. cit., Chapter 10.

55. Ibid., p. 587.

56. Even public assistance cases were organizing to protest against investigators hired to report on their private lives. Research questionnaires used in projects funded by the government were scrutinized for invasion of privacy.

Legislation was contemplated against the use of bugging devices.

CHAPTER 2

1. The parts of this book that were written by Paul Bohannan are based on research carried out between 1963 and 1966 under grants MH 06551-01A1 and MH 11544-01 of the National Institute of Mental Health, and grant No. GS-61 from the National Science Foundation.

CHAPTER 3

1. Rangell, Leo. 1963. "On Friendship." *Journal of the American Psychoanalytic Association* 11:3–54.
2. Freud, Sigmund (1921). 1949. *Group Psychology and the Analysis of the Ego*. New York: Liveright Publishing Corp.
3. Alexander, Franz. 1930. "The Neurotic Character." *International Journal of Psychoanalysis* 11:292–311.
4. Freud, Sigmund (1910). 1948. "Contributions to the Psychology of Love. A Special Type of Choice of Object made by Men." *Collected Papers* 4:192–202. London: Hogarth Press.
5. Blos, Peter. 1962. *On Adolescence: A Psychoanalytic Interpretation*. New York: Free Press.
6. Freud, Anna. 1946. *The Ego and the Mechanisms of Defense*. New York: International Universities Press.
7. Erikson, Erik H. 1956. "The Problem of Ego Identity." *Journal of the American Psychoanalytic Association* 4:56–121.
8. Alexander, Franz. 1930. Op. cit.
9. Gitelson, Maxwell. 1963. "On the Problem of Character Neurosis." *Journal of the Hillside Hospital* 12:3–17.
10. Fenichel, Otto. 1945. *The Psychoanalytic Theory of Neurosis*. New York: W. W. Norton & Co.

Chapter 4

1. Hunt, 1966, p. 144, believes that nearly all men and about four-fifths of the women ultimately have post-marital coitus.

2. Kinsey, A.; Pomeroy, W.; Martin, C.; and Gebhard, P., 1953. *Sexual Behavior in the Human Female.* Philadelphia: W. B. Saunders.

3. Technically, such calculations are labeled "age-specific" and may be made for incidence and frequency of behavior.

4. Christenson, C. and Gagnon, J., 1965. "Sexual Behavior in a Group of Older Women." *Journal of Gerontology.* Vol. 20, No. 3, p. 352.

5. This agrees with what we learned in our prior analysis of female sexuality (Kinsey et al., 1953).

6. This means that only 3 per cent of the divorced had had extramarital coitus but *not* in the final year of the marriage.

7. This agrees with Hunt, 1966, p. 144, who feels that most postmarital women resume coitus within a year.

8. Kinsey et al., 1953, p. 292, in speaking of married women who had had premarital coitus, state that 46 per cent had had such coitus only with the fiancé.

9. Terman, 1938, p. 418, also found that about 82 per cent of the divorced and remarried women in his sample had had postmarital coitus with their subsequent spouses.

10. Kinsey et al., 1953.

11. Hunt, 1966, in his excellent book on the formerly married notes that there is evidence that the widowed are much less permissive sexually than the divorced. Lack of permissiveness and lack of response often go hand in hand.

12. Kinsey et al., 1953. Page 736 reports the average of onset of menopause as 46.3. Thus a moderate number would experience menopausal symptoms in age-period

41–45 and we know such symptoms have a depressant effect (largely psychogenic) on the sexual activities of many females.

13. Kinsey et al., 1953. See Table 106 on page 404 for marital coitus. One may draw some crude inferences regarding nonmarital coitus from Table 121, p. 443 and Table 90, p. 343 (use Protestants only).
14. Kinsey et al., 1953. Table 106, p. 404. About 40 to 50 per cent of the married women reached orgasm in their marital coitus 90 per cent of the time or more.
15. Gebhard, 1966, p. 90.

CHAPTER 5

1. Mead, Margaret. 1935. *Sex and Temperament in Three Primitive Societies*. New York: William Morrow & Co. [Reprinted 1963, Apollo A–67, Morrow]
2. Mead, Margaret. 1935. *Sex and Temperament.*
3. Fortune, R. F. 1932. *Sorcerers of Dobu; The Social Anthropology of the Dobu Islanders of the Western Pacific.* New York: E. P. Dutton & Co.
4. Mead, Margaret. 1949. *Male and Female.* New York: William Morrow & Co. [Reprinted 1955, Mentor MD150, New American Library and by the University of Nebraska Press]
5. Mead, Margaret. 1949. *Male and Female.*
6. Cohen, Yehudi A. 1964. *The Transition from Childhood to Adolescence.* Chicago: Aldine Press.
   Parsons, Talcott. 1954. "The Incest Taboo in Relation to Social Structure and the Socialization of the Child." *British Journal of Sociology* 5:101–17.
   Mead, Margaret. 1968. "Incest" for the *International Encyclopedia of the Social Sciences.* New York: Macmillan and Free Press.
7. Henry, Jules. 1941. *Jungle People.* New York: Augustin. [Reprinted 1964, Vintage V521, Random House]
8. Landes, Ruth and Zborowski, Mark. 1950. "Hypotheses

Concerning the Eastern Jewish Family." *Psychiatry* 13:447–64.

9. Aberle, David F.; Bronfenbrenner, Urie; Hess, Eckhard H.; Miller, Daniel R.; Schneider, David M.; and Spuhler, James N. 1963. "The Incest Taboo and the Mating Pattern of Animals." *American Anthropologist* 65:253–65.

10. Weinberg, S. Kirson. 1955. *Incest Behavior*. New York: Citadel Press.

11. Mead, Margaret. 1962. "Outdoor Recreation in the Context of Emerging American Cultural Values." In *Trends in American Living and Outdoor Recreation*. Reports to the Outdoor Recreation Resources Review Commission No. 22 (pp. 2–25). Washington, Government Printing Office.

12. Wolfenstein, Martha. 1946. *The Impact of a Children's Story on Mothers and Children*. Monographs of the Society for Research in Child Development, Vol. 11, Ser. 42. Washington: National Research Council.
Mead, Margaret. 1955. "Implications of Insight—II" in *Childhood in Contemporary Cultures*. Margaret Mead and Martha Wolfenstein, eds. (pp. 449–61). Chicago: University of Chicago Press. [Reprinted 1963, Phoenix P124, University of Chicago Press]

CHAPTER 7

1. A comprehensive presentation will, it is hoped, be published shortly. Special Studies published so far are the following:
Rheinstein, M. "Trends in Marriage and Divorce in Western Countries." 18 Law and Contemporary Problems 3 (1953); Rheinstein, M. "The Law of Divorce and the Problem of Marriage Stability." 9 Vanderbilt Law Review 633 (1956);
Rheinstein, M. "Lectures on Marriage and Divorce" (in Japanese with English summary). Tokyo, 1963;

Rheinstein, M. and Watanabe, Yozo. "The Family and
the Law. The Individualistic Premise and Modern
Japanese Family Law," in A. von Mehren (ed.),
*Law in Japan: The Legal Order in a Changing So-
ciety* (1963);

Rheinstein, M. "The Code and the Family," in: New
York University Institute of Comparative Law.
*The Code Napoleon and The Common Law
World.* 1956.

Rheinstein, M. "Modern Civil Law. Family Law and
Succession," in: Yiannopolous (ed.), *Civil Law in
the Modern World.* 1965.

Rheinstein, M. "An Inquiry into the State of Marriage
Stability in the Swiss and the Italian Parts of the
Italian-Swiss Border Region," in: Festschrift für
Hans Ficker; in press.

Wolf, E., Lüke, G., and Hax, H. *Scheidung und
Scheidungsrecht.* 485 pp., Tübingen, 1959;

Rheinstein, M. "Divorce and the Law in Germany." 65
Am. J. of Sociology 489. 1960 (review of the book
just listed).

Mueller, G. W. "Inquiry into the State of a Divorceless
Society. Domestic Relations Law and Morals in
England from 1660 to 1857." 18 Univ. of Pitts-
burgh Law Rev. 545 (1957).

Two international conferences were sponsored by the
University of Chicago Comparative Law Research Center. The first was held in 1956 in Santiago de Com-
postela, Spain. Papers were presented to it by W. Czachorski (Poland), J. L. Aguilar Gorrondona (Spain),
L. de Luca (Italy), P. L. Vallindas and others (Greece),
J. Limpens (Belgium), R. H. Graveson (England),
G. Marty (France), C. J. Arnholm (Norway), K. Red-
den, T. Esener and N. Seymen (Turkey), B. T.
Blagojevic (Yugoslavia), G. M. Swerdlov (U.S.S.R.)
and M. Rheinstein (U.S.A.). They are published in

Revista del Instituto de Derecho Comparado, No. 8–9, Barcelona, 1957, pp. 467–725.

The second conference convened in 1957 at the University of Chicago. Papers were submitted by H. Ficker (Germany), H. Hinderling (Switzerland), J. M. Mogey (England), T. Sameshima (Japan), G. Marty (France), J. Melander (Finland), G. Karlsson (Sweden), B. T. Blagojevic and W. Bonac (Yugoslavia), W. Czachorski (Poland), and W. L. McCurdy, Q. Johnstone, P. V. Alexander, A. Platerifs, E. W. Burgess, J. P. Spiegel, Q. Johnstone, H. G. Foster and M. Rheinstein (U.S.A.). They are published in *Annales de la Faculté de droit d'Istanbul,* tome IX, 1960, 379 pp.

2. In the presentation of the Swedish law of divorce the author could draw upon an extensive report prepared at the University of Chicago Comparative Law Research Center by Mr. Sven Beckman of Stockholm.

Other principal sources were: Sellin, Johan Thorsten. "Marriage and Divorce Legislation in Sweden" (doctoral dissertation presented to the University of Pennsylvania), 1922. English translation of the Swedish statute, with explanation.

Schmidt, Folke. *Äktenskapsrätt,* Stockholm, 1964.

Schmidt, Folke. The "leniency" of the Scandinavian Divorce laws. 7 *Scandinavian Studies in Law* 107 (1962–1963).

Nylander, Ivar. *Studier Rörande den Svenska Äktenskaprättens Historia.* Upsala, 1961.

3. This idea is neatly expressed in the formula prescribed to be used by the pastor or the secular official by whom the marriage is performed. As prescribed by the Royal Proclamation of 3 December 1915, the secular officiant has to address the parties as follows:

"The end of marriage is the welfare of the individual and the maintenance of society. You have expressed your desire to enter matrimony. Do you, A.B., take C.D. as your wife for better or for worse?— Do you, C.D., take A.B. as your husband for better or for worse? Take each other's hands in confirmation. By virtue of my office, I declare you husband and wife. Never forget the promise of lifelong faith, which you have now made. Live together in mutual love, confidence and respect, and consider your responsibility to future generations. May happiness and unity be yours and bless your home."

Two ends of marriage are stated in this formula, the welfare of the individual and the maintenance of society, but significantly, the first place is given to the individual.

4. U. S. Department of Health, Education, and Welfare. Public Health Service, Vital and Health Statistics; Divorce Statistics.

5. Sipilä, Helvi. *Bor Lagstiftningen om Äktenskapskilnad Reformeras?* Vammala (Finland), 1957, p. 41.

6. Nordic Council, Yearbook of Nordic Statistics, 1965, p. 25; 1967, Table 22.

7. The determination of what right of maintenance, if any, one party has against the other, is an incident of the action for judicial separation.

8. In Sweden 99 per cent.

9. On Swedish attitudes toward sex, see the article on "L'amour en liberté," in *L'Express*, no. 708 (January 1965), 1.34.

10. In seventeenth-century Sweden a letter of divorcement would be issued to a married person if her or his spouse had left the realm with the intent permanently to terminate the marital community of life. A letter of divorcement would also be issued if a party to a marriage had left home for a legitimate reason but had not been heard of for seven years. No divorce was available if a spouse willfully deserted the home and remained inside the realm at a known address or drove the other spouse out of the home. In such cases, the procedure was to be that applicable to "quarrelsome couples." Through the

means of church discipline, the clergy had to reconcile the parties. In case of refusal, punishment would be meted out by the secular court.

11. The first was King Christian V Law, enacted for Denmark in 1683 and for Norway in 1687. The Swedish Code, profoundly amended many times is, in form, still in effect in Sweden as well as in Finland, which at the time of the Code's enactment was a part of the Swedish realm.

12. The jurisdiction belongs to the Parliament of the Dominion rather than that of the Province, because under the British North America Act, 1867, which still operates as Canada's constitution, jurisdiction to legislate on matters of marriage and divorce belongs to the Dominion rather than to the Provinces (see Art. 91).

13. See Blake, Nelson M. *The Road to Reno*. New York: Macmillan (1962), 48 et s.

14. The Danish data for the period from 1954 to 1960 were as follows:

| | DIVORCES GRANTED BY | | |
	Local admin. authority	Ministry of Justice	The courts
1948	6777		549
1954	6193	15	478
1955	6290	19	462
1956	5997	10	492
1957	5978	8	450
1958	6069	15	487
1959	5937	9	511
1963	5935	3	522
1964	5970	0	513

Source: Danmarks Statistik Ärbog 1960; 1966, Table 24

15. A typical consent divorce is described by August Strindberg in his play, *The Tie* (Bandet).

16. See page 20a.

17. Percentages of Population occupied in

	1870	1920	1945	1950
Agriculture	51.6	38.4	28.2	23.4
industry, commerce, and communications	12.5	44.2	57.0	63.0

SOURCE: *Handwörterbuch der Sozialwissenschaften,* vol. 9, p. 162 (1956).

18. See Ekeberg, Birger. "The Scandinavian Co-operation in the Field of Legislation," in *Institut international pour l'unification du droit privé,* Unification of Law, vol. 1 p. 321, 1948; Bagge, Algott. "The Uniform Laws of the Nordic Countries," in the same publication, Yearbook 1961, p. 179.

19. The *Nya Jordabalken* was promulgated as Law of 1. June 1907.

20. Until 1781 marriage could not be celebrated in any way other than by ceremony in the Lutheran State Church By Royal Decree of 24 January 1781, Catholics and members of other "alien faiths" were granted the freedom to form congregations and with it the privilege of concluding marriages in accordance with their rites. In 1782, Jews were given the same privilege; but not until 1863 was intermarriage permitted between Jews and Christians. It was for such marriages that the possibility of a nonreligious ceremony was for the first time provided in Sweden. For other persons, the possibility of secular marriage was opened through the Dissenter Law of 1873 and a law of 1908.

21. See Karlsson, G. "Social Policies and Marriage Stability in Sweden," *Annales de a Faculté de droit de l'Université d'Istanbul,* tome IX, p. 240 (1960).

22. Swedish law of 17 June 1938.

23. The term *divorce faillite* is widely used in French parlance. It refers to the view in which divorce is regarded as an escape from a marriage that has become bankrupt

in contrast to a *divorce sanction,* i.e. the view under which divorce is treated as the punishment meted out by an innocent party to a partner who has become guilty of adultery or other marital misconduct. The corresponding German terms are *Zerrüttungsprinzep* and *Verschuldensprinzep.*

24. See Law of 28 May 1959 (SFS nr. 287) 13 § 2.
25. See *supra,* p. XXX.
26. See Borum, O. A. *Familieretten,* 2 ed., 1946, p. 112.
27. Sipilä, 1.c. 2.
28. See *supra.*
29. Marriage Law, Chapter 11. § 24.
30. Sec. 29. A different standard is stated for the wife's separate maintenance before divorce. Since she is still his wife, the husband has to maintain her on the same standard on which she would live if there were no separation. But allowance is to be made for the increase in cost due to the necessity of supporting two separate households. It would be interesting to know how this provision works out in the case of a man whose income just suffices to maintain one household.

CHAPTER 8

1. (Befu, 1964; Ben-Dor, 1966; Damas, 1963, 1964; Gradburn, 1964; Guemple, 1965, 1966; Heinrich, 1960, 1963; Hughes, 1958, 1960; and Lantis, 1946, 1960.)
2. The studies most relevant to this paper are the following, only a portion of the total literature on North Alaska: Burch, 1966; Gubser, 1965; Heinrich, 1955a, 1955b, 1960, 1963; Pospisil, 1964; Pospisil and Laughlin, 1963; and Spencer, 1959. For a general description of the life of the people living in the northern portion of this region, see Chance, 1966.
3. In this and subsequent diagrams, a triangle indicates a male and a circle a female. An equal sign indicates a marital tie. These symbols are in common use among anthropologists.

4. *Actually*, of course, the relationship was a crucial one for the society from a number of points of view.

5. In everyday American speech, we are accustomed to using the term "polygamy" to refer to the situation of a man having two or more wives. Technically, however, such a situation is known as "polygyny." Its counterpart, where one woman has two husbands, is called "polyandry." Both polygyny and polyandry are included under the rubric "polygamy," which means simply "plural marriage" of any kind.

6. It has sometimes been claimed that baby girls were frequently put to death at birth in the traditional society. This situation would have resulted in more men than women, a further limitation on the possibilities for polygyny. The *actual frequency* of infanticide of any kind has been questioned (Burch, 1966), however, at least insofar as the North Alaskan Eskimos are concerned. On the other hand, it has been suggested that the hazards of hunting would have resulted in a higher death rate for men than for women. This would have increased the opportunities for polygyny. While this seems a reasonable proposition, it is one that has yet to be examined with sufficient thoroughness to permit definite statements on the subject one way or the other. Consequently, we must assume that males and females were roughly equal in number in the society until it is demonstrated to have been otherwise.

7. The field research which formed the basis for the "breakthrough" in our understanding of this custom was conducted by Albert Heinrich (1955a, 1955b, 1960, 1963). Heinrich's work was followed by a study in which Guemple (1961) reviewed the entire literature, both published and unpublished, dealing with exchange practices. Subsequent field research of my own has confirmed the general conclusions reached by Heinrich and Guemple, and has started to fill in the details.

8. Heinrich, 1955a: 134 ff.

9. The North Alaskans were apparently more extreme in their treatment of strangers than were other Eskimo groups.

10. As is true of most aspects of kinship, the Eskimos divided siblings along different lines than we do, a matter which cannot be more fully explored here.

11. After a time, almost everyone in an Eskimo village could become related through this process if carried on over even a few generations. There were, however, various social mechanisms for getting around this problem when necessary. In addition, certain factors operated to counteract this unifying tendency, so that actual situations were generally less complicated in this respect than one might be led to suspect.

12. Heinrich, 1955a: 170.

13. This greatly minimized the possibility of a wife being "exchanged" or "loaned" by her *ui* to another man. If she did not approve, she could divorce her husband on the spot.

14. Hunt, 1966: 203.

15. This raises the question of where the *relatives* of the spouses fit into the divorce situation. This question, which is not often dealt with, would probably be a most interesting one to consider, especially in any sort of cross-cultural analysis of marriage, divorce, and their implications.

16. Levy, 1952: 256.

17. I do not mean to imply by this remark that economic functions alone were served by this relationship. On the contrary, numerous others, many of them crucial for the operation of the society, were also fulfilled through the operation of the *ui-nuliaq* relationship, but on the whole they seem either to have been unrecognized or were simply considered relatively unimportant by the Eskimos themselves.

18. The North Alaskan Eskimos seem to have been more extreme in this respect than their relatives to the east in

Canada and Greenland. This is possibly a consequence of the fact that subsistence conditions were generally more favorable in Alaska than they were to the east, hence this particular ideal would have been more easily attained there.

19. Spencer, 1959: 182 ff.
20. My remarks on the postdivorce situation in the United States are based largely on Goode's study *After Divorce* (Free Press, 1956), and Hunt's *The World of the Formerly Married* (McGraw, 1967). The discussion is most applicable to the middle and upper levels of United States society, and less so at the lower levels.
21. Precise data are lacking but the "between-marriage" period for the traditional North Alaskan Eskimos was probably measured in terms of days, weeks, or months, but rarely, if ever, in years. This is in sharp contrast with our own system.
22. This brings up an important point which should not be overlooked, namely, that the Eskimos did have other, non-marital relationships which were very strong indeed. Among the Eskimos, parent-child, sibling, and cousin relationships *at least* were all much stronger than are the comparable relationships in our own society.
23. Goode, 1956: 207, 216.
24. Hunt's (1966) more recent account of the postmarital situation indicates that the patterns which are now beginning to develop to guide behavior during this period are overwhelmingly oriented to getting people over the trauma of their divorce, and to the location and recruitment of new spouses. In other words, the "formerly married" state remains highly unsatisfactory to most people involved in it even though some sort of structure is beginning to evolve. This suggests that it is not lack of definition that is the key to remarriage. On the contrary, I see it as another affirmation of the great strength which marriage has in our society.

25. Goode, 1956: 306.
26. Hunt, 1966: Chapter 7.
27. Even though the postmarriage situation is becoming increasingly structured in the United States with respect to husband-wife interaction, I have yet to hear of any satisfactory developments along these lines as far as children are concerned.

CHAPTER 9

1. Ardener, E., 1962. *Divorce and Fertility: An African Study*. Nigerian Social and Economic Studies, No. 3. (Nigerian Institute of Social and Economic Research.) London: Oxford University Press.
2. Cohen, Ronald, 1966. "The Bornu King Lists," in *Boston University Publications in African History*. Vol. II. J. Butler, ed. (pp. 41–83). Boston: Boston University Press.
3. Greenberg, Joseph H., 1954. "Studies in African Linguistic Classification." *Southwestern Journal of Anthropology* 10:405–15.
4. Cohen, Ronald, 1967a. *The Kanuri of Bornu*. New York: Holt, Rinehart & Winston.
5. Cohen, Ronald (in press). "From Empire to Colony: Bornu in the Nineteenth and Twentieth Centuries," in *The Impact of Colonialism*. Victor W. Turner, ed. Stanford: The Hoover Institute.
6. Cohen, Ronald, 1967b. "Social Stratification in Bornu," in *Class and Status in Sub-Saharan Africa*. A. Tuden and L. Plotnicov, eds. New York: The Free Press.
7. Levy, R., 1957. *The Social Structure of Islam* (2nd ed.) (p. 98, Koran 4). Cambridge: University Press.
8. Cohen, Ronald, 1967a. Op. cit. (pp. 39–40).
9. Cohen, Ronald, 1967a. Op. cit. (p. 40).
10. Cohen, Ronald, 1967a. Op. cit.
11. Bohannan, Paul and Huckleberry, Karan, 1967. "Institutions of Divorce, Family and the Law," *Law and Society Review*, Vol. I, No. 2, pp. 81–102.

12. Cohen, Ronald, 1967b. Op. cit.
13. Pushkin, A. and Cohen, Ronald, 1967. "The Values of Modernization," *Journal of the Developing Areas*, Vol. 2, pp. 7–22.

CHAPTER 10

1. The Report of the Governor's Commission on the Family (Sacramento, California: December 1966). Pages 124–44 contain an annotated bibliography on the legal articles dealing with the family court. This report will be quoted at numerous places in the text, and when no specific references for quotations are given, it is this report that is quoted. For those readers who are interested in the legal references, another version of this article prepared for the legal specialist is published in 56 Calif. L. Rev. 1205. (1968.)
2. Alexander, P. *Family Life Conference Suggests New Judicial Procedures and Attitudes Toward Marriage and Divorce*, 32 J. Am. Jud. Scc'y. 38, 41 (1948). *See also* by the same author, *The Family Court—an Obstacle Race?* 19 U. Pitt. L. Rev. 602 (1958); *Legal Science and the Social Sciences: The Family Court*, 21 Mo. L. Rev. 105 (1956); *Let's Get the Embattled Spouses out of the Trenches*, 18 Law & Contemp. Prob. 98 (1953).
3. 387 U.S. 1, 87 S.Ct. 1428 (1967). *Gault* involved the commitment of a fifteen-year-old boy to an Arizona training school because his participation in a lewd telephone call to a married woman indicated to the juvenile court judge that the boy was habitually involved in immoral matters. The commitment was intended for the duration of the boy's minority, although the maximum penalty under Arizona law for an adult who made lewd telephone calls was a fine of from $5.00 to $50 or imprisonment for not more than two months. No notice of their son's arrest or detention was given to his parents,

and they did not learn of the court hearing until the evening before it was held. Neither the boy nor his parents were represented by counsel during the proceedings, nor were they advised of their right to counsel. No record was kept of the hearings. The juvenile court judge committed the boy to the training school. His decision was upheld by the Supreme Court of Arizona, but the United States Supreme Court reversed. The case has created a revolution in juvenile court law and has been widely discussed. *See generally*, C. Tenney, *The New Dilemma in the Juvenile Court*, 47 Neb. L. Rev. 67 (1968); O. Ketcham, *Guidelines from Gault: Revolutionary Requirements and Reappraisal*, 53 Va. L. Rev. 1700 (1967); G. Parker, *The Century of the Child*, 45 Can. B. Rev. 741 (1967); M. Paulson, *The Constitutional Domestication of the Juvenile Court*, in 1967 Supreme Court Review 233 (P. Kurland, ed.) Univ. of Chi. Press, 1967; S. Rubin, *The Juvenile Court System in Evolution*, 2 Valparaiso U. L. Rev. 1 (1967); Comment, *Children are People*, 55 Calif. L. Rev. 1204 (1967). The Court's opinion itself contains a detailed review of recent literature criticizing the juvenile court; *see* 387 U.S. at 14–31; 87 S.Ct. at 1437–43.

4. The President's Comm'n. on Law Enforcement and the Administration of Justice Task Force Report on Juvenile Delinquency and Youth Crime 7 (1967). A study cited by the Task Force Report indicated that of the 1564 juvenile court judges who responded to a questionnaire (70 per cent of the total), half had not received undergraduate degrees, a fifth had received no college education at all, and a fifth were not members of the bar. The very scarcity of juvenile court judges is also a serious problem. For a thoughtful study of the use of referees to supplement judges in the California juvenile courts, see A. Gough, *Referees in California's Juvenile*

Courts: A Study in Sub-Judicial Adjudication, 19 Hastings L. J. 3 (1967).

5. *In re Gault, supra* n. 3, 387 U.S. at 17–18, 87 S.Ct. at 1438–39.

6. Rheinstein, M. *The Law of Divorce and the Problem of Marriage Stability,* 9 Vand. L. Rev. 633, 639 (1956). *See also id.,* at 635–40.

7. Clark, H. The Law of Domestic Relations in the United States 280–85 (1968); Madden, J. Handbook of the Law of Persons and Domestic Relations, 256–61 (1931); McCurdy, W. *Divorce—A Suggested Approach with Particular Reference to Dissolution for Living Separate and Apart,* 9 Vand. L. Rev. 685 (1956).

8. *Beeby* v. *Beeby,* 1 Hagg. Ecc. 789, 790; 162 Eng. Rep. 755, 756 (1799). Compare Cal. Civ. Code §§ 122–23 (West, 1954).

9. Philips, I. "*Mental Hygiene, Divorce and the Law.*" 3 J. Fam. L. 63 (1963); Watson, A. "Psychoanalysis and Divorce," in *The Marriage Relationship* 321, 332 (Rosenbaum S., & Alger, I., eds., 1968); *see generally,* Despert, J. L. *Children of Divorce* (1953).

10. Wadlington, W. "Divorce Without Fault, Without Perjury," 52 Va. L. Rev. 32, 82 (1966); *see also* Bradway, J. "The Myth of the Innocent Spouse," in Selected Essays on Family Law 937 (Association of American Law Schools ed. 1950).

11. *DeBurgh* v. *DeBurgh,* 39 Cal.2d 858, 863–64; 250 P.2d 598, 601 (1952).

12. Armstrong, B. *California Family Law* 123 (1953). *See also* Armstrong, B. "Family Law: Order Out of Chaos." 53 Calif. L. Rev. 121, 122–24 (1965).

13. Divorce in California: "Initial Complaints for Divorce, Annulment and Separate Maintenance," 1966, Table 63, p. 175; Tables 3 & 4, pp. 116–17 (State of California, Department of Public Health, Bureau of Vital Statistics, 1967).

14. Report 119–20, n. 23. For similar examples of the form language used in uncontested divorces in other jurisdictions, see Foote, C.; Levy, R.; and Sander, F. *Cases and Materials on Family Law* 683–701 (1966).

15. *See generally* Rheinstein, M. *supra* n. 6 at 634–35; Rheinstein, M. *The Law in Action Versus the Law of Books.* 9 University of Chicago Law School Conference Series 39 (1962).

16. Virtue, M. *Family Cases in Court.* 86091 (1956).

17. Report of a Group Appointed by the Archbishop of Canterbury. *Putting Asunder: A Divorce Law for Contemporary Society* papa 23. (S.P.C.K., 1966) (hereafter cited as *Putting Asunder*); see also Report 26–29.

18. 39 Cal.2d at 863–64; 250 P.2d at 601.

19. REPORT 91: Two bills were introduced into the California Legislature in 1967 for the purpose of proposing the commission's recommendations: S.B. 826, introduced by Senator Grunsky, and A.B. 1420 introduced by Assemblyman Shoemaker, both members of the commission. The bills were reintroduced during the 1968 session as S.B. 88 and A.B. 230. Both bills had the same section numbers on each occasion and will henceforth be cited simply by section. The standard for dissolution is found in § 4716. The bill was reintroduced in 1969 as S.B. 252. For a discussion of the final version of S.B. 252, which was enacted in 1969, see text at Note 40.

20. REPORT 83; § 4707. The caseload of the family court may make group counseling advisable. For an interesting analysis of the confidentiality to be accorded group sessions, see Note, *Group Therapy and Privileged Communication.* 43 Ind. L. Rev. 93 (1967).

21. Foster, H. *Conciliation and Counseling in the Courts in Family Law Cases.* 41 N.Y.U. L. Rev. 353, 357–58, 363–64, 381 (1966).

22. Bohannan, P. and Huckleberry, K. *Institutions of Di-*

vorce, *Family and the Law*. 1 Law and Society Rev. 81 (1967).

23. Simon, A. *Stepchild in the Family*. (1964.)

24. Despert, J. L. *Children of Divorce*. (1953.)

25. Kubie, L. "Psychoanalysis and Marriage," in *Neurotic Interaction in Marriage*. 10, 14–15 (Eisenstein, V., ed., 1956); Eidelberg, L. "Neurotic Choice of Mate," in *id.*, 57, 63 (1956). *See also* Watson, A. *supra* note 9, at 328–29.

26. *E.g.*, Eidelberg, L. *Id.*, at 63–64; Reider, N. "Problems in the Prediction of Marital Adjustment," in *id.*, 311, 320–25; Bergler, E. *Divorce Won't Help*. (1948.)

27. Green, S. "Casework Diagnosis of Marital Problems," in *Neurotic Interaction in Marriage*. 235–43 (Eisenstein, V., ed., 1956); Gomberg, M. "Present Status of Treatment Programs," in *id.*, 269–89.

28. *Cf.* Rheinstein, M. *supra* n. 6 at 640; Paulsen, M. *Divorce: Canterbury Style*. 1 Valparaiso U. L. Rev. 93, 97 (1966).

29. *Putting Asunder*, par. 66, p. 53.

30. *Putting Asunder*, par. 64, p. 48.

31. *See* Kanowitz, L. *Sex-Based Discrimination in American Law: Law and the Single Girl*. 11 St. Louis L. Rev. 293, 326–30 (1967); Cal. Advisory Comm'n. on the Status of Women, California Women 17–26 (1967); President's Comm'n. on the Status of Women, American Women 27–34 (1963). *See generally, Symposium, Women and the Labor Force*. 7 Indust. Relations 187 (1968).

32. Cal. Civ. Code § 146 (West, 1954). *See generally* vol. I, Armstrong, B. California Family Law 791–96 (1953).

33. *See generally*, Foster H. and Freed, D. *Child Custody*. 39 N.Y.U. L. Rev. 423, 615 (1964).

34. 258 Iowa 1390, 140 N.W. 2d 152 (Iowa 1966), *cert den.*, 385 U.S. 949 (1966). The Iowa judgment awarding custody to the maternal grandparents was modified in California by an order appointing Harold Painter, the

boy's father, guardian of his son's person and awarding him custody of his son. *In re Painter*, No. 22077 (Superior Court, Santa Cruz County, Aug. 28, 1968).

35. See Kay, H. and Phillips, I. *Poverty and the Law of Child Custody.* 54 Calif. L. Rev. 717, 720–22 (1966). Judge Byron Lindsley: Report to the Assembly Judiciary Committee on A.B. 1420, The Family Court (unpublished manuscript, August 1967).

36. Parsons, T. "The Normal American Family," in *Man and Civilization: The Family's Search for Survival.* 37 (S. Farber ed. 1965).

37. Foote, C.; Levy, R.; and Sander, F. *Cases and Materials on Family Law.* 769–95 (1966).

38. Harper, F. and Harper, M. *Lawyers and Marriage Counseling.* 1 J. Fam. Law 73, 74 (1961).

39. Landis, J. "The Family and Social Change: A Positive View," in *Man and Civilization: The Family's Search for Survival.* 173–82, at 179–80 (S. Farber ed. 1965) (reporting a study of 330 university students, all children of divorced parents). *See also* F. Nye. "Child Adjustment in Broken and Unhappy Homes." 19 *Marr. and Fam. Liv.* 356 (1957).

40. Calif. Stats. 1969, ch. 1608, § 4506.

41. *Id.,* at § 4507.

42. Calif. Stats. 1969, ch. 1609, § 4509.

43. Calif. Stats. 1969, ch. 1608, § 4508(a).

44. REPORT 93; § 4718. See also text at note 28, *supra.*

45. *Divorce in California,* op. cit. *supra* note 13, at p. 175, Table 63.

46. Calif. Stats. 1969, ch. 1608, § 4800.

47. *Id.,* at § 4600.

48. Ibid.

49. Calif. Stats. 1969, ch. 1609, § 4509.

50. *E.g., In re A.J.,* 274 A.C.A. 225, 78 Cal. 880 (1969), *In re Raya,* 255 C.A.2d 260, 63 Cal. 252 (1967).

51. Calif. Stats. 1969, ch. 1608, § 4001.

52. Dyson E. and Dyson R. *Family Courts in the United States*, 8 J. Fam. Law 505 (1968).

CHAPTER 11

1. Bohannan, Paul. *Love, Sex and Being Human*. New York: Doubleday. 1969. pp. 88–91.

REFERENCES

Aberle, David F.; Bronfenbrenner, Urie; Hess, Eckhard H.; Miller, Daniel R.; Schneider, David M.; and Spuhler, James N. 1963. "The Incest Taboo and the Mating Pattern of Animals." *American Anthropologist* 65:253–65.

Alexander, Franz. 1930. "The Neurotic Character." *International Journal of Psychoanalysis* 11:292–311.

Ardener, E. 1962. *Divorce and Fertility: An African Study*, Nigerian Social and Economic Studies, No. 3. (Nigerian Institute of Social and Economic Research.) London: Oxford University Press.

Befu, Harumi. 1964. "Eskimo Systems of Kinship Terms—Their Diversity and Uniformity." *Arctic Anthropology* 2:(1):84–98.

Ben-Dor, Shmuel. 1966. *Makkovik: Eskimos and Settlers in a Labrador Community. A Contrastive Study in Adaptation.* St. John's, Newfoundland: Memorial University of Newfoundland, Institute of Social and Economic Research. Newfoundland Social and Economic Studies No. 4.

Bergler, Edmund. 1948. *Divorce Won't Help.* New York: Harper & Row.

Bernard, Jessie. 1942. *American Family Behavior.* New York: Harper & Row.

Bernard, Jessie. 1956. *Remarriage, A Study of Marriage.* New York: Dryden Press.

Bernard, Jessie. 1964. "Adjustments of Marital Partners," in Harold T. Christensen, *Handbook of Marriage and the Family.* Chicago: Rand McNally.

Bernard, Jessie. 1969. "Infidelity, A Moral or Social Issue?" *Science and Psychoanalysis*, vol. 16.

Blos, Peter. 1962. *On Adolescence: A Psychoanalytic Interpretation.* New York: The Free Press of Glencoe.

Bohannan, Paul and Karan Huckleberry. 1967. "Institutions of Divorce, Family and the Law." *Law and Society Review,* vol. I, no. 2, pp. 81–102.

Burch, Ernest S., Jr. 1966. "Authority, Aid and Affection: The Structure of Eskimo Kin Relationships." (Unpublished Ph.D. dissertation, Department of Anthropology, University of Chicago.)

Chance, Norman A. 1966. *The Eskimo of Northern Alaska.* New York: Holt, Rinehart & Winston.

Christensen, Harold and Barber, Kenneth E. 1967. "Interfaith versus Intrafaith Marriage in Indiana." *Journal of Marriage and the Family.* 29, August, pp. 461–549.

Christenson, Cornelia and Gagnon, John. 1965. "Sexual Behavior in a Group of Older Women." *Journal of Gerontology,* vol. 20, No. 3, pp. 351–55.

Cohen, Ronald. 1966. "The Bornu King Lists," in *Boston University Publications in African History,* vol. II, J. Butler, ed. (pp. 41–83). Boston: Boston University Press.

Cohen, Ronald. 1967a. *The Kanuri of Bornu.* New York: Holt, Rinehart & Winston.

Cohen, Ronald. 1967b. "Social Stratification in Bornu," in *Class and Status in Sub-Saharan Africa.* A. Tuden and L. Plotnicov, eds. New York: The Free Press of Glencoe.

Cohen, Ronald. In press. "From Empire to Colony: Bornu in the Nineteenth and Twentieth Centuries," in *The Impact of Colonialism.* Victor W. Turner, ed. Stanford: The Hoover Institute.

Cohen, Yehudi A. 1964. *The Transition from Childhood to Adolescence.* Chicago: Aldine Press.

Cuber, John F. and Harroff, Peggy. 1966. *Sex and the Significant Americans.* Baltimore: Penguin Books.

Damas, David. 1963. *Iglugligmiut Kinship and Local Group-*

ings: A Structural Approach. Ottawa: National Museum of Canada Bulletin No. 196.

Damas, David. 1964. "The Patterning of the Igluligmiut Kinship System." *Ethnology* 3:(4):377–88.

Despert, J. Louise. 1962. *Children of Divorce.* New York: Doubleday & Co. (Dolphin Books).

Erickson, Erik H. 1956. "The Problem of Ego Identity." *Journal of the American Psychoanalytic Assoc.* 4:56–121.

Fenichel, Otto. 1945. *The Psychoanalytic Theory of Neurosis.* New York: W. W. Norton & Co.

Fortune, R. F. 1932. *Sorcerers of Dobu; The Social Anthropology of the Dobu Islanders of the Western Pacific.* New York: E. P. Dutton & Co.

Freud, Anna (1936). 1946. *The Ego and the Mechanisms of Defense.* New York: International Universities Press.

Freud, Sigmund (1910). 1948. "Contribution to the Psychology of Love. A Special Type of Choice of Object made by Men." *Collected Papers* 4:192–202. London: Hogarth Press.

Freud, Sigmund (1921). 1949. *Group Psychology and the Analysis of the Ego.* New York: Liveright Publishing Corp.

Gebhard, Paul. 1966. "Factors in Marital Orgasm." *The Journal of Social Issues,* Vol. 22, No. 2, pp. 88–95.

Gitelson, Maxwell. 1963. "On the Problem of Character Neurosis." *Journal of the Hillside Hospital* 12:3–17.

Goode, W. J. 1956. *After Divorce.* Chicago: Free Press.

Goode, W. J. 1963. *World Revolution and Family Patterns.* New York: Free Press.

Gradburn, Nelson H. H. 1964. "Taqagmiut Eskimo Kinship Terminology." Ottawa: Northern Co-ordination and Research Centre, Department of Northern Affairs and National Resources.

Greenberg, Joseph H. 1954. "Studies in African Linguistic Classification, VIII." *Southwestern Journal of Anthropology* 10:405–15.

Gubser, Nicholas J. 1965. *The Nunamiut Eskimos: Hunters of Caribou*. New Haven: Yale University Press.

Guemple, D. L. 1961. *Innuit Spouse-Exchange*. Chicago: Department of Anthropology, University of Chicago.

Guemple, D. L. 1965. "Saunik: Name-Sharing as a Factor Governing Eskimo Kinship Terms." *Ethnology* 4:(3): 323–35.

Guemple, D. L. 1966. "Kinship-Reckoning among the Belcher Island Eskimo." (Unpublished Ph.D. dissertation, Department of Anthropology, University of Chicago.)

Heinrich, Albert C. 1955a. "An Outline of the Kinship System of the Bering Straits Eskimos." (Unpublished M.A. thesis, Department of Education, University of Alaska.)

Heinrich, Albert C. 1955b. "A Survey of Kinship Forms and Terminologies Found among the Inupiaq-Speaking Peoples of Alaska." (College, Alaska: Unpublished manuscript in the University of Alaska library.)

Heinrich, Albert C. 1960. "Structural Features of Northwestern Alaskan Eskimo Kinship." *Southwestern Journal of Anthropology* 16:(1):110–26.

Heinrich, Albert C. 1963. "Eskimo-Type Kinship and Eskimo Kinship: An Evaluation and a Provisional Model for Presenting the Evidence Pertaining to Inupiaq Kinship Systems." (Unpublished Ph.D. dissertation, Department of Anthropology, University of Washington.)

Henry, Jules. 1941. *Jungle People*. New York: Augustin. [Reprinted 1964, Vintage V521, Random House]

Hughes, Charles C. 1958. "An Eskimo Deviant from the 'Eskimo Type' of Social Organization." *American Anthropologist* 60:(6):1140–47.

Hughes, Charles C. 1960. *An Eskimo Village in the Modern World*. Ithaca: Cornell University Press.

Hunt, Morton M. 1966. *The World of the Formerly Married*. New York: McGraw-Hill Book Co.

Jacobson, Paul H. 1959. *American Marriage and Divorce*. New York: Rinehart & Co.

Kinsey, Alfred C.; Pomeroy, Wardell B.; and Martin, Clyde
E. 1948. *Sexual Behavior in the Human Male*. Philadelphia: W. B. Saunders Company.

Kinsey, Alfred C.; Pomeroy, Wardell B.; Martin, Clyde
E.; and Gebhard, Paul. 1953. *Sexual Behavior in the
Human Female*. Philadelphia: W. B. Saunders Com-
pany.

Komarovsky, Mirra. 1966. *Blue-Collar Marriage*. New York:
Random House, Inc.

Landes, Ruth and Zborowski, Mark. 1950. "Hypotheses
Concerning the Eastern European Jewish Family." *Psychiatry* 13:447–64.

Lantis, Margaret. 1946. *The Social Structure of the Nunivak
Eskimo*. Transactions of the American Philosophical Society, ns., Vol. 35, Part 3.

Levy. M. J., Jr. 1952. *The Structure of Society*. Princeton:
Princeton University Press.

Levy, R. 1957. *The Social Structure of Islam* (2nd ed.).
Cambridge: The University Press.

Levy, Robert. No date. *Uniform Marriage and Divorce Legislation: A Preliminary Analysis*. Prepared for the Special
Committee on Divorce of the National Conference of
Commissioners on Uniform State Laws (mimeographed).

Liebow, Elliott. 1967. *Fathers Without Children*. Boston:
Little, Brown & Co., Inc.

Mead, Margaret. 1935. *Sex and Temperament in Three
Primitive Societies*. New York: William Morrow & Co.
[Reprinted 1963, Apollo A-67, Morrow]

Mead, Margaret. 1949. *Male and Female*. New York: William Morrow & Co. [Reprinted 1955, Mentor MD150,
New American Library]

Mead, Margaret. 1955. "Implications of Insight—II" in *Childhood in Contemporary Cultures*. Margaret Mead and
Martha Wolfenstein, eds. (pp. 449–61). Chicago: University of Chicago Press. [Reprinted 1963, Phoenix
P124, University of Chicago Press]

Mead, Margaret. 1965. "Outdoor Recreation in the Context of Emerging American Cultural Values," in *Trends in American Living and Outdoor Recreation*. Reports to the Outdoor Recreation Resources Review Commission No. 22 (pp. 2–25). Washington: Government Printing Office.

Mead, Margaret. 1968. "Incest" for the *International Encyclopedia of the Social Sciences*. New York: Macmillan and Free Press.

Nimkoff, M. F. 1952. "Contributions to a Therapeutic Solution to the Divorce Problem: Sociology," paper in Conference on Divorce: The Law School, University of Chicago, 9, pp. 55–62.

Nye, F. Ivan and Hoffman, Lois W. 1963. *The Employed Mother in America*. Chicago: Rand McNally & Co.

Parsons, Talcott. 1954. "The incest taboo in relation to social structure and the socialization of the child." *British Journal of Sociology* 5:101–17.

Peshkin, A. and Cohen, R. 1967. "The Values of Modernization." *Journal of the Developing Areas*, vol. 2, pp. 7–22.

Pospisil, Leopold. 1964. "Law and Societal Structure among the Nunamiut Eskimo," in *Explorations in Cultural Anthropology: Essays in Honor of George Peter Murdock*, Ward H. Goodenough, ed. (pp. 395–431). New York: McGraw-Hill.

Pospisil, Leopold and Laughlin, William S. 1963. "Kinship Terminology among the Nunamiut Eskimos." *Ethnology* 2:(2):180–89.

Rainwater, Lee. 1966. "Some Aspects of Lower-Class Sexual Behavior." *Journal of Social Issues*, vol. 22, April.

Rangell, Leo. 1963. "On Friendship." *Journal of the American Psychoanalytic Assoc.* 11:3–54.

Rubel, Arthur J. 1961. "Partnership and Wife-Exchange Among the Eskimo and Aleut of Northern North America." *Anthropological Papers of the University of Alaska* 10:(1):59–72.

Spencer, Robert F. 1959. *The North Alaskan Eskimo: A Study in Ecology and Society*. BAE Bulletin No. 171. Washington: Government Printing Office.

Sumner, William Grant. 1906. *Folkways*. Boston: Ginn & Co.

Sussman, Marvin. 1955, 1963. *Sourcebook in Marriage and the Family*. Boston: Houghton Mifflin Co.

Terman, L. M. and Wallin, Paul. 1949. "The Validity of Marriage Prediction and Marital Adjustment Tests." *American Sociological Review* 14 (August).

Terman, L. M. 1938. *Psychological Factors in Marital Happiness*. New York: McGraw-Hill Book Company.

Tumin, Melvin. 1965. "The Functionalist Approach to Social Problems." *Social Problems*, Spring, p. 383.

United States Government National Center for Health Statistics. 1969. *Monthly Vital Statistics* Report, March 12.

United States Government U. S. Census of Population. 1960. *Employment Status and Work Experience*. Washington: Government Printing Office.

United States Government U. S. Census of Population. 1960. *Marital Status*. Washington: Government Printing Office.

United States Government U. S. Census of Population. 1960. *Persons by Family Characteristics*. Washington: Government Printing Office.

United States Government U. S. Department of Health, Education, and Welfare, Public Health Service. 1963. *Divorce Statistics Analysis*. Washington: Government Printing Office.

United States Government U. S. Department of Health, Education, and Welfare, Public Health Service. 1969. *Divorce Statistics, 1966*. Washington: Government Printing Office.

Vernier, Chester G. and Frank, R. A. 1938. *American Family Laws*. Stanford: Stanford University Press.

Weinberg, S. Kirson. 1955. *Incest Behavior*. New York: Citadel Press.

Wolfenstein, Martha. 1946. *The Impact of a Children's Story on Mothers and Children*. Monographs of the Society for Research in Child Development, vol. 11, Ser. 42. Washington: National Research Council.

CONTRIBUTORS

JESSIE BERNARD: Foremost American family sociologist; professor emeritus of Penn State University, associate of UNESCO, Paris; author of *American Family Behavior, Remarriage,* and many other books.

PAUL BOHANNAN: Professor of Anthropology at Northwestern University; author of *Africa and Africans, Social Anthropology, Love, Sex and Being Human.*

ERNEST BURCH, JR.: Anthropologist, University of Manitoba; author of technical papers.

RONALD COHEN: Anthropologist, Northwestern University; author of many technical papers and case studies.

PAUL GEBHARD: Director, Kinsey Institute of Sex Research, Indiana University; author (with Kinsey, Pomeroy, and Martin) of *Sexual Behavior of the Human Female,* and (with others) *Sex Offenders.*

HERMA HILL KAY: Professor of Law, University of California, Berkeley; specialist in family law and in the legal rights of children; member of California committees investigating divorce law and other family matters.

MARGARET MEAD: Curator, American Museum of Natural History; author of *Male and Female,* and many other books and articles.

ARTHUR A. MILLER, M.D.: Training psychoanalyst; Chicago Institute for Psychoanalysis; Professor of Psychiatry, University of Michigan.

MAX RHEINSTEIN: Professor of Law, University of Chicago; internationally known specialist on family law and conflict of laws.

Index

ANCHOR BOOKS

SOCIOLOGY

SOCIOLOGY (cont'd)

DATE DUE

DEC 1 2 2000		
OCT 2 5 2001		
OCT 2 2		
FEB 1 6 2009		

The Library Store   #47-0114 Peel Off Pressure Sensitive   1